PENGUIN BOOKS

THE CAMERA AGE

Michael J. Arlen is the author of
Living-Room War (1969), *Exiles* (1970,
nominated for a National Book Award),
An American Verdict (1973), *Passage to
Ararat* (1975, winner of the National
Book Award in Contemporary Affairs),
The View from Highway 1 (1976), and
Thirty Seconds (1980), which is also
published by Penguin Books.

THE CAMERA AGE

ESSAYS ON TELEVISION

MICHAEL J. ARLEN

PENGUIN BOOKS

Penguin Books Ltd, Harmondsworth,
Middlesex, England
Penguin Books, 625 Madison Avenue,
New York, New York 10022, U.S.A.
Penguin Books Australia Ltd, Ringwood,
Victoria, Australia
Penguin Books Canada Limited, 2801 John Street,
Markham, Ontario, Canada L3R 1B4
Penguin Books (N.Z.) Ltd, 182–190 Wairau Road,
Auckland 10, New Zealand

First published in the United States of America by
Farrar, Straus and Giroux 1981
First published in Canada by
McGraw-Hill Ryerson Limited 1981
Published in Penguin Books 1982

LIBRARY OF CONGRESS CATALOGING IN PUBLICATION DATA
Arlen, Michael J.
The camera age.
Reprint. Originally published: New York:
Farrar, Straus and Giroux, 1981.
1. Television broadcasting—United States—
Collected works.   I. Title.
PN1992.3.U5A87   1982   791.45′0973   81-17902
ISBN 0 14 00.6107 X   AACR2

Printed in the United States of America by
Offset Paperback Mfrs., Inc., Dallas, Pennsylvania
Set in Bodoni

*This book is dedicated to
my father, Michael Arlen (1896–1956),
novelist, playwright, short-story writer,
screenwriter, and perhaps unsurprisingly, for
two months toward the end of his gifted
and bittersweet life, host of his own
short-lived television show on NBC*

AUTHOR'S NOTE

All these essays (with the exception of the introduction) were originally published in *The New Yorker*, though many of them have been substantially revised for inclusion in this volume. Few of the changes have been aimed at updating details or at trying to give a topical passage written some years ago the appearance of contemporaneity—forms of textual face-lifting, it seems to me, that usually leave the patient in a condition of belonging properly neither to the past nor to the present. In one or two cases where I thought additional information might interest the reader, I have provided it in a kind of postscript. But for the most part the revisions have been directed at trying sometimes to expand upon, and more often to compress and clarify, those ideas that continued to evolve since the pieces were first published. Once again, I extend my considerable thanks to William Shawn, the editor of *The New Yorker*, who has edited my work for the magazine for close to twenty years, and also to Michael di Capua, my editor at Farrar, Straus and Giroux.

CONTENTS

THE CAMERA AGE

INTRODUCTION

THE ESSAYS collected here are about television in America and especially about the experience of watching television in America—this huge, shared, strangely experienceless experience as it sometimes seems to be.

Television today sits in the center of American homes and none too far from the center of American lives—a companionable though unsettling kind of house pet. Here and there, somebody will scornfully announce: "I never watch television!" Or even: "I don't own a television set!" But these defiances matter little. You don't really need to have this pet in your house to be affected by it.

Of course, since television is so close to home, as it were, a lot of people don't seem to know quite what to make of it. It's too close, too intimate an experience. At any rate, it's not one that bears thinking about very much.

TV is entertainment, isn't it? Yes.

George likes to watch the football. Yes.

I'm crazy about *Dallas*. Yes.

It tells me what's happening in the world. Yes.

Television is hard to pin down, almost impossible, but still some people are always trying to pin it down. Television is full of paradox, after all, and this is an age that seems to be rather more comfortable with the terrible swift sword of generalization. Clichés about the magic of mass media drip from the ceiling like stalactites. Stern, sweeping, and apocalyptic pronouncements on the evils of TV rain like pebbles upon the heads of insouciant citizens. Thus, television is variously defined as all-powerful, manipulative, hypnotic: a dark electronic necromancer who can as easily sell refrigerators to the Eskimos as elect Wintergreen to the Presidency. Or as a despoiler of youth. Or as an inciter to national violence. Or as a false messenger: a source of dangerously biased news and censored information. And so on.

Naturally, these generalities have a certain amount of truth to them, at least some of the time, at least now and then. Where there's smoke there's fire, as the saying goes, though sometimes it is Paris burning and sometimes only a piece of smoldering rutabaga in the kitchen. As usual, the particular instance is probably what counts.

Television is certainly a powerful authority. On the other hand, it is surely just as true that television is also the most intrinsically *porous* medium of communication that man in his peculiar wisdom has yet devised. Consider for a moment the unusual relationship that the ordinary viewer maintains with this almighty force—for example, an American family gathered in, or rather drifting in and out of, the proverbial living room, watching the set. Think how hard it is even to read the sports page in the morning newspaper while carrying on a conversation with one's wife about vacation plans; how altogether difficult it is to work on office business or an algebra assignment while seated in a theater, attending to a play; how virtually impossible it is to read a decent novel or listen to a concert or look at a painting with coherent interest while at the same time talking with a client or best friend or faraway parent on the telephone. But on most evenings of the year, in most households of the land, it is a safe bet that the nation's favorite television programs are being viewed not only happily but satisfactorily while a myriad of such parallel activities are going on—and not so much around these programs as right through them.

Do we then seem to have a porous authority, an oddly permeable wizard? Still other paradoxes abound. For instance, television has created sports while it has destroyed sports. Television has broken down traditional voting patterns, based on party allegiance; at the same time it has brought into being a new, fluid, shifting electorate of videoconscious voters.

Television helped promote our involvement in Vietnam with its simplistic, uncritical, combat-oriented reporting. But these same news reports also fueled the protest movements that turned the country against the war.

Studies by social scientists (George Gerbner et al.), based on national statistical samples, suggest that the more television an individual watches, the more he or she is likely to be inclined to violence, alienation, anomie, etc., though studies by other social scientists (Paul C. Hirsch et al.), *based on the same national statistical samples*, indicate just as clearly that among the individuals most prone to violence, alienation, anomie, etc., are those who don't watch any television at all.

In social terms, television is commonly regarded as a poor substitute for human contact. But is it a poor substitute for a world without human contact? Consider: television did not itself bring about the fragmentation of modern family life, as a result of which old people are often separated from the rest of society and left to themselves. Television, however, ministers to these seniors, cast adrift and bobbing on the ebb tide in their Centers, Homes, and Resurrection Cities, connecting them, if not alas to Wayne Jr., newly married and too busy to visit, then at least to Phil Donahue and *All My Children*. Consider: in its dealings with the young, television often plays a sleazy Pied Piper to children, will sell them anything, addle their minds, and teach them bad grammar in the process. (The Pied Piper, one should remember, first came to Hamelin town at the invitation of the grownups.) But television also meets the young on their own terms, gives them choice as well as freedom of access, and also provides them—within the glowing, flickering perimeter of the TV set—something that throughout history the young have badly needed: a place of their own to exist in, temporarily untalked to, undefined, unimproved.

Is television then a window on the world? Or is it a space we have found to hide in from the twentieth century? The fact is that television sometimes has a way of answering questions that nobody knew were being asked, so perhaps a not unimportant function of a television critic in these times is at least to scan the answers being given by his TV set in order to learn some of the questions.

Last but not least: I titled this volume *The Camera Age* because I believe that some of the most interesting questions being raised right now by television have to do with fundamental matters of perception. It has been evident for some time in this country that we have gradually shifted to television as the primary source for our perceptions of the world. In other words, our view outside the window is increasingly defined by television's view: television's news, television's sports, television's level of talk, television's social values, etc. At the same time, television itself has been steadily shifting its own perceptions so as to be in tune with the visual-cinematic era we now live in.

More and more, we see what the cameras see. Our interests become determined by what the cameras are interested in. Our news programs, for example, are under pressure to show us what the cameras deem newsworthy. Our cultural programs reshape dance, theater, painting, or literary material according to the camera's eye, as if the formal essence of particular works in nonvisual (or nonfilmic) areas were somehow neutral, waiting to be recast in the new medium.

In important ways, it is a time of liberation; just as in other important ways it is bound to be a time of loss. For one hundred years or so, across the Western world, visual forms and crafts have been emerging from their lengthy servitude to the demands of trying to express nonvisual information. Painting gave up storytelling; photography has shaken free of journalism; movies abandoned the stage play. Finally, television, the most conservative of all the popular arts, the most hidebound, the most deeply rooted in the logic of nonvisual information, and the most massive, has been moving its great weight into the new terrain. Right now, it is in midstride: one foot still planted in the Old World, where visual signs exist mainly to express narrative stories or writerly information, and one foot now pressing into the New World, where visual forms have their own logic.

Is the camera eye but an extension of the human eye, or does it have its own perceptions? Already, to a remarkable extent, the television cameras stare out across the world, peering into politics, into space, into back yards, into courthouses, casting their eyes at family life, public life, sports, sex, revolution, war, famine as well as plenty, while we stay home, also staring—living our lives in terms of what we think the cameras tell us.

CAMERAS IN COMMAND

I HAVE a friend who is a bachelor from time to time and who at present resides in an enormous new apartment building, constructed of pale-blue brick and named after a Wagner heroine, that has a video camera mounted in each of its elevators. These cameras are not the swiveling kind, such as may be found in giant drugstores, whose roving eye scans the cosmetics counter and magazine rack and garden-accesories display with the rhythmic, inquisitorial, and easily outwittable manner of a Mr. McGregor searching his lettuce patch for Peter Rabbit. The cameras in my friend's elevators make no such claim to restless curiosity. Instead, they are stationary, sure of themselves, each fixed in place upon a little shelf high in the left rear corner of the elevator, with its lens pointing more or less directly at the front of the car, although I've noticed, riding up and down from my friend's apartment in the company of other residents of the Wagnerian building, that we all generally tend to flatten ourselves ever so casually against the back of the elevator; out of sight, as it were, if not out of mind. It is a tendency, one might add, that affords an endearing example of mutual trust among urban strangers, for if our elevator group some afternoon should happen to contain a burglar-rapist-maniac he would clearly be able to wreak his dreadful havoc upon the rest of us unobserved by the vigilant though farsighted camera, his depredations as well as our gallant struggles unrecorded on the downstairs monitor screen, which is situated next to the mail room in the lobby and is supposed to be monitored by Raoul, the doorman: a descendant of a past more spiritual and humanistic than our own cool, Japanese electronics culture, who thus passes most of his time on a stool near the air vent just inside the front door, discussing night life with delivery boys and giving unsound advice to Haitian domestics.

I've thought of these elevator cameras every so often, not only last summer, when I used to drop by my friend's place fairly frequently, but this fall and winter, as the Iranian crisis prolonged itself (as the newscasters say) into its second and third month, because in certain ways they seem so representative, so emblematic, of the camera era that we are all living in. For some time, that is, we have been surrounded by camera images, and in the past decade we have started to actually live by them: to revere what the camera reveres, to see what the camera sees, to be guided by what the camera shows us. Long ago, in 1930, Christopher Isherwood wrote in *A Berlin Diary*: "I am a camera with its shutter open, quite passive, recording, not thinking." Such a lovely sentence, but how quaint and inexact and literary (dread modern pejorative!) it sounds today, in the context of the camera's looming and forceful presence in our midst. With what irony does Isherwood's tender phrase "quite passive" echo in the years that have seen the rise of photojournalism, *The March of Time*, paparazzi, *60 Minutes*, and the dialectics of *auteur* cinema and young filmmakers. And now there is Iran: Iran, Day 67 or 76— for the networks seem to have discovered the pleasures of linear time, with the result that each night's report has been introduced by a logo to remind us of the consecutive, or perhaps Newtonian, nature of the event. Or possibly it is not so much the pleasures of linear time which have been discovered as the homespun satisfactions of fidelity; that is, for many years network news departments have been wearing themselves thin in the service of a kind of hyperactive news promiscuity, careering from crisis to crisis, setting up their cameras at a new trouble spot before the rubble has been cleared away from the last one, so that now, having decided to *stick with the story*, they have been covering it with the relentless predictability of a Don Juan who has decided to stay home for a few evenings. Was any man ever so consistently, so regularly, so admirably *at home* as this fellow? Day after day, night after night, the networks have brought us the news from the streets of Teheran, even when there was no news, or when what there was of it had been more or less produced by the host nation for the purposes of worldwide television coverage.

Such fidelity to an important news event is a fine thing, to be sure; nor is steadfastness in covering a television beat such a commonplace occurrence that one should be impatient for a return to the old promiscuity. But what has obtained in our Iranian coverage, for the most part, seems less a matter of steadfastness of thought or action than a matter of rigidity of camera view. Let us even take this small thought a step further and say what has surely been in the minds of many persons over the past sixty-seven or seventy-six Iranian days: that there appear to have been two sets of prisoners taken in the Iranian crisis. Most explicitly and affectingly, of course, there are the fifty or so men and women of the American Embassy who are being held hostage in Teheran; apparently, they are not being physically brutalized, but they are being held against their will, are not free to go, and are presumably being compelled, or at least encouraged, to channel their thoughts along lines selected by their captors. Not altogether dissimilarly, the American news audience (decidedly more comfortable but also, while not actually brutalized, not entirely free to go either, and with its conscious thoughts being shaped by its captors) has been held captive by the TV cameras. One could say that it is the network news organizations that own the cameras and direct their placement, but in a sense the network news organizations have been held captive, too. The cameras are in command, as they have been so often in recent history. Cameras, for example, largely determined the selection of the American President, Jimmy Carter, who is trying to deal with the Iranian crisis, and though cameras didn't exactly topple the Shah, a close cousin of the camera—the cassette tape recorder—brought the Ayatollah Khomeini to power, and cameras have most certainly been determining the shape of the hostage crisis, both on the Iranian side and on our own. The mighty Wurlitzer of "the news" supposedly speaks with many voices, many *words*—the words of newscasters and voice-over correspondents and government spokesmen trying to describe the situation and define their views of it—but the single, focusing message that the public has lately received has been the camera's message: the belligerent, chanting, menacing Iranians in the streets of Teheran outside our Embassy. In earlier times, when people lived in oral or print eras, they could be focused and controlled by slogans (like "God for Harry! England and St. George!") or print messages (as from Tom Paine or Harriet Beecher Stowe). In the late nineteen-thirties, as Christopher Isherwood was to discover, whole nations could be rallied and controlled by loudspeakers and radio: a distanced version of the human voice, yet one that became even more powerful than the real thing. Now it is the camera that provides our points of reference, our focus. Indeed, our sense of great events has become so over-whelmingly visual—Mrs. John F. Kennedy reaching out across the back of that car in Dallas—that many people (whose forebears were doubtless once as widely deprived of man-made imagery and color as their progeny are now inundated by them) appear to believe that the visual plane is the only plane that life itself happens on. Consider, for instance, those fragments from the vast network news coverage of Vietnam, which were never really stories as such (those reiterated glimpses of helicopters landing, of men fanning out in the tall grass, of distant planes and puffs of smoke and napalm, of Westy Westmoreland in his little cap, and of visiting dignitaries touring the war zone), but which come down to us as *scenes*: symbolic messages of the war, even more powerful and haunting, I think, than the exaggerated flourishes of such recent epics as *The Deer Hunter* and *Apocalypse Now* (though, alas, not quite so "real").

For most of the public, Vietnam *was* those scenes, and is remembered not only through them but in terms of them; lately, they have passed as actual experience into the moviemakers' own cameras. Then came the "boat people," who had *their* scenes: capsizing hulks and heart-rending waifs. Then the Cambodians, though the starving and decimated Cambodians unfortunately lacked both cameras and scenes; there were print reports and articles and some pictures of Mrs. Carter at refugee camps in Thailand, but no *scenes*. And now the Iranians and the hostages: our nightly glimpse of Teheran. For many years, it must be recalled, our cameras unsuccessfully visited Iran: nodding politely at the Shah, who would usually dress up for the occasion (as if dressing up produced a scene!); or going to sleep over the Shah's land-reform program; or waking up somewhat over the Shah water-skiing (the Shah in a bathing suit; not a scene, either); and simply going out to lunch at the mention of repression (no scene there) or SAVAK (there is such a thing as *too much* of a scene) or the power of the Muslim priesthood (be serious; how can there be a scene about priests; old, bearded priests?). But now the cameras are back and are presumably happy, for they finally have their Iranian scene: the mobs in the streets outside the Embassy. At first, who would have thought it? Such an unlikely film location: the outside of a captured embassy, with the presumed subject of the story inside and out of sight! The network news directors couldn't have hoped for much: eventually, maybe a small war, of course, or, better still, a little armed conflict, with those far-off planes and tiny puffs of smoke; but, if not armed conflict, then what? The usual nothing. That only goes to show you what network news directors know, or ayatollahs, for that matter, because, though Khomeini certainly knew a lot about tape recorders and cassettes, maybe as much as Oriana Fallaci (since it was by cassette that he transmitted the Good Word from the suburbs of Paris to the Muslim faithful in Iran), he couldn't have really known that much about cameras, about what our cameras would see. The young Iranian activists, however, were quick to see what our cameras saw, and so began to speak to *them*, commune with the cameras. At this point, the network news directors, remembering their solemn journalistic mission and also the expensive reportorial talent on their payrolls, dispatched their heavy hitters to Iran: Mike Wallace to Qum! But why should the Iranians bother with the heavy hitters when they could speak directly to our cameras?

It was a dilemma, admittedly; a modern dilemma. By this time, virtually everyone disliked the Iranians. The government disliked the Iranians. The citizens disliked the Iranians. The news directors, being citizens too, certainly disliked the Iranians. But the cameras loved them. The cameras and the Iranians were pals. Of course, the Iranians didn't get the affection of the cameras for nothing. They had to put in a day's work now and then: raise the old fist, chant the old chant, march the old march down to the gates of the Embassy compound. But it was worth it, because of the scene. An interesting point, too, is that it wasn't what you would call a surefire, terrific scene. It didn't leap out at you from the pages of the script and say: Film me, young filmmaker. It was more the kind of scene you don't really notice at first, while you're blocking all the other, really important scenes; but then afterward, in the notorious cutting room, when the celebrated *auteur* film editor is telling you that none of the other really important scenes work, you suddenly notice: Hey, man, *this* is the really big scene. All those swarthy faces, all those hands and arms, all those beards. No matter that there's no fancy dialogue, no exploding ammo dumps, no little planes in the sky. This one *works*. It all sort of flows together, naturally cinematic, and, besides, you can hang things on it, cut to the subplot: cameo appearances by the Foreign Minister of the moment, attacking the criminality of our foreign policy; or nice Mr. Waldheim, of the United Nations, huddled in the back of his car; or even, now and then, a glimpse of the old Ayatollah, sitting on his carpet up in Qum murmuring "Rosebud" into a blank tape cassette. The only problem with the scene, I guess, is that it's incomplete; it tends to leave things out. It lacks the hostages, for one thing, though that's rather to be expected, considering the circumstances. Mostly, I imagine, it lacks *information*. Who are those people in the streets, anyway? Who are these militants (referred to as "students" on television, presumably in the spirit of palship) who hold our people prisoners in our Embassy? What did the Shah do, good or bad, that made a number of Americans happy to watch him water-skiing and a larger number of Iranians want to kill him? There are many more questions that might be asked and could be answered, even on television, but to ask and answer them would doubtless detract from the scene, make it unworkable. The cameras would begin to blink their eyes in ambivalence and confusion, and sulk, and lose their pleasure, and leave Iran again.

So the moral, if there is one, is that we must probably learn to live with our cameras, at least for the time being (whether they are mounted in elevators or in drugstores or in wars or in political conventions or in Teheran), and learn to understand the scenes and images they choose to bring us. Only God's love, as the saying goes, is complete. I should point out, though, that my friend in the blue-brick building has been burgled twice since July— nothing really serious, if you know what I mean: his cuff links and Cuisinart the first time, his stereo speakers the second time—and has been giving serious thought to moving to a different neighborhood and a less contemporary building, with bars on the windows and one of those Prisoner of Zenda locks on the front door. He says that he will miss Raoul, who is of the opinion that both heists were inside jobs, but he won't miss the cameras that always pretended to be looking after him but never told him what he really needed to know. The trick now, one imagines, is to figure out which neighborhood to move to.

(1980)

THE ANCIENT MARINER
AND THE
WEDDING GUEST

IN AN AGE that has virtually pickled itself in guilt but appears to have no sense of shame at all, it must have seemed to the managers of NBC's *Today* show (whose once mighty ratings have been lagging behind ABC's *Good Morning America*) to be no more than just another eminently reasonable, competitive, and self-justifying broadcasterly move when they decided to lead off their fall programming with a week-long series of appearances by former President Richard Nixon. Mr. Nixon did not, of course, receive the ultimate deference that is paid by media warlords to our noblest citizens—namely, a "roast" in his honor—nor, for that matter, possibly for seasonal reasons, was he granted his own Christmas Special (which might be broadcast, in keeping with the traditions of the genre, either from the Holy Land or from an aircraft carrier in the Persian Gulf). But he was certainly accorded the kind of top-drawer, blue-ribbon interview treatment that in the past has been commonly reserved for such esteemed and beloved national figures as Lyndon Johnson, Georgia O'Keeffe, and Anwar Sadat. In other words, there was no kicking around of the doughty ex-Prexy by summoning him at dawn to Rockefeller Center, there to wait in sodden torpor in the *Today* show's greenroom, drinking filthy coffee from a Styrofoam cup in the company of dour tennis champions and publicity-crazed nonfiction authors. NBC's Nixon interviews were nothing if not statesmanly: a class operation in the spirit of the Higher Electronic Journalism, complete with *separate taping date, home setting, distinguished interviewer* (the author and journalist Theodore H. White), and *two matching chintz-covered armchairs*, in which interviewer and interviewee might face each other—comfortably, even cozily, though with no loss of dignity to the historic occasion.

I was rather sorry to see the sturdy Teddy White sitting in one of those chintz-covered chairs. White has enjoyed a lengthy and often distinguished career in journalism, and NBC apparently now considers him its leading candidate for supra-journalistic nuncio—to provide that special, lofty Cronkite or Walters tone which networks are fond of bringing to affairs of state. But this time it was not a happy part to play—not a jewel in White's diadem, so to speak. For Nixon—as he has managed to do fairly consistently since that sunny afternoon in August 1974 when he choppered off the White House lawn—more or less resolutely cast himself as the Ancient Mariner, and so left White with little more than the role of the Wedding Guest. As in the poet Coleridge's prescient lines:

> *The Wedding-Guest sat on a stone:*
> *He cannot choose but hear;*
> *And thus spake on that ancient man,*
> *The bright-eyed Mariner.*

Granted, not even Torquemada himself could have steered more than an occasional query safely clear of the self-serving maelstrom of the Nixonian mind. (White: "You're the— I wouldn't call you the *child* of TV. It's a little late in life to call you the child of anything. But you're the—" Nixon: "The *orphan*.") The chief difficulty, though, seemed to be that what might charitably be called the informational content of the Nixon-White dialogues appeared so thin—scarcely substantial enough to warrant having brought the old boy back from Elba and having sent Teddy White to chat him up.

Here, for example, the former Chief Executive shared with White and us his thoughts about the upcoming elections:

> NIXON: I would confidently predict that Reagan will win all the Mountain States. He will win all the Plains States, because the farmers are—
>
> WHITE: The Plains States? You mean going through Indiana?
>
> NIXON: No, no, I mean the other side of the Mississippi.
>
> WHITE: Yeah.
>
> NIXON: From the Mississippi on.
>
> WHITE: That's the Kansas–Nebraska belt.
>
> NIXON: That's right.

The network news managers only added to the unreality of the proceedings by pretending to believe not merely that Mr. Nixon should have been there in the first place, proffering advice and comments about our political institutions from the special perspective of someone who had nearly reduced them to rubble, but that he and White were also producing news. Thus, on another occasion, when Nixon—in response to one of the rare questions from White that he deigned to answer directly—conceded that, despite his belief in the two-party system ("I happen to believe in the two-party system"), he would include Representative John Anderson in the Presidential candidates' forthcoming debate, this morsel of ex-Presidential waffle was extracted as precious ore from the program and edited into NBC's nightly news, where it appeared as one of the day's serious news events: an example of recombinant news splicing, as it were.

But, in fairness to NBC, it must be said that the week-long early-morning Nixon show was not a total loss. True, Teddy White, after a lifetime in the presence of great men, seemed to find it hard to take a less than courtly tone with our ex-Commander in Chief. For instance, "Mr. President, only two people in all our history have ever run in five national campaigns from coast to coast. One was Franklin D. Roosevelt, the other was Richard M. Nixon. Is it possible to talk sense to the country about the complicated issues of our time in a Presidential campaign? We're going to be talking this morning about problems here at home. How would you list them? Where would you start, as the most serious problem?" In response to which sonorous and probing query, our precipitately resigned ex-President was heard to murmur, "Well, I would say that our most serious problem is the problem of inflation, and close behind it is the problem of unemployment." Still, a few flashes of the classic Nixon style shone through the fog of Higher Journalistic blather. For example, "I must say, I've got to give Carter's people high marks. They are tough. They are subtle. They are ruthless." And, "They're a tough bunch, believe me, these Georgia boys. They may play softball down in Plains, but they play hardball in the country." And, "The real question is whether the Reagan staff can get organized, can toughen itself, will be selfless enough to combat them." And, last but not least, "The one rule, let me say, Ted, that I would say to staff members all over. *You never knock your own man.* The candidate makes a booboo, you go out and take the heat yourself." One wonders which particular booboo our Ancient ("I am not an albatross") Mariner had in mind. The Watergate-break-in booboo? The Ellsberg-break-in booboo? The eighteen-and-a-half-minute-tape-erasure booboo? Or perhaps some new and altogether different booboo, not yet disclosed on network TV?

Well, never mind. As the French philosopher Jacques Ellul observed, "The man who lives in the news is a man without memory." Small thanks, though, to NBC's news managers, whose fear of a ratings drop has led them in recent months to steadily undermine the *Today* show's once admirable sense of proportion—first by the introduction, earlier in the year, of that noisy, unfunny, phony-grass-roots weatherman Willard Scott, and then, last week, by the spectacle of our notorious unindicted ex-President discoursing on the State of the Union from a chintz armchair while the nation munched on its morning bagels. Unfortunately, not the least of the ravages wrought by these trendy and injudicious media masterstrokes has been to erode still further the journalistic integrity of *Today*'s competent news team, Tom Brokaw and Jane Pauley, who are compelled—by common courtesy, if not by network fiat—to accommodate themselves respectfully to what takes place on the rest of the show. This morning (as on most recent mornings), a strained and miserable attempt at a smile struggled across Mr. Brokaw's face in response to the latest of Mr. Scott's inanities, while at the end of at least one of the Nixon interviews both Pauley and Brokaw came on camera, first to acknowledge that protests against Nixon's appearance had been received and then to dutifully defend the network's shabby venture as "interesting in its own right." What is interesting about it, of course, is that the Nixon Pardoning Process, which was gratuitously begun six years ago by the genial President Ford (speaking the immortal words "My conscience tells me clearly and certainly that I cannot prolong the bad dreams that continue to reopen a chapter that is closed"), and was subtly advanced a few years later by the media entrepreneur David Frost, has now apparently been completed by the NBC peacock.

(1980)

THE LAME DEER

EVERY SO OFTEN, some dismal weeks turn up when there seems to be even less of interest than usual on the TV screen, and little point in being a so-called critic of television programs, and, indeed, slight social value in the fact of television itself. Should one, after all, waste time and paper on composing a polemic against *Hello, Larry*? Or attempt a Jungian analysis of *Fantasy Island*? Or pay sullen homage to the BBC? Or none of the above? None of the above, I thought a few days ago, and went off instead—there being intimations of spring in the air —to spend a day or so with friends in the country. These friends I have known for fifteen years or more. Bill is a sculptor of considerable renown, at least among the art departments of Southwestern banks and Latin-American universities. His wife, Mary, is a smart, sinewy woman who once climbed Mt. McKinley in her youth (when, she says, it was not so steep), and who has since raised three children, two of them now off at school and college, and also found time to develop an innovative instructional program at a nearby school for the deaf, where she teaches. They are fine people, at once gentle and stubbornly uncompromising, and I suspect that, despite certain temperamental differences between us, we have liked each other well over the years because we somehow fill up, or complement, the blank spaces in each other's sensibilities.

That is, Bill and Mary are irredeemably rural, at least in the modern manner (their new wood-burning stove, I have noted privately, stands beside what must surely have been the Shah of Iran's personal collection of stereo equipment): partial to all things natural, at ease with animals, and moderately tolerant of, or at least entertained by, my soft and superficial city ways, and certainly by my occupation of television critic, which they try to be kind about, though as one might be in the case of a once promising friend who had gone to medical school only to end up as a dealer in patent medicine. And I, for my part, while irredeemably citified, am always warmed by their hospitality and made to feel, after even a brief stay on their Connecticut hillside, ever so slightly more in touch with those blessed "basics" that have been eluding me all my life and that I know will be snatched away again, presumably by the Triborough Bridge toll attendant, as soon as I try to reenter the city.

Indeed, the area of western Connecticut that they live in is as lovely, it seems to me, as any spot in New England. It is a place of small dairy farms, and old wooden fences, and roads without signposts which keep taking you in circles, and villages where the postmaster sells candy bars and potato chips on the side, and streams that look as though they might be fun to fish in if only one liked to fish. Above my friends' house, there is a broad, rough field belonging to a nearby farmer in which for years a half-dozen large, ancient, swaybacked horses have shuffled about like elderly out-of-work stevedores. Below the house, there are some woods: not dark, impenetrable, depressing woods, such as one finds in Maine or in the serious parts of New Hampshire, but green and leafy woods—in summer, that is—full of birch and maple and such, where animals, small and not so small, rustle about, in and out of sight. On the whole, except for

Mr. L——, a half mile down the road, who owns a power saw that he exercises on Saturday morning, and Mr. and Mrs. McK——, who board a large male youth, possibly a son, who owns a Kawasaki motorbike of stupefying resonance, it has been a region of relative isolation and tranquillity, where raccoons and porcupines forage in the underbrush and deer occasionally appear right out on the hillside, once barren, that now each springtime blooms with Mary's tulips. Bill and Mary (he from a suburb of Boston, she from Grand Rapids) have become good conservators and groundskeepers. They are proud of their wildlife, of their shared place in the ecology of the hillside. They have become learned about the birds, the permanent constituency as well as the transients. For years, they have bought hay each summer from one of the farmers in order to feed the deer in winter. Sometimes, when the deer have then trampled or eaten too many of the tulips, there has been mild grumbling, followed by inconclusive discussions about wire fencing, but it is clear that Bill and Mary would rather have the deer than the tulips. The deer, as one or the other of them has periodically remarked, were there first, before the house and long before the tulips. The deer are a part of their lives and of their children's lives; in fact, it was largely so that their children might have what they describe as "this natural relationship with wildlife" that my friends moved to their hillside twelve years ago —to the real countryside rather than the artificial suburbs.

But, alas, in recent years, and especially in the past two or three years, even this remote corner of the state has experienced changes—the usual changes: first, a green, windowless factory for manufacturing filtration systems, three miles away; then a shopping center down near the crossroads; then a traffic light on North Street to replace the old flashing yellow beacon, and, of course, more traffic; and then a new "access road" to Route 22, so that the new traffic might have access. To be honest about it, the past few times I have visited Bill and Mary I have noticed a change in their place, too: not so much on their actual property—for their hillside has yet to be "improved" by new construction—but in the feel of the place. What not so long ago felt wild now feels less wild. Last August, for instance, the green and leafy woods were there, as always—to be looked at and listened to and roamed around in as their eight-year-old Jimmy chased after squirrels—but one was aware, through not entirely extrasensory means, that not so very far away (though technically invisible) was rapidly a-building an apparently quite elegant "condominium village" for senior citizens, on the other side of the trees.

This month, when I came out, the condominium village seemed to be completed. Hawthorne Estates is what it's called, perhaps in honor of the famed novelist, who unfortunately died too soon to live there. On the surface, Bill and Mary professed to be taking their new neighbors in stride. "I think they really tried to be careful about the environment," said Bill, and Mary said, "Even a community like this one has to have growth." But clearly their hearts were more than a little broken. We were standing together just outside the kitchen door, looking at the first buds and thinking our various thoughts. I remarked that, from the sound of things in the underbrush, the raccoons and porcupines were as plentiful as ever. "For the time being," said Mary. The number of migrating birds had noticeably lessened, she thought, and one species had simply not appeared.

"Maybe they're late," I said.

Mary said, "They're not late. They had a haven here, a safe place, and people spoiled it, as they usually do —people and their machines and their technology."

What made them saddest of all was what seemed to be happening to the deer population. All winter long, Bill and Mary had put hay out, but only a few deer had shown up, and for one long stretch of three weeks none had shown up. "The senior citizens probably shot them all," said Bill.

Mary said, "That's not funny. You know, we always used to speak of them as *our* deer, even though I knew they weren't our deer. But now that they're gone, or nearly gone, I feel we've all—especially Jimmy—lost something that *was* ours, and was priceless."

We went back inside the house—into the large, old-fashioned kitchen, where Mary had some things she was getting ready for dinner. Outside, the light was fading from the sky, now thick with gray-white clouds that hung heavily above the treetops: an autumnal sky. We all felt in need of cheering up. Bill disappeared down the stairs to the basement in search of beer. Mary was slicing carrots with a deft, rhythmic stroke. Suddenly she said, "Look! Look!" I peered with her through the window above the sink. At the edge of the tree line, perhaps two hundred feet away, quite motionless, stood a solitary deer. Then its small, fine head turned, sniffing the air. It took a few short, tactful steps parallel to the tree line, seeming to limp a little as it did, and then stopped. "It's the lame deer," Mary said, in a whisper. "I thought we'd lost it." Then, "Bill, go get Jimmy!"

Bill was still out of sight and hearing, rummaging for beer, so, thinking the moment was an urgent one, I went myself in search of Jimmy. I found him where I thought I might: in what is called the ironing room, watching television. Bill and Mary, I should explain, while not entirely disapproving of television in recent years—at least, not to the extent of refusing to let it into the house —have nonetheless managed to maintain what I suppose is a certain degree of perverse integrity on the point by permitting only an antiquated, sixteen-inch Zenith (certainly not part of the Shah of Iran's collection), which they have stuck into the small, austere chamber, just off the washer-dryer alcove on the second floor, where Mrs. Cooney sometimes hangs out of a Tuesday or Thursday afternoon, reading the paper, drinking coffee, folding an occasional item of laundry, watching *The Young and the Restless*, but definitely not ironing. Thus, whenever members of the family wish to eat of the forbidden fruit (be it *The MacNeil/Lehrer Report* or *Great Performances*), they must do so in the same austere circumstances: a Presbyterian approach to worship which, as I have vainly pointed out, only emphasizes the basic spirituality of the occasion. "Jimmy," I now said in what I meant to be a sincere voice, "the lame deer is outside on the hill."

Jimmy swiveled his head, as if on ball bearings, and cast a bleary eye at me. "There's sea elephants fighting here," he said.

And so there were. On the Zenith's small and fuzzy screen, two hefty walruslike creatures were battering each other, with noisy grunts, against a picturesque background of rocks and ocean. A narratoı's voice, cultivated and slightly European, intoned, "Once again, the age-old ritual of dominance is reenacted among the larger bulls."

"There's a deer outside in the field," I said to Jimmy.

"I've seen the deer," said Jimmy.

And ɛo, together, we watched the sea elephants. Now dozens of them, flopping and waddling around on the beach. "Ungainly on the land," the distinguished-sounding narrator observed, "they are nonetheless uniquely streamlined for life in the ocean." Now babies: strange little blue-black things shaped like Marisol sculptures. "This baby must find a cow willing to nurse him or face certain death," the narrator said gloomily. Now a baby flopping about in the surf. "A baby sea elephant not more than a day or two old struggles to stay afloat," said the narrator.

"Oh, look at that!" said Mary, who had just come into the ironing room. "What are they doing to it?"

A good question, for at that moment two men, each with a beard and a woolen hat, appeared on the beach and started to wrestle with the baby sea elephant. "Members of the expedition spot him and move in to help," said the narrator as the two men carried the baby sea elephant from the water and dumped it into a group of sea elephants on the sand. "The milk the pups consume —estimated at half a gallon a day—is extremely rich in fat," said the narrator.

Mary said, "Imagine that."

And so it went. The sea elephants, both small and large, waddled and flopped about on the beach. Some grunted. Some swam in the water. The distinguished-sounding narrator—a learned but invisible presence on the remote and rock-strewn beach—spoke to us with a subtle mixture of charm and scientific detachment: "This old bull swims with an apparent lack of effort, yet he is capable of diving to a depth of one thousand feet and can suspend breathing for five minutes before coming up for air."

"That's extraordinary," said Bill, who had also come into the room, carrying a six-pack of beer.

"Five minutes isn't long," said Jimmy. "The humpback whale can stay down for forty-five minutes."

The assembled sea elephants now grew even noisier. "Responding to the seductive calls of the females," said the narrator, "a bull heads into the frenzy of mating."

Enormous sea elephants now crashed and bumped about on the beach. One huge creature, doubtless a bull, slumped peacefully over a rock, looking something like a beanbag chair.

In the half darkness of the room, I was aware of the three other faces watching the television screen. At first, I was struck by a certain obvious irony in the situation. Here we were, after all, gathered in this windowless room watching filmed scenes of distant animals while actual animals wandered about in the fields below, begging for attention. I wondered what had happened to the lame deer on the hillside, and guessed the unbeguiling answer. It had vanished as quickly and discreetly as it had arrived; nor, it occurred to me, had it been exactly begging for attention. I thought: in any case, there will be other deer coming to the hillside, to eat the hay or the tulips, to visit, to be part of Jimmy's priceless heritage. And then I thought: perhaps not, or perhaps not for long; certainly not forever.

I remembered, long ago, as a child of more or less Jimmy's age, visiting, with my mother, some of her kinfolk who lived in the French countryside. There was a large, cold, stone house; fireplaces and fires; snow on the fields and trees. One afternoon of a slow December day, my grandfather and I went on a jaunt together, up the hill back of the house, across endless fields, through woods where pine branches spilled snow on our heads. He was a tall, white-haired gentleman of few words, and wore knickerbockers, as I remember, and immense boots. At last, we came through the woods and into a clearing. The sky was piercing blue. There was another stand of dark trees on the horizon, about a mile away. On our journey, some snow had got in between my socks and my boots, for the boots were borrowed from a cousin and were much too large, and now I tried to squidge my feet around inside the boots without attracting attention. I felt my grandfather's hand on my shoulder and stopped squidging my feet. He was pointing across the clearing, to the right. Perhaps two dozen deer were crossing the snowy field: dark, delicate animals with spindly legs. And now, breaking off from the herd, a large stag came toward us. He stopped not far from where we stood. I remember him as huge, with flowering antlers; he seemed to float above the snow. He stood there for I don't know how long, staring, it seemed, at my old grandfather, and my grandfather stared at him, and then the stag moved away, drifting back to the herd, and led the herd slowly across the clearing and into the fastness of the woods, and then my grandfather turned me about and we trudged home. Ten years later, after the war, with my grandfather dead, and the woods cleared to make way for an army supply depot, and with the old stone house sold to an executive of a nearby chemical company, we went back there briefly to pick up some things, though what things I can't recall. I remember my grandfather's hunting trophies—mounted heads of deer and mountain sheep, and even one water buffalo—lying in a jumble on the floor of an empty room. "He loved hunting," my mother said. "He could have taught you a lot about it." I was eighteen at the time and full of sensibility, and those dusty animal heads seemed to me quite horrible and wasteful; I felt ashamed for my grandfather. But in due course a stronger memory took over: a residue of the emotion I had been aware of in that long-ago winter meeting between the old hunter and the stag, standing in the snow. It was nothing, I imagine, so sentimental as love of wildlife, for there had been too much killing for much love to have survived, but, rather—so I like to think, anyway —the mysterious fellow-feeling (that doubtless does not exclude either love or fear or wonder) of one earthly species for another.

In fact, in the end, it seems to me that it is this deep fellow-feeling that transcends all the obvious and commonplace ironies of man's recent relationships with animals, whether the relationship occurs nobly or murderously (depending on one's current point of view), as it is said to occur between hunters and their quarry; or awkwardly and trivially, as generally happens when a city parent takes a city child to observe the despondent inhabitants of the local zoo; or somewhat pompously, in a manner redolent of utilitarianism and scientific superego, as in the current vogue for subjecting animals to scientific study on behalf of humankind. It is as if man still could not get rid of animals from his soul, though he has killed them for his food and exploited them for his work and made amusements of them for his sport, and steadily reduced their territories through the growth of his own territories, and implacably reduced their population by the enlargement of his own population. Each step along the path that he has taken in his push to reduce the wilderness seems to have brought with it a counterstep, so to speak—never, of course, adequate to what has been taken away but expressive, often in bizarre and unlikely ways, of the guilt and loss he appears to feel for the "others." For instance, after the Americans had stripped the buffalo from the plains (as Neil Harris has pointed out), they created a strange modern totem to the power of the vanished beasts in the form of Buffalo Bill Cody and his hugely popular Wild West show. And, at a time when the white man was beginning to impose his will in earnest upon the "dark continent" of Africa and its wildlife, the totemic figure of Tarzan was created, speaking to us of a land whose animalism was supposedly so potent that it could transform an English gentleman into an ape (or, at least, a half ape) in a few years; and, later, King Kong, whose primitive power was supposedly nearly equal to that of a modern state (at any rate, minus its air force). And all the while, the strange, haunted, sometimes brutal, sometimes well-meaning process of the ghettoization of wild animal life has continued. First, after the advanced peoples cleared their own territories of wildlife, came the zoos and menageries and animal shows of the last century. Then, as the advanced peoples pushed farther into remote territories, notably into Africa, came the segregation of those animals in areas where they might be hunted. Then, as the number of huntable animals was dangerously reduced, and as the number of transportable, nonhunting, animal-interested tourists increased, came the establishment of nonhunting (or photo-safari) ghettos. Indeed, many, perhaps most, nations, recognizing the impossibility or inadvisability of wild animals continuing to run wild, have erected their own animal ghettos, be they, as in this country, large and government-operated, like Yellowstone National Park, or small and commercial, like Sea World or Marineland. There are ghettos now for waterfowl, for alligators, for elk, for sea otters; although, as in the case of human ghettos, many of the animal ghettos are under increasing pressure from the rising numbers and commercial demands of the surrounding populations. According to recent reports, for instance, the clam diggers in California are up in arms against the protected sea otters off Pismo Beach; in Kenya, farmers, both black and white, are putting pressure on the government to do something about the obstreperous elephants in the Tsavo game park, which have been breaking out of the park and trampling farmland underfoot. Thus, finally, it seems, not so much owing to his wisdom (which is not greatly to be relied on in these matters) as perhaps in response to these age-old and persistent stirrings in his soul, man, who apparently cannot do *without* wild animals and cannot live *with* them, has devised the last animal ghetto: the television zoo.

Or so I thought, watching the sea elephants cavorting on Bill and Mary's television screen, and so I have thought since, remembering the beauty and oddity, however "distanced" by camera lens or electronic transmission, of the many images of wildlife that I have seen on other television screens. In some ways, doubtless, it is not such a great accomplishment. Man has killed off most of the wildlife on the planet, so now he dispatches little bands of TV explorers to remote islands or far-off rain forests, from which they return with images of wildlife, which they can bring to us at home. We stay put; the zoo comes to visit. Still, in other ways—and not unimportant ways, either—the new process seems but another link in what one rather hopes is a never-ending chain of man's attempts to deal with not only his presence but the implications of his presence on this planet. I even thought (mindful that in the stern temple of the ironing room such a thought might be construed as close to blasphemy by my hosts) that television itself, despite its frequent trashiness and steady banality, may perhaps be already serving as a socializing (dare one say civilizing?) force, in ways that modern peoples can so far scarcely imagine.

At any rate, on the rocky island of the sea elephants, our TV explorers were winding up their activities, and trying to have the last word, as usual. One of the bearded and wool-hatted men advanced along the beach, carrying a loudspeaker that was emitting sounds that seemed to be driving the sea elephants into the water. "The noise of the loudspeaker is regarded as a threat by the bulls," explained the distinguished narrator. Then there were some beautiful sequences of sea elephants swimming underwater: giant Marisol sculptures gliding through the deep. Then, above water, a parting shot of the rocky island and of the sea elephants once again flopping around in the surf, as the narrator, no stranger to the poetic impulse, declaimed, "We salute you, our ancient cousin of the sea!" Soon afterward, the zoo closed for the night.

Somebody switched on a light in the room; it had grown dark outside.

"I want to see the deer," Jimmy said.

"The deer left," said Mary. "But don't worry—he'll be back."

"I wasn't worried," said Jimmy, who may even be right, for the time being.

(1979)

SMOOTH PEBBLES AT SOUTHFORK

IT'S EASY to see why *Dallas* is one of the most popular shows in the country. It's juicily wicked, with plenty of Hollywood-style shimmer: all those designer dresses and helicopter-mounted hunting parties. Larry Hagman as bad J. R. Ewing is a most satisfying villain, especially in an era when heroes, anointed with the blessings of ambivalence, have all the good lines and evil is commonly represented by inarticulate psychopaths; Hagman's J.R. has a touch of Tennessee Williams's mean-weak young Southern gentlemen, a touch of old, snarly Dan Duryea, and a good deal of his own soft, spacey charm. Even the *Dallas* women hold their positions on the court better than most TV-pretty actresses, though the young ones all rather look alike; there's nothing really sexy ever going on, but there's a sort of subdued, genteel, panting quality in most of the episodes that keeps things interesting.

A lot of people seem to think of *Dallas* as soap opera —"prime-time soap opera" is what one of the news magazines called it a while ago—and one can hardly blame them. The hour-long scripts abound in infidelities and double-dealings of various kinds, and few of the principal characters appear to enjoy many moments of serenity—even a quiet evening at home now and then— free from the ravages of treachery and tantrum. Of course, "soap opera" has come to be one of those catch-all terms, applied to just about anything that seems to have a strong emotional or melodramatic tilt to it; I remember, for instance, President Nixon's "final days" and the BBC's version of *Anna Karenina* both being described as soap operas. But what is interesting, I think, about *Dallas* is the degree to which it *doesn't* resemble soap opera—at least, classic soap opera. In classic soap opera, after all, the fun is in the interaction of the characters, but what makes the whole thing work is the stability of the social framework: what used to be called the "manners" of society. In the early radio soaps, and in the famous television soaps of the nineteen-fifties and sixties, these social conventions provided a framework not only for the story but also for the characters' emotions—an electrical field of force, as it were, that remained in place and that the characters bounced off (usually into one another) in a more or less continuing process. The key element was the *stability* of the framework, the established and agreed-upon nature of the rules. Thus, in classic soap opera, when a wife was unfaithful to her husband she knew with reasonable exactitude (as did the audience) how her husband and the community would respond to her infidelity. Frequently, the "manners" of the soap-opera story didn't correspond precisely to the "manners" of the audience, but that wasn't the point. The point was that for the story to make sense it needed limits; then the fun could begin, as the wife contrived to make a fool of her husband, or was tormented by guilt, and so forth. In this sense, all drama of manners—be it American soap opera, British drawing-room comedy, or Japanese *Noh* play—is a story of prisoners in a jail whose walls proclaim that certain things are *done* and certain things *not done*. Think of *As the World Turns*, or the plays of

Noël Coward, or *All in the Family*. Ostensibly, this last program enjoyed its tremendous success because of Norman Lear's masterly creation of the Archie Bunker family, because of the funny, pungent scripts, and because of the first-rate ensemble acting of the four principals. But surely the series worked as well as it did, and for as long as it did, because Lear had the good sense to preserve the social essence of Johnny Speight's *Till Death Us Do Part*, the BBC series on which *All in the Family* was based, and which was intrinsically a comedy of manners: a drama of prisoners, first of the larger world of social conventions, then of the smaller world of family roles. At any given moment in *All in the Family*, you knew exactly where Archie stood, where Edith stood, where Meathead stood, where Gloria stood. There were playful surprises but no real surprises. The framework was in place; the situation was stabilized.

Dallas seems to be different. Here it's not that the drama lacks "manners" but that the "manners" don't constitute a framework; at any rate, it's not a framework of any strength or consistency. In *Dallas*, when a wife cheats on her husband, neither she nor her husband nor anyone else, including the audience, can be sure how the other parties will respond. For example, when Bobby (J.R.'s more or less good brother) suspects that his wife, Pam, is planning to have an affair with her boss during a forthcoming business trip to Paris, he neither confronts her with his suspicions nor believes her unsolicited protestations of fidelity; then, on her departure, he takes up with an old girlfriend who happens along— and rather stoically won't sleep with her. What behavior pattern is this? Mere ambivalence? What code of manners is Bobby plugged into? Obviously, a code full of loopholes, but then most codes of manners contain a few loopholes. Essentially, one imagines, it is a code whose specifics are in a state of flux or suspension—a code in which the rules have become destabilized and the players are making them up as they go along.

Sometimes this improvisational quality adds a certain laid-back contemporaneity to the proceedings; at other times, though, it introduces an almost goofy absence of logic into an otherwise rational structure. Sue Ellen and J.R., for example, clearly have one of the worst marriages in North America. He constantly lies to her, betrays her, threatens her, and for the rest of the time has nothing to do with the poor woman. In turn, she lies to him, betrays him, is desperately trying to get a divorce, and is currently having him tailed by a private investigator. It is scarcely the relationship of two lovebirds; moreover, the wretched condition of their marriage is no secret to anyone else in the family. But when one evening, out of the blue, Sue Ellen, with inexplicable sweetness, gives a surprise anniversary party for her swinish mate (her secret motive is that she will use the party as evidence of wifely loyalty in the divorce proceedings), not one of the other characters so much as blinks an eye or seems to think the homey little event at all strange or out of the ordinary. Family, in-laws, and friends stand about complaisantly, holding their cocktail glasses, like a new kind of Greek chorus that isn't into tipping off the audience about what's really going on; or like townspeople in a Western movie who have temporarily lost track of the moral drift of the situation. In fact, as an indication of the vagueness that shrouds the Ewings from time to time, J.R. not only doesn't find the party at all strange himself but suddenly concludes that it's a jolly invitation from Sue Ellen (whose private investigator he has just laid a trap for) to a lovers' roll in the hay, which he thereupon proposes —and is astonished and resentful at being turned down.

The characters in *Dallas* are liberated from having to relate to a consistent perspective. They're also free to reinvent themselves, even from moment to moment. Consider the rapid and rather whimsical shift in what had seemed to be a close relationship between Ray and Donna. Ray is the blond, good-looking manager of Southfork, the Ewing ranch, and Donna is the equally blond and good-looking young widow whom he has long had a crush on. At the beginning of their courtship, Ray appears very much the confident, laconic Westerner. He's the kind that don't say much, though he's strong and decent—a likely match for Donna, who is described as "active in state politics." But no sooner does he get things going with Donna than he starts turning into Hamlet. Donna gives a party—not a real party; a cozy little dinner, with Ray and a couple of political friends, both of them Texans, real easy folks, not exactly your Galbraith and Schlesinger crowd—and before you know it, Ray has become all shy and dithery. First, he murmurs that the only thing he knows to talk about is ranch management. Then, he allows as how he feels all out of place, and so forth. If a Texas cowboy could pout, Ray comes close to pouting. The fact is that he has suddenly stopped being a Texas cowboy, even a Texan. The framework has bent again, which means that Donna is soon floating off into undiscovered or improvised territory. Since Ray won't marry her—being true to his new Hamlet role, and apparently unaware of the thousands of cowboys who have had working wives, sometimes even educated working wives—a still more unlikely scene ensues when she goes to Ray's boss, old Jock Ewing, the family patriarch, and tries to persuade *him* to lean on Ray a little bit. Fortunately, Jock's role is still stabilized at this point, so he sends her packing.

Soap operas are almost never dreams. Daydreams, maybe: suppose the handsome doctor falls in love with the nurse; suppose the cute secretary steals the boss's affections. But most soap operas are too pragmatic to exist on a dream plane; they are too full of the nuts and bolts of daily life. A good example of a classic, down-to-earth soap was the English *Upstairs, Downstairs*: that finely detailed rendering of the comings and goings of the Bellamy family and their servants in Edwardian England, which was such a hit with the American vid-lit audience when it was rebroadcast here by the Not Yet Ready for the Public television system a few years back. I've seen it suggested (I think by the Washington *Post*'s perceptive Richard Cohen) that *Dallas* is a sort of home-grown, American version of *Upstairs, Downstairs*. It's certainly true that *Dallas* is *ours*, and though a case might be made for the fact that *Upstairs, Downstairs* was also ours, the comparison is an interesting one. All the same, my guess is that a closer kin to *Upstairs, Downstairs* might be *All in the Family*, for the two dramas share not only a rigid and coherent structure of manners but also a fondness for the grit and texture of social detail. When Lady Bellamy went on a trip, everything was done just right: the trunks, the packing, the right clothes for the voyage, the right clothes for the bottom of the trunk, the tissue paper for inside the sleeves. Similarly, when Edith Bunker gave a Tupperware party, not only did she have a complete set—and of the newest

line—of Tupperware laid out on the table, but the
Tupperware lady herself was on hand to make sure that
Edith arranged things properly. But, unlike *Upstairs,
Downstairs* and *All in the Family* and any number of
recent television series that seem resolutely prosy, even
journalistic, in their attention to detail, *Dallas* for the
most part seems happily unfactual, undetailed, smooth,
dreamlike. Some of the dream, of course, derives from
the movie version of Edna Ferber's *Giant*: that huge
Victorian house rising out of the flat Texas landscape in
the middle of nowhere. The Ewings' ranch house is certainly cast in the same image, but, as the advertising
people say, it is definitely downscale from *Giant*. Large
but not huge; white, serene, and grandly suburban, the
Ewing domicile floats on a lake of pale-green lawn beneath a pale-blue sky; a dream not so much of oil or
Texas or ranching as of American executive life. The
Ewing driveway looks like one of those tasteful car
commercials. Meals are genteelly taken on the Ewing
patio. Now and then, as if surprised by the camera, a
Chicano servant is glimpsed in the background (somebody, presumably, has to pick up after the Ewings), but
fleetingly, shyly, as if "they" weren't really there, or
at least all took the bus back to town after work. It
could be anywhere. Lake Forest: the Ewings of Lake
Forest. It's hard to imagine that people watch *Dallas*
because it's so American; there's no "downstairs" in
evidence at Southfork, and the "upstairs" is alternately
neurotic and criminal. Still, all the people in the audience who *aren't* corporate executives can probably get
off on seeing what a mess those upscale Ewings make of
things. All that boozing and sleeping around and driving
full-size cars with rock-bottom EPA ratings. Gold Amer-

ican Express cards sure don't buy a person happiness, do they?

Dallas isn't grainy, like real soap opera. It's smooth, like a river pebble, like a dream. Its characters don't so much lack manners as lack a stable relationship to manners. Young and old, new rich and old rich, good and bad share this stripped-down, improvisational quality. People make up "conventional" behavior on the spur of the moment. Consider, for example, the curious matter of the paternity complications that surround Sue Ellen's baby. What's not especially curious are the paternity complications themselves, for we've been led to believe from the beginning that there was something fishy about the fathering of that child. In the first place, J.R. is as unspeakable a father as he is a husband; then, he and Sue Ellen rarely seem to be in a family-forming mood, what with his philandering and her long addiction to the bottle; then, too, there is Cliff, who is Sue Ellen's handsome and manly former lover, and who keeps popping up in the series like a jack-in-the-box. At any rate, for a variety of reasons, a story to the effect that J.R. is not the real father appears in the newspaper. So far, so good; a typically juicy *Dallas* imbroglio. But then Miss Ellie gets into the act. Miss Ellie, of course, is the beloved matriarch of the Ewings. Once upon a time, if memory serves, Barbara Bel Geddes, the daughter of the designer Norman Bel Geddes, was a movie starlet who risked the wrath of the Hollywood production code by speaking the word "virgin" aloud in a comedy called *The Moon Is Blue*. Now she plays Miss Ellie, a Texas lady of the old school. She has piles of money, sure; but she has standards, too. Miss Ellie rules the roost. She sets the tone. She has more than values; she has *old* values. What then is Miss Ellie's response to the paternity crisis concerning the birth of her grandchild? She gives a cocktail party. That's right. Miss Ellie, supported in her gallant moment by J.R., Sue Ellen, Bobby, Pam, etc., gives a cocktail party at Southfork, to which all Dallas society is invited. All Dallas society naturally shows up, with the result that another goofy scene takes place, in which the elegantly gowned and coiffed ladies of *tout* Dallas mill around the Ewing house with their prosperous husbands (all of them making Sue Ellen so nervous that she spends much of the party on the phone to Dusty, her current lover) until the arrival of the Ewing lawyer with the latest blood-test results. These are quickly announced to the hushed and assembled cocktailers, and prove to the surprise of everyone (not least Sue Ellen and J.R.) that J.R. is indeed the father of his child.

The character of Miss Ellie, in this instance, was clearly destabilized; old values, new values, and no values were whirling around as in a kitchen blender. But what's interesting is the degree to which *Dallas* has managed to attune itself to an intrinsically destabilized view of manners and social conventions while remaining perfectly on-target with its audience. The Ewings are our foremost pioneers in this new field of behavioral improvisation, though they are no longer alone. For example, not only does Billy Ikehorn, the heroine of the mini-series *Scruples* (based with extreme and scholarly fidelity on Judith Krantz's novel of that name), travel light—another pebble-smooth, untextured creature hurtling through time warps of social convention with no aerodynamic drag—but her behavior patterns seem to be imprinted on a continually changing assortment of re-placeable computer chips. To begin with, we are told that Billy is by birth "a Winthrop"—albeit a poor Winthrop. Aside from the fact that to be even a poor Winthrop in America is presumably to carry with one a greater imprint of social definition than, say, a Rocke-feller (at least, as Rockefellers have reportedly found out from time to time on marrying Winthrops), from a less genealogically specialized point of view there are still a number of possibilities for good old-fashioned melodramatic conflict: for instance, the girl of simple virtue who rebels against the upper-crust pretensions of her rich relatives. But no such luck. Billy is quite happy being a Winthrop; the only problem is being a poor Winthrop. Accordingly, she marries a tough old Jewish tycoon from Southern California and becomes rich; and when he dies she opens a fancy Beverly Hills super-boutique called Scruples and becomes even richer.

As success stories go, this is a fine one, and in other times, one imagines, a best-selling novelist might have focused on Billy's fairly remarkable journey from Win-throp Country to Mr. Ikehorn's bed and then to Scruples. But in our present era of social aerodynamics such journeys are apparently no problem, nothing special, not really interesting. The content level is probably too high or else too grainy. What we see of Billy's story, at any rate, are endless scenes of Billy's rich, good life, pre-sented mostly in the form of a continuing sequence of quasi-television commercials in which the stylishly dressed participants give surface evidence of belonging to recognized social groups and being connected to com-prehensible systems of manners while in fact they are floating free—not merely of background but of behavior. The computer chips seem to get switched in and out as the occasion warrants.

At one point, for example, Billy, recently widowed and visiting in the South of France, is invited to a dinner party given by some swanky Hollywood people. Billy's arrival at the party is a car commercial. Billy herself is a clothes commercial. The setting for the party is a champagne commercial. Clearly, it is a fancy affair, with all the guests dressed to the nines, and with the social-minded hostess fussing around about the seating arrangements for dinner. Billy, being a Winthrop by birth and educated at the poshest of schools, normally takes a back seat to no one in matters of etiquette; just by looking at her, one knows she is a lady who can tell a fish knife from a salad fork. But just before dinner—the much-discussed seated dinner—Billy bumps into a young fellow she takes a fancy to, and off they wander to spend the evening by themselves. Granted, there's a venerable Hollywood tradition that enables high-spirited young lovers to turn up their noses at stuffy old people's parties, but in this case there's nothing very rebellious or high-spirited about Billy's departure. The two of them would just rather be somewhere else—in a French bistro commercial, as it turns out. Neither Billy nor her well-dressed escort seem to see anything worth remarking on in their casual departure from the party. For that matter, the fussy hostess doesn't seem to care much either that two of her favorite guests have disappeared, so to speak, into the bushes. Evidently, by then she's floating, too.

Like Miss Ellie and the *Dallas* gang, Billy Ikehorn, the hostess, and the rest of the *Scruples* crowd drift in and out of various conceptions of proper behavior as if they were trying on clothes. Since the characters are destabilized, they can do anything. But since they answer neither to God nor to any known framework of social conventions, it's hard to know whom or what they do answer to. "Themselves" is probably the missing word, but since these new selves consist of such replaceable circuitry it's not easy to know what that means, either. In an earlier scene in *Scruples*, when Billy is in California with her husband, who is barely alive after a stroke, she tires of hanging around the house and one evening accepts an invitation from her sick husband's male nurse to an all-night party that he and some pals are giving—which she blithely attends, and where she is drugged and messed around with. I guess it's possible that the wife of a barely alive Southern California industrialist might accept from someone who was not only an employee but also a virtual stranger an invitation to an all-night party in another stranger's house. Still, one imagines that there might be a certain eccentricity attached to the act. Where there's no framework and no code, however, there can't be eccentricity. In any event, Billy Ikehorn, as far as one can tell, is regarded by herself and all the other characters in *Scruples* as completely normal, well-behaved, even proper. Once a Winthrop, as the saying goes, always a Winthrop. Similarly, the Ewings of Southfork, while periodically prone to helpless bouts of infidelity and private naughtiness, nonetheless seem to regard themselves, at least in social terms, as models of decorum and correctly observed convention. When nothing has a place of its own, then everything just possibly may have a place *somewhere*. We're living in strange, smooth times, aren't we? Travelin' light, gathering no moss, making up new identities as we go along. Out in the audience, our citizens reconstitute themselves ever more rapidly according to fashion "looks" (proletarian, Russian, Chinese, Navajo, cowboy, preppy), and search for texture in the feel of denim, in imported whole-wheat bread, in the vibrations of stereo tracks. Meanwhile, our new television favorites float free above their glossy plots: figures without background or definition, without entries in their passports. In other words, ourselves aerodynamically advanced, we cheer the streamlined, destabilized characters we so resemble. Who'd want it any other way?

(1980)

HYPE IN THE SNOW

ALTHOUGH it's hard to pick a Special Sportscasting Moment from this winter's Olympic Games, a likely candidate might be the time, a few evenings ago, when one of the knowledgeable TV commentators up in Lake Placid remarked knowledgeably to his companion that "the great thing about the Olympics this year is that everyone gets to have a different favorite Olympic event," thus giving the lie, if you will pardon the expression, to an idea that many of us were brought up on, though clearly in less complex times; namely, that everyone always has to have the *same* favorite Olympic event. Such as the exciting downhill ski race, which this year, to judge from ABC's clever use of advanced tape-editing techniques, was dominated by Franz Klammer's 1976 victory at Innsbruck. To have seen the splendid yellow-suited Klammer once, hurtling and bouncing downhill on his skis, is to have seen him a hundred times, accompanied by the breathless four-year-old commentary of Bob Beattie and Frank Gifford, all of it fresh as a daisy and none the worse for wear after being packed on ice and lightly salted for the past four years. No matter that the event is somewhat archival. Klammer is a great competitor, and since his trip down the mountain in 1976 lasted less than two minutes, one can hardly begrudge him a Proustian share of viewing time in 1980. But perhaps you were wondering about my own favorite Olympic event. Was it the speed skating, *par exemple*? After all, how splendid for America, at a time when the old bald eagle is beset by sinister forces abroad and the incredible shrinking dollar bill at home, to watch that unbelievably muscular young Eric Heiden gliding along on the icy oval, and gliding along, and gliding along, and gliding along, and gliding along. Somebody (was it August Strindberg?) once asked why there was such a scarcity, almost a dearth, of great novels—or, certainly, plays—on the subject of speed skating, and though there is no ready reply even now to the famed Swedish dramatist's question (should he have been the one, after all, to raise it), it is possible that sports that contain an excess of *gliding along* are not easily translatable to the imaginative realm. So much for the strange fascination that Eric Heiden held for August Strindberg, though the two never, to the best of my knowledge, actually met. Ships that pass in the night, as it were. For a while, I thought that my favorite Olympic event was going to be ski jumping, but it appears that somebody has changed the design of ski-jump courses in recent years so as to minimize the effect of *thudding* from great heights onto the snow—an effect that was long an intrinsic source of awestruck fascination to spectators of the sport. Of course, today's ski jumpers hurtle down a fearfully steep incline, and they could always thud onto that, but instead they usually soar out and out—not an unthrilling spectacle by any means—and because, alas, somebody (the jump designers, or possibly the ski jumpers' parents) has somehow either raised the landing ground or lowered the soaring angle, the spectacle is altogether different. Very skillful, to be sure. Generally excellent. But somehow deficient in the possibility of *thudding*. Another instance, if you will, of the careless demolition of old values in the service of a new technology. Briefly, I considered transferring my favorite-event allegiance to pair figure skating. This was while I believed that *we* stood a chance in the competition. This was while I was being led to believe that *we* did *not* stand a chance in the hockey, which is also very exciting, even though it lacks background music. This was while I was being nudged and chivied and generally pushed around by the ABC commentators to put my spectatorly emotions on the line for America's leading pair-figure-skating duo, Tai Babilonia and Randy Gardner. The rest is part of pair-figure-skating history, as everyone knows. I put my emotions on the line, or I was all set to put them on the line. They were very close to the line. And then occurred that dreadful moment in pair-figure-skating annals, when Tai Babilonia and Randy Gardner had to withdraw on account of injury! I'm telling you, I thought ABC handled its disappointment very well. As things were, I was extremely sorry not to see Tai Babilonia and Randy Gardner do their stuff, but later I realized (possibly no more than a rationalization) that it would have been even worse—wouldn't it?—to have watched them, and to have listened to all those wonderful semiclassical selections, and then perhaps see them lose to the stuck-up Russians, with their murkily recorded disco.

So let me tell you my this year's favorite Olympic event. It is the cross-country biathlon; I may not have got some of those words quite right. At any rate, it is clearly a fascinating event that combines, according to a report I am reading in *TV Guide*, elements of cross-country skiing and rifle shooting. Imagine that! The best of both possible worlds. On the one hand, a little small-arms fire definitely raises the interest level of cross-country skiing, while all that vaguely lyric, somewhat frostbitten whoosh-whooshing along on the snow on tiny, *thin* skis certainly softens and enhances, in my opinion, some of the horrider aspects of popping off guns in the woods. Mind you, I have not watched the cross-country biathlon at present writing, but I am very much looking forward to it. Indeed, it occurs to me that when the next Winter Olympics are held, in 1984 (Aha! An irony there!), the sagacious Olympic Committee, meeting, as it does, in the watery caverns of Atlantis, may see fit to combine many—even *all*—of the events with a bit of rifle shooting. Speed skating, for example. Or that peculiar giant slalom, with all the zigging and zagging and whooshing and zigging and zagging and whooshing, and with the little numbers showing the giant slalomers' time being displayed so interestingly and so accurately against the snow. Imagine how a couple of random rifle shots would add to the mystery and drama of that event! But it would have to be done *just right*, keeping true to the Olympic ideal, and not pushing too far into the shadowy realms of entertainment-for-its-own-sake, which I know even the ABC sportscasters are very much against. Still, I bet we are the nation that could pull it off. Also, there is always the possibility that, armed to the teeth and firing cheerfully from the hip, as it were, we might win a freedom-loving-though-defense-minded superpower's proper quota of medals, for a change.

(1980)

THE BIG PARADE

THE OSCAR ceremonies have come and gone, drawing the usual enormous television audience, and afterward evoking the usual round of learned exegesis from various quarters. For instance, Mr. Vincent Canby, the *Times*'s estimable cinema scribe, has found in the latest awards ceremony a sort of medieval, or perhaps Oriental (or perhaps medieval Oriental), parable wherein television is the devouring beast and the movie industry is the main dish, thus ending up as "a large lump in the belly of the python called television." On the other hand, Miss Glenda Jackson, the actress, while detecting no indications of pythonlike engorgement in the event, or being too ladylike to mention them if she did, discovered a certain "public hanging" tone in the ceremonies, whereby, so she thought, members of the television audience were placed in the position of voyeurs observing the pain or embarrassment of the losers. Clearly, the Oscar ritual lies very close to what Mr. William Gass once described, though in a different context, as "the heart of the heart of the country," with many of those who watch seeing in it whatever they choose to see, be it a python or a gallows or pie in the sky.

Still, I appreciate Mr. Canby's vision of the gobbling up of the mighty motion-picture industry by the apparently even mightier process of television. Television has been widely observed to have taken over many of the native ceremonies of American life—notably, politics and sports—and surely countless citizens share Mr. Canby's feelings about the monster in our midst whose appetite is so gargantuan that it must relentlessly consume everything within sight. In fact, it's hard to challenge the basic truth of such a view, for obviously something has been happening to ceremony and ritual since television came on the scene. In sports and politics, for example, it is clear that things were one way before television and now are a different way after its arrival. In both cases, traditional and once venerated rituals appear to have been overwhelmed by television and then reshaped and redefined according to television's forms and time requirements. The Oscar ceremonies, too, like the national political conventions, have become increasingly fine-tuned and overdirected, until the point of both events often seems to be no more (and no less) than their televisability: having all the participants there on schedule, looking right and saying the right kind of thing for the right length of time. In this regard, I can't say that I really agree with Miss Jackson's observations—at least, not on the basis of historical Oscar scholarship—for it strikes me that year by year, as Mr. Canby's python has ingested more and more of the Academy Awards into its gullet, there have been fewer and fewer opportunities for voyeurism on the part of the audience. In the first place, today's show-business celebrities, major and minor, are much better trained at bringing off public ceremonial than they used to be. Gone are those annual Hollywood parodies of golf-club trophy dinners, with their cheery, blowsy atmosphere of booze, smoke, bad jokes, and overstuffed gowns. Nowadays the actors and actresses sit there, row by row in the Chandler Pavilion, as if dressed in crinolines and velvet suits and balancing teacups on their knees, staring straight ahead or now and then making discreet conversation with their companions.

In the second place, if by chance an embittered and rejected nominee for Best Supporting Actor should be pushed beyond the limits of reason—like the Phantom of the Opera—to the point of attempting to saw off a chandelier above the assembled multitude or of biting a veteran producer on the arm, it seems certain that the TV cameras (which at the Oscar ceremonies appear to be operated by the same men who work the sidelines at a football game and who always know when to swivel their lenses away from injuries or painful moments) would never give us a look at it but instead would quickly cut to a commercial, and then back to Johnny Carson, who would produce an off-the-cuff, quite funny joke while the poor fellow was being carted off to the Chandler Institute for Deranged Best Supporting Actors.

The truth is, though, that if Mr. Canby's simile of devourment seems accurate in a number of ways, in certain other ways it is probably a bit misleading, because what it implies is that television is some sort of *deus ex machina* that has landed from who knows where upon our peaceful planet and has begun to work its will rapidly and inexorably upon the sacred institutions of American life—for instance, taking the mystery out of political conventions, messing around with the hallowed orthodoxy of the baseball schedule, and either banalizing or overproducing the Oscars. This view of technology as the proverbial monster that threatens to get out of control and destroy its master has a certain surface logic to it, in the sense that technology does seem to change one's life, sometimes for the better and sometimes for the worse, and that the people in charge of it don't always know what they're doing. But, alas, although it would probably be reasonably comforting, at least to the re-

maining Calvinists in our midst, to believe it was technology that brought human incompetence and arrogance
to our planet, there seems little real evidence that these
are novel aspects of man's nature, recently called into
being by mechanical invention, or that mankind's enduring penchant for creating monsters—be they Medusa or
Dr. Frankenstein's creature or The Thing From Outer
Space—indicates anything but its enduring effort to
distance and thus somehow deal with its own fears about
itself. Television has certainly marched into American
life with what seems to be an imperial authority, yet
what is worth noting is the degree to which it clumsily
struggles to adjust to the changing ethos of our society.
Obviously, this isn't so in every respect. Despite the
ongoing prattle of network philosophers to the effect that
television gives the public what it wants, in all too many
instances its alleged gifts to the public are shoddy or
self-serving or at any rate do minimum justice to the
intellectual and emotional resources of the vast audience. We don't see on television an exact mirror image
of what we are, or even of what we want. But for the
most part what we get is a general version, a crude but
by no means inaccurate approximation, of what our society perceives as being important.

Thus, the Oscars. To all appearances, this is a purely
theatrical event, taking place in a theatrical setting and
involving theatrical (i.e., show-business) participants.
But think for a moment of the Oscar ceremonies as a
slightly different form of ritual: a parade or procession;
in fact, a ceremonial parade. The other day, as it happens, while leafing through some old books I had brought
down from the top shelf of my bookcase, I came across
a singular volume that I don't think I had opened since

I'd picked it up years ago for ninety-five cents at some secondhand bookstore. The book is long and narrow, bound in some kind of blue leather, but very faded and rather tattered, and its title is: *A Record of Events Connected with the Death and Funeral of Her Late Majesty Queen Victoria and the Accession of His Majesty King Edward VII.*

The book itself is of no literary consequence; indeed, I don't imagine that it has much collector's value either, since they must have printed them up by the board foot at the time. What it is, in fact, is a fifty-nine-page account of the parades and processions with which the British commemorated two of the events that seemed important to them at the beginning of this century, and I mention it here because its dry, formal contents seem to speak so clearly (and in such a self-confident, matter-of-fact voice) of a period not all that long ago when things were done so differently from the way we do them now. What's interesting, I think, isn't so much the specifics of royal death and accession as the glimpses provided of the forms and rituals that people employed for honoring the serious things of life. Chiefly, this was by parades. All across Europe in its imperial age, parades were held not out of quaintness or a nostalgia for the picturesque as they are now, but as a matter of course. Consider the structure of these lengthy, over-dressed, and unwieldy processions. Essentially, of course, they were huge linear displays, wherein the spectators remained stationary, aligned on either side of the great avenues, while the participants (who were perceived as being the important persons of their era) passed by and displayed themselves. And who were these important persons? In the first rank there were

Sovereigns; then Royal Highnesses; then Serene Highnesses; then military grandees; then troops; then military animals; then military machines. At Queen Victoria's funeral, for example, the relatively modest Burial Procession at Frogmore (the last of five Processions that had been held in a space of four days) consisted of such carefully ranked diverse elements as the Grenadier Guards, the Highlanders, the Royal Servants, the Bishop of Winchester, a Gun Carriage drawn by eight horses of the Royal Horse Artillery, four Sovereigns, one Queen, twenty-five Royal Highnesses, four Serene Highnesses, several Dukes, various Excellencies, select Visitors such as Count de Filcaho, Flügel-Adjutant Kraemer, the Munshi Abdul Karim, C.V.O., the Dean of Windsor and the Choir, and a battery of Royal Horse Artillery and eighty-one guns that were fired preceding a rendering by the Choir of the anthem (surely an endearing choice) "Man That Is Born of a Woman." Well, that was in February 1901, and while it is often hard to tell whether or not we have greatly advanced in time from that era, we commonly appear to be in a very different place. At any rate, we still have parades, but they seem to have changed greatly in form as well as content. In fact, we have parades constantly, and I don't mean those folkloric, largely anachronistic parades on St. Patrick's Day and Armed Forces Day and the like, but the real parades of our era—the parades that the populace wholeheartedly turns out for: the Emmy ceremonies and the Grammys and the Tonys and, of course, the big one, the Oscars. For, as has been well noted, our important persons are no longer sovereigns, or even heads of state (who are presumably tainted by too much secularism or bloodshed or boringness), but figures from the entertainment world. And our processional avenues are no longer the streets of our great cities but the airwaves above the continents and oceans, through which images of the paraders are now displayed—in some ways closer to the audience than those dimly glimpsed figures in the gilded horse-drawn carriages, and in some ways farther away. Thus, though television appears to have changed our folk customs by transforming, for example, the Oscar ceremonies into the self-important, slickly sentimental TV package they were a few weeks ago, what seems more interesting is the way *we've* changed (while also staying the same), now goggling en masse at Raquel Welch, wafting by in a red satin jump suit, instead of, say, Her Imperial and Royal Highness the Duchess of Saxe-Coburg and Gotha, gliding by, doubtless, under thirty-five kilos of taffeta and rubies. Nowadays, at our electronic parades, nobody plays those dreary national anthems, unless you count the primitive sports events where anthems are still played, though somewhat in the nature of mantras, presumably in order to calm the athletes before the fray. Instead, through the airwaves, the studio orchestras transmit the new "Internationale" of pop music; indeed, at the Oscars five such "anthems," from five currently important "nations" (or categories) of pop music, were played at stated intervals. And these days our important persons, presumably in consequence of the same post-religious anxiety that was already evident in the Victorian era (to the effect that since one can't count on God to provide suitable rewards in the Hereafter, man had better rustle up something down here on earth), receive awards of minuscule statuary instead of medals, which (in keeping with the spirit of our superficially pacifist and only clandestinely martial epoch) are given for entertainingness on the screen rather than for valor on the field of battle—and whose recipients are revealed to the public by means of a "secret casket" (or envelope) that is first guarded by an accountant and then entrusted to a movie star or a TV celebrity.

But in the end, as is perhaps the nature of parades, the one thing that has remained more or less the same, through the passage of time and the advent of television, is the desire, at least on the part of the parade's governors, to have the parade *run right*. Thus, in 1901, after Queen Victoria's death, the great warships of the British fleet—about forty of them, accompanied by eight warships from foreign fleets—passed in their own procession from Cowes to Portsmouth, each ship first having been moored in exactly the right fashion ("Battle Ships and Cruisers moored with six shackles, Gun Boats with four shackles"), and then proceeding in exactly the right order of line, firing the right kind of guns ("Minute Guns") at the right moment ("3 o'clock p.m.") from the right place ("the side of the Ship furthest from the Procession"), with all the ships' bands instructed to play "the Funeral Marches of Chopin and Beethoven *only*." Not altogether dissimilarly, seventy-eight years later our own Personages and objects of national reverence waited at their carefully prescribed moorings in the Chandler Pavilion to float by on the stage, in the proper order, and fire off their well-timed salutes, and speak the words on the prompting machine *only*, and in general display themselves according to the present strict standards of media etiquette. Happily, however, one gathers that the veil of royal primness has not yet completely descended on our new nobility, for there is testimony that after the recent Oscar ceremonies—backstairs, as it were, out of sight of the crowds and in the presence only of the servants—the Grand Duchess of Fonda noisily berated the Marquess of Cimino for the "racist" quality of his movie *The Deer Hunter*, which, as it turned out, she had not yet seen. The Marquess's reply has become lost in the mists of time (and the servants have dutifully kept their lips zipped), but doubtless it was in keeping with the intrinsically mythic nature of the evening. Future generations, whose processions will surely take place on computer consoles in the form of a regal grouping of numbers, will doubtless make of it what they can.

(1979)

THE MOON MEN

DID YOU SEE those five Soviet dissidents on TV, the day they arrived in New York? I'd read in the *Times* that morning of their sudden release from Soviet prisons and of their hasty passage over here, but somehow I wasn't expecting them quite so routinely, so *televisably*, on the TV. Five men in dark suits, seated all in a row behind one of those familiar press-conference tables laden with wires and microphones and glasses of water, the whole scene sidling into the evening news while my wife cooked dinner. The suits had been made in Bulgaria, the *Times* reported, as if that explained something one way or the other, and maybe it did. At the televised press conference, nobody said anything about the suits, which seemed too thick and woolly to be really comfortable under the television lights; doubtless, the Bulgarian tailors had not been thinking about problems of media exposure as they stitched away at the five vestments in their proud, uncompetitive tailoring factories. The Soviet travelers sat in silence while a State Department spokesman discussed their future travel plans. There were numerous enthusiastic questions from the press, as after a notable sports triumph. No one drank the water in the glasses on the table. One would have to say that it was a mysterious though not altogether untypical contemporary event; at any rate, it felt strange to be witnessing it from the kitchen. There we were, after all, an American household in our shirt-sleeves, with our hair down, with the happy whine of the Cuisinart in the background, face to face, so to speak, with these five pale, sad men who had been living, as it were, on the moon for a significant portion of their adult lives. Let us push the metaphor a little further and state that these were moon men from the dark side of the moon. In the paper that morning there had been a wirephoto taken abroad of the five dissidents, with the picture all gray and fuzzy as wirephotos often are, giving the appearance of having been transmitted across great distances by imperfect means, and with the men themselves distinctly gray, fuzzy, and hollow-eyed in their demeanor, as well they might be considering the kind of life style they had been following until moments before the photographer showed up. But that evening on the news, the ashen-gray quality seemed to have vanished from the men around the conference table; the sense of the harsh unusual, the grainy, grim look that had peered out from the newspaper page seemed to have receded to the point of scarcely being visible. Was it gone for good, briskly scrubbed away by the color cameras and the beaming immigration officials? It seemed hard to believe that such a look in the eyes could have gone away so quickly. Of course, the travelers were now *ours*. The Soviet Union had provided them with birthplaces and hollow eyes. Bulgaria had provided them with suits, although a suit, even a Bulgarian suit, is no longer the mark of civilization that it once was. Consider that a suit is what the generous citizens of San Francisco gave to Ishi, the Stone Age Indian who stumbled out of the Sierra foothills in 1911. Today our Ishis take their suits for granted, and why not? What is so terrific or civilizing about a suit? Besides, what counts for most in the modern process of assimilation is not being suitably dressed but being properly televised. The truth is, you moon men and Stone Age warriors can no longer be really ours (and so run the risk of being practically homeless!) until you have been publicly debriefed on television; until you have sat down, alone sometimes or in a row with others to be initiated, with microphones in front of you, and TV cameras not far away, and perhaps a pitcher or so of water and some glasses on the table (a good host always offers the weary traveler a drink from his well), and then have permitted us to steal your souls. No, I hasten to correct that last suggestion. Not steal, for stealing implies a definitely covetous energy. Borrowing is probably more like it, as in our recent attempts to borrow Mr. Solzhenitsyn's soul, although that earlier moon traveler remains noticeably reluctant to lend it, preferring, one gathers, to keep it safe in his Vermont *dacha*, behind a tall wire fence, and instead to give us perverse and hardly compensatory glimpses of his attempts to be *more like us*: for example, the evolution of the Solzhenitsyn tennis game, as recently pictured in one of the news magazines, or last June's venture into Midwestern Calvinist oratory at the Harvard commencement. But what is there in Solzhenitsyn's soul, you may ask, and in the souls of these new refugees that we want to borrow? What is it we lack that these political immigrants might have to lend us? Secrets? Top-level information? Scientific know-how? Sometimes one hears solemn reference to such important considerations when moon men arrive in our midst, though it's hard to believe that any of these recent space travelers have brought with them much privileged information about valuable moon rocks or hidden moon canals to hand over to our notorious and indefatigable Bureau of Moon Secrets. Perhaps, then, our welcome is extended from pure compassion, for it is surely a well-known historical fact that our nation has been justly famous, at least from time to time, for its compassionate regard for immigrants. Still, pure compassion is possibly a sound of such delicacy as not to have been heard too frequently amid the bureaucratic grindings and clankings of even this most benign and beatific government. In the last century, for instance, our widely reported compassion for the poor and down-trodden of Europe was coincidentally and significantly alloyed with our growing need for labor. Lately, we seem to have evolved a new compassion for the politi-cally disadvantaged from all over the world (though, as before, rather more for certain species than for others; at least, there seem to be few Kurdish exiles tending bar in Miami). One wonders, then, what it is that we now need that makes us so hospitable. Of course, there is no reason to rule out generosity; generosity is bound to be present in some measure, as it was in our welcome of the European laborers in the nineteenth century. But might not the underlying psychic need now be for this: for acceptable touchstones of pain and pathos in what has come to be increasingly a smooth, trouble-free, green-golf-course countryside. We don't want too much pathos or too stark a variety of pain. We certainly don't want a whole lot of bad vibrations dumped like a sack-ful of hot potatoes into the national lap. We don't want the problems to be really *ours*. We don't want to actually taste the ashes. But to have a little distanced pain around —somebody else's, out of sight behind a wire fence in Vermont—is probably not such a bad idea; and to be able to still feel pathos—glowing somewhere out there in the American landscape—may have become almost a necessity.

At any rate, a few hours after the five dissidents had been processed through their television debriefing, my wife and I sat down to watch the television version of Maya Angelou's *I Know Why the Caged Bird Sings*, which CBS was presenting as its Saturday Night Movie. I didn't think of it as a professional assignment. It was more a matter of our having decided to stay in that evening and keep company with the kids (who naturally went out), and, if possible, watch something passably interesting on the TV. On the whole, it was one of those not-so-bad, early-summertime city nights. A small breeze blew in the open window. The cars and buses rolled rhythmically by on the avenue below. A sort of lazy quiet seemed to hover in the warm air: the Cuisinart had been hushed and put away for the night; even from the apartment next door there was a rare silence from the Stereo Bully, whose horrid sound equipment had conceivably fused itself into meltdown. In the spirit of woolgathering on the back porch, we sat at the kitchen table in our fine New York apartment and watched the story of Maya Angelou: a black girl growing up in nineteen-thirties Arkansas.

I remembered Angelou's autobiography from a few years back as having been a warm, passionate book, full of the sweetness of young spirits and the harshness of hard times. Evidently, Angelou and her co-screenwriter, Leonora Thuna, had caught the essence of the story in their television adaptation, which was narrower in range than the book but was still faithful to its original spirit. The tone of the television movie was nostalgic and affectionate. The primary relationship lay between Maya (Constance Good) and her grandmother (Esther Rolle), and the screenplay's emphasis was on the details and texture of a poor-but-honest black sharecropper's life in rural Arkansas during the Depression. With the exception of a couple of notably theatrical moments, the narrative was a simple one populated by country schoolrooms, farm chores, kitchen tables, and long dusty roads. Indeed, so little was happening on the screen, though the movie was certainly well done and pleasing, that I found time to wonder what the real focus of the drama might be: what did this story tell us? Now we were watching the old, stout grandmother bending low over the sparse fields. We watched her as she picked peas, watched the green pea pods piling up in the wood basket, watched her old gnarled hands as she worked. Now we watched her sweeping up the kitchen floor as little Maya did her homework, poring over the tattered textbooks that the teacher has lent her. The camera drifted slowly around inside the little sharecropper's kitchen, pausing on the ancient floorboards, on the battered utensils, on the wood-burning stove. One had a feeling not only of hard times but of hard times so affectionately, so fondly, re-created.

At about this time, I got up to find a beer in the refrigerator. The grandmother had finished sweeping up the floor and was now performing some new chore close by the dilapidated kitchen sink: shelling peas. As I walked back to the table with my beer, I noticed the expression on my wife's face. She was staring with what could only be described as utter raptness at Esther Rolle as she worked over those peas. And what was I doing? I, too, was staring, had been staring over my shoulder as I went to the refrigerator, both of us now staring, husband and wife, settled in our shiny Formica kitchen with the recently tiled floor and last year's butcher-block carving table, watching a scene in a television movie in which an energetic and capable black character actress fussed around a painstakingly accurate stage-set version of a tumbledown kitchen, shelling peas! What could either of us have been watching with such attentiveness? Action, character, incident? I rather doubt it. I think we were having one of those media-induced pathos experiences. We were keeping in touch with the sensibility of pain.

Granted, it's nothing new for audiences to find vicarious pleasure in depictions of other people's pain or pathos. Hogarth went to Gin Lane, and Goya to the battlefields, and Dickens to the law courts. But what is strange in modern America, I sometimes feel, is that we have worked so hard and so successfully at banishing the appearance of hardship from our countryside that we seem to have come close to getting rid of meaning, too. Thus, to remind ourselves of those things that are supposed to matter (or that once mattered), we poke around in the past, and not carelessly by any means but with a loving, almost loopy fidelity to surfaces, to grit, to texture. Are our sensibilities really as smooth as the quasi-childlike screenplays of most cinema and TV movies indicate? Then, to remind ourselves of our unsmooth past, we probe history for acceptable examples of harsh reality: *Roots*, for instance, with its stirring whiff of the nastiness of slavery; or *Holocaust*, with its careful intimations of Nazi atrocities; or now Maya Angelou's story, with its loving, almost lyric, portrayal of nineteen-thirties rural poverty. (The Depression, it's worth noting, seems to have edged out the Jazz Age as the most popularly nostalgic moment of recent history.)

Naturally, there is plenty of pain and pathos in the

real American present, but not much of it is acceptable
on an audience level any more than on a citizen level,
and most of it seems to be almost too strong for meaning. The life of the American underclass (ghetto life, as
it is usually called) certainly exists out there, but for
the most part it flits by on our television screens as stage-
set pastiche: background for some hard-boiled cop show.
The better kind of drama series periodically deals with
problems (social, emotional, and so forth), but their
effect is invariably to let the problem have its day, its
say, its moment in the limelight, and then to have the
offending matter swallowed whole into the stomach of
the genial beast, which slowly lumbers off toward next
week's show. Right now there are probably two types of
American pain that seem to be allowed a presence of
their own in mass entertainment, and one of them is the
pain of the disabled Vietnam veteran and the other is
the pain of the mentally unstable. These are our home-
grown moon men, after all. They're not quite part of the
mainstream (or so we tell ourselves). We find them in
tide pools, in nooks and crannies at the edge of the sea,
and hold them up in our large and clumsy hands in the
manner of endangered species. We don't exactly love
these furious paraplegics or sad crazies but they are too
remote from the heartland of the audience to threaten it.

Prosperous and unthreatened, we should be content.
Why then do we fondle the misery of the past or of
faraway nations? One imagines it must be because of
the need to remind ourselves of our other selves, our
former lives, when pain and pathos were admitted into
every household, and meaning was something most
people took all too much for granted and didn't have
to search for. On the television screen in front of us,

I Know Why the Caged Bird Sings was drawing to a close, with little Maya, now eighteen, seated in a white dress on the porch of the country schoolhouse, about to graduate. Maya's grandmother, fresh from the fields, sat in the front row, close to tears. The camera showed us close-ups of the fat and sweating black minister who was making the graduation speech, then moved to show the paint peeling off the schoolhouse porch, the broken planks, the tatty little graduation dresses, then finally swung wide to show the arid and dusty Arkansas land-scape. Such hard country! It was strange to realize as we sat there in our kitchen, our very nice American kitchen, that we were looking at our new Arcadia. Of course, it was a different Arcadia from that green and sunny land of the old tales, where tranquillity reigned and everything was in its place and nobody went without what they needed. This was the country, so beautiful in its remoteness and so lovely in its unattainability, that poets in harsher times used to reach out to in their dreams. The New World had once been such an Arcadian vision, hadn't it? And then we reached it, gained the vision, for without a doubt it was that most agreeable and prosperous and even scenic land that we now lived in. Here we are, having made Arcadia real; and behind us, through the haze of nostalgia, like an island rising out of the sea mists as we sail away from it, we begin to glimpse our new Arcadia: that dream-memory of the other, harsher place we left behind, where (as only the Old People dimly remember) toil prevailed over leisure, where instead of convenience there was effort, where in-stead of smoothness there was grit, and where instead of enough or more than enough there was never enough. Is it possible, one wonders, to ever truly leave behind such a place, which was home for so many of the race, and for so long. In time, perhaps one can; doubtless, leaving it is well worth the effort. In the meantime, from our gleaming kitchens, from our effort-free houses, from our smooth-as-silk countryside, we look out with a certain longing to that island, receding in the haze, where Maya Angelou and so many others grew up: that place where even today our moon men still live until we snatch them up, transporting them through space, parachuting them to earth so that we may see them right in front of us on our television screens, so close really as to make us think that we could reach out a hand and almost touch them.

(1979)

THE MODULATING OF
THE PRESIDENCY

OUR Presidential candidates are lost somewhere out there in America. They've been lost for weeks, for months, maybe for years—two mainstream candidates, one independent candidate, a baker's dozen of peripheral candidates. Bill Moyers found some of the peripheral candidates the other evening—wandering bleakly like trappers in the dark woods where the media sun never shines—and warmed them briefly in the glow of public television's lights; but soon they wandered off again (their faces pink and glowing) and are lost once more. Of course, our independent and peripheral candidates are always lost—trappers trudging through the wilderness, stubbornly trapping for extinct or near-extinct species. But in this autumn of an election year, in a nation whose politics (so virtually everyone agrees) have been taken over, veritably subsumed, by television, our mainstream candidates are also lost—not entirely out of view or altogether out of mind, for they pop up constantly on the news, addressing factory workers here or chatting with Hispanics there, but nonetheless as good as vanished, *perdu*, lost from sight, and right in front of the all-seeing, all-powerful eyes of the mighty network cameras.

To listen to the political people and the network people talk about the election coverage, you'd think that there was nothing wrong with it that a little more fiddling with the controls and components wouldn't cure. If there's a problem, it is apparently a problem of *modulation*; at any rate, these days everybody is bent on fine-tuning. Some weeks ago, when the networks were riding hard on Governor Reagan for a careless remark he'd made about our China policy (in other words, they were modulating their coverage of the Reagan campaign so as to bring out the special vibrato of his China statement), a Reagan aide observed to a correspondent—in the manner of one engineer talking shop with another—that henceforth Reagan's campaign staff would be "doing a little more fine-tuning" of the governor's press encounters; in short, they'd be modulating *their* controls so as to excise unplayable Reagan statements before they got locked into the soundtrack.

There are times, of course, when the modulation problem is mainly in the video side of the equipment, as took place the other day when an unexpected visual malfunction occurred over at CBS News—a problem of graphics overload, as it might be described. What happened was this: In an attempt to clearly demonstrate (i.e., fine-tune) candidate Reagan's penchant for changing his mind, CBS News flashed little white Xs over an image of the governor while a voice-over tracked the candidate's about-faces on the issues. The network's modest foray into early newspaper-art design seemed inoffensive enough at the time, and scarcely the point at issue compared with the governor's record of rhetorical instability. But clearly the network's efforts at visual fine-tuning had taxed the system. (Doubtless, good Republicans in the television audience, close in spirit to primitive peoples in their concern for the well-being of the soul, had feared that those little white Xs presaged an X'ing out not only of their leader's discarded enthusiasms but of their leader as well.) Alarm bells rang. Red lights flashed in secret control rooms. *Graphics overload on Channel 2!* The next evening, no less a totemic figure than the venerable Walter Cronkite, sage and elder of CBS News, apologized on camera for the mistake—not a mistake of accuracy or reporting but a mistake in graphics. The red lights blinked off. Gradually, the system returned to harmony—sputtering, fizzling, steaming, cooling. Only the governor and what he stood (or didn't stand) for were left somehow out of focus.

Most of the time, however, the modulation trouble seems to lie in the audio components: problems of sound mixing, so to speak. For example, when President Carter (who had visually fine-tuned himself out of the primaries by staying in the White House) attempted to fine-tune himself into the campaign by criticizing Reagan, his criticisms made news less for their substance than for what might be thought of as their audio qualities —qualities that were measured and noted by the press on a daily basis, and whose generally perceived "harshness" soon became the principal journalistic point of reference for the whole Carter campaign. As a result of poor audio notices, Carter then decided to change the sound of his campaign—or at least the sound mix. This new audio-engineering decision to sound less harsh (which was announced appropriately by the candidate in a Barbara Walters interview) then became the next press reference point for the President's efforts to retain the Presidency. In fact, Carter had probably meant what he had said in his attacks on Reagan, in his admonitions to the effect that Reagan would divide the country, would turn "race against race," and so forth. That was Carter talking, but the press didn't seem to be listening to what he was saying—only to the sound of what he was saying: a "harsh" sound, a *bad* sound. Perhaps Carter shouldn't have put the word "race" into the soundtrack; the sound of the word "race" seems to grate on everybody's ears this year. Perhaps he should have introduced a little sociology into the mix, thereby providing that kind of soft, blurry, statesmanly sound that makes for easy listening. One imagines, however, that some savvy Carter media strategist—one of the President's fine-tuners —had heard somewhere of the terrific sound produced years ago by Harry Truman in his "Give 'em hell" campaign, and thought, Hey, if we could just get President Jimmy to put on the bib overalls and raise a little hell and play some of that down-home music, we'll be at the top of the charts by Halloween. The Harry Truman sound! The sound of the once and future country-and-western Presidency! *Good* sound! It was the right general idea but with the wrong particulars. What they got instead was that *other* country music: that dry-lipped Appalachian sound—quavering reeds and somber, God-fearing plainsong: harsh, albeit authentic.

Similarly, when Governor Reagan, early in the campaign, was making all those discordant sounds about China and the Ku Klux Klan and God knows what else, those were *his* sounds, too. They weren't nice sounds, either, of course, and this posed a special kind of problem. The video equipment indicated the governor to be a uniformly nice fellow, but the audio equipment registered an awkward mixture: a lot of bad sounds were coming through. Evidently, the equipment was at fault; it was another problem of modulation. Audio engineers were called in to fine-tune the governor after the China sounds played poorly, but there are some sounds so sharp and strange that they can't easily be mixed. Possibly the equipment is still primitive in certain ways; it amplifies some things when you least expect it. For instance, your candidate is being cool, just bopping along in the recording studio, laying down a little warm and easy candidacy music, doing his thing, figuring that if there's a real soft spot somewhere the engineers can always put in a couple of mariachi tracks after the session, or maybe some echoes, or church bells, or a whole defense-department percussion section, but then suddenly—whoooee! *Ku Klux Klan!* Oh, man. *Ku Klux Klan?* A very bad sound. Just about jams the machine. More alarms. Red lights everywhere. *Bad-sound overload!* No engineer can wipe that kind of sound once it gets on the track. You have to cancel the recording session. Delay the tour. Send everybody back to Malibu and figure out how to get that bad sound out of there.

Sooner or later, nowadays, the bad sound disappears, even if you have to fine-tune the candidate out of the campaign to do it. Television anchormen, like the great stone heads on Easter Island, have had their day. This is the day of the modulating engineers: the cutters, splicers, mixers, editors, and so on. Listen to the hum of our modern political campaigns: the whir of tape on editing and mixing machines—forward, stop, reverse, snip, snip, splice, forward, stop, snip, whir: our new montage actuality. The candidates wander the country, like trappers—or perhaps like rock bands, in full view of everyone but seen by no one. Who are those men behind the painted faces and fright wigs onstage, and what actual music is buried in their wires, cables, consoles, and amplifying systems? Today, both the politicians and the networks are caught up in the same dance of technology. The real power is the power of the men and women who control the montage effects—the technologists who instinctively understand the truth of Eisenstein's statement: "The basic fact was true, and remains true to this day, that the juxtaposition of two separate shots by splicing them together resembles not so much a simple sum of one shot plus another shot as it does a *creation*." One shot plus another shot; one sound plus another sound: *Creation!* These engineers are the new creators, our political kingmakers. The other day, President Carter was on a speaking tour in Nashville, in the course of which, for a brief moment, he criticized the three networks for not having shown on their news programs a few nights before that part of a Reagan interview where the governor strongly disavowed the SALT II treaty. Carter, in other words, was speaking to the issue of network editing, fine-tuning—scolding them for having declined to transmit a more creative Reagan montage. In rebuttal, however, the CBS technicians employed montage on Carter. They fine-tuned his Nashville remarks so that, in their presentation, the President seemed to have little on his mind beyond attacking the three networks. Then they employed montage on one of their earlier news broadcasts and thus extracted a brief CBS reference to Reagan's disavowal of SALT II. Now they put it all together: a new montage— a new creation. How clever, one thought. Such energy of technique! It was more than an interesting example of television byplay. What we had witnessed was a journalistic-political dialogue entirely focused on montage—on the technology of video-and-sound modulation. The only thing missing, of course, was a coherent sense of the candidate: of either one, or of both candidates, for that matter, who seem destined to dart perpetually through factories, airports, slum-housing projects, municipal parades, etc., always beneath the camera lights —beautifully framed, expertly recorded—but somehow never *seen*. It's as if the love that politicians once bore the public has been transferred to the new machines, and the machines have lost sight of the one thing about these strange, complex, and driven people that anyone ever really cared about: who they are.

(1980)

UPRIVER IN
SAMURAI COUNTRY

THOUGH Anglo-Saxons aren't the only people who are attracted to captivity stories (consider, for example, the worldwide popularity of that earliest captivity story, the Book of Exodus), there seems to be a special racial and sexual self-consciousness close to the center of the Anglo-Saxon temperament which remains deeply fascinated not merely by tales of captivity but by tales of the captivity of whites by darker-skinned and mythically potent "heathen." In early America, so-called captivity narratives based on the capture of white settlers by Indians formed the first real body of native American literature. Tales such as Mary Rowlandson's *The Sovereignty and Goodness of God: A Narrative of the Captivity and Restauration* (1682) and John Williams's *The Redeemed Captive* (1706) went through printing after printing and, together with their numerous imitators and progeny, virtually dominated American publishing lists for at least forty years; in fact, of the four most widely read books in America between 1680 and 1720, three were captivity narratives (the fourth being *Pilgrim's Progress*).

The earliest and probably the best of these tales were what we would now describe as nonfiction: authentic accounts of the actual captivity of certain unlucky settlers. Puritan clerics and authors, however, were quick to note the special appeal of these narratives of lonely travail in the wilderness, and in short order a literary manufacturing operation was under way in New England, producing manuscripts that were then published both in Boston (from which they were distributed to the New England colonies) and in London (from which they were distributed to the Southern colonies as well as to the English reading public). As in most literary genres, these numerous captivity tales varied in certain obvious surface details, but the underlying psychological force of the stories remained the same, for these were, above all, narratives of chastisement and humiliation. From their pulpits, the Puritan clerics spoke of the superiority of the Puritan colonist to the Indians, and of the Christian duty of the white settler to bring religion and morality to the benighted savages. But in their earliest literature—in these widely read captivity narratives —the Puritans seemed drawn to a quite different concept of values and relationships. In these stories, the white-skinned and God-fearing Puritan was invariably a lost and doomed figure in the dark and inhospitable wilderness—a prisoner of mythically powerful dark-skinned savages (sometimes referred to as "black men" in Puritan narratives)—and was compelled to stoically submit to the twin sufferings of wilderness captivity: first, physical suffering from hardship, privation, and, sometimes, torture; then the deeper psychic suffering from having to undergo both Indian "marriage" and Indian "communion."

Thus, the woods and forests of early New England were the original "heart of darkness" for the Anglo-Saxon sensibility, where white men and women, isolated by accident or force from white society, were compelled by the fabulous potency of the dark-skinned savage to betray not only the Christian God but the Christian marriage bed. In time, of course, as both the frontier and the Indians moved westward and spilled across the Plains States, the Puritan captivity narratives were replaced by more up-to-date American literary genres, such as the numerous Daniel Boone stories. But the hypnotically powerful theme of Anglo-Saxon punishment in the wilderness didn't so much vanish as reappear in another place and in another context: the nineteenth-century narratives of English intruders into Africa, the Middle East, and India. In the writings of Sir Richard Burton, to take an early example, or of T. E. Lawrence, to take a later example (to say nothing of Kipling, Conrad, and the adventures of Lady Hester Stanhope in between), we have the same idealization, as it were, of humiliation and chastisement, the same powerful *frissons* of the white man in the presence of the inevitably potent and darker-skinned natives—all those "manly Turks" and "cruel, splendid sheikhs," and so forth, who dot English and American fiction up to this day.

Today, in fact, we have *Shogun*: first, a widely popular novel by James Clavell (an Englishman, naturalized an American) and, more recently, a widely popular— or, at least, widely watched—NBC television series (with Clavell as executive producer, Eric Bercovici as producer and screenwriter, and Jerry London as director). I have heard *Shogun* the novel described fondly in various ways—as an adventure story or a historical novel of feudal Japan—but what it seemed to be more than anything else was a reworking of the theme of Anglo-Saxon captivity in the inhospitable wilderness. Its interior structure, at any rate, was a fairly simple one that stuck close to the classic genre: a seventeenth-century seafarer, John Blackthorne, journeys "upriver," as it were, and becomes lost, and intrudes into the "wilderness" of feudal Japan. There he is humiliated and chastised by the mythically powerful yellow-skinned Japanese, whom he soon comes to respect for their manly ways and stern code of manners. Later, he is more or less compelled to betray his English wife and children back home and submit to Japanese "marriage" in the form of a romance with Lady Mariko, and to Japanese "communion" in the form of espousal of the samurai code. Naturally, the novel purported to be about many other matters: the rivalries and alliances between various Japanese warlords, who are constantly jockeying for position in the absence of a national military leader, or Shogun (the title thus refers to a character who doesn't ever appear); periodic machinations on the part of the wily Jesuits; Blackthorne's love affair with Lady Mariko; and so forth. On a superficial level, Clavell's enormous book was a hodgepodge of royal princes, musketeers, scheming cardinals, and alarums and excursions, such as Alexander Dumas might have concocted—and if this were all there was to it, one doubts whether any more people would have read it than normally read Dumas these days. But the energy of *Shogun* the novel was somewhere else: not exactly out of sight but not in the overblown and rather confusing sweep of historical pageantry, either. The book's energy—and a considerable energy there was, to account for those millions of readers —lay close to its opening scenes: in the captivity of our pale-skinned Blackthorne and in his romantic attachment not so much to Lady Mariko as to the idealized and powerful samurai.

The book, in fact, was another in the long line of Anglo-American raptures over a dark-skinned superrace. Clavell's Japanese were, almost to a man, immensely strong, beautifully conditioned, splendidly cruel, and yet possessed of an instinctive sense of justice and fair play. In the novel, not only were heads lopped from necks at an awesome rate, but the blows were always clean, swift, and true. Clearly, there were no feeble wrists or rusty swords in feudal Japan. And no bad sports among the samurai, for not only did the samurai commit *seppuku* (suicide) with a frequency that makes one wonder how the Japanese had any population problem at all by the twentieth century, but they did so each time with unimpeachable dignity, courage, and, of course, that same manual dexterity. In other words, while the surface of the narrative frothed along merrily and interminably with the comings and goings of Lords Yabu, Toranaga, Ishido, etc., and their henchmen, the novel's real drive proceeded from Blackthorne's captivity fantasy: the time-honored white man's descent into the fascinating world of spectacular punishment (one of Blackthorne's crew is boiled alive, by numerous immersions over a space of many pages), bitter humiliation (a samurai pees on the stoic Blackthorne's prostrate back), alienation, and isolation, with, at all times, an idealization of his manly captors.

This is the old-fashioned Puritan literary dream that powered *Shogun* the novel and accounted for its special hold on readers. What accounts, I think, for the much looser hold of NBC's *Shogun* on its viewers is that the television team chose to blunt or blur the captivity theme when it transferred the novel to the screen. Granted, NBC's *Shogun* has been an enormous success, at least in terms of ratings. It is the most costly television production ever made, and its promotional budget was commensurately extravagant. NBC even managed to badger certain educational associations so that *Shogun* material might be introduced into school classrooms—Feudal Japanese Night in Soc. Sci. 102, so to speak. Still, my guess is that NBC's vast, ambitious, and often finely made production somehow missed its target—not in numbers but in effect. Many of the people I spoke with who had watched the series seemed confused and vaguely disappointed. Even sympathetic viewers spoke of too many characters and a bewildering narrative. The plot of television's *Shogun* was in fact somewhat less confusing than the novel, but I think it was perceived as a cumbersome chronicle-play by much of its audience for the reason that this quasi-historical superstructure was what mostly remained of the novel when it was transferred to the screen.

Shogun in television terms was more than ever a story of feuding barons—Lord This against Lord That, junior warlord against senior warlord—though *who* was against *whom* seemed sometimes neither very clear nor even important. Every so often, the clever, elegantly costumed Jesuits would troop on and then troop off—to be forgotten in the march of partly authentic and partly fabricated Japanese history until they were summoned once again into their robes. Lady Mariko was now a major character—she, too, being elegantly costumed—with scant mention of Blackthorne's wife at home, and thus scant sense of his betrayal, and, indeed, with Blackthorne and Mariko's romance having the aspect less of an Englishman's "going native" than of a romantic interlude between D'Artagnan and Milady de Winter. On NBC's *Shogun*, virtually everyone was elegantly costumed, the exception being Blackthorne's crew, who were picturesquely folkish during the few moments that they appeared. Where the novel had concentrated, in its crude and boyishly clever way, on pain and cruelty and perpetual head-loppings, television's *Shogun* became an epic of elaborate and expensive wardrobe changes.

In many ways, the production was quite beautiful. Rarely in a television series—even in such an ambitious one as *Roots*—has there been a comparable amplitude of graceful cinematography. This is not to say that new visual ground was broken in *Shogun* but that TV's normally skimpy visual menu of monotonous long shots, ping-pong close-ups, and haphazard composition was here sumptuously expanded to include a whole variety of cleverly conceived panoramas, overheads, subtle tracking shots, and well-punctuated close-ups. Unfortunately, the point of all these expensive camera settings and of Andrew Laszlo's elegant cinematography often seemed to miss the mark. Clavell, after all, had written a captivity story from which he was now filming a historical drama, but Laszlo (doubtless with Clavell's approval) was photographing, for the most part, a series of midcult "artistic" tableaux. The more the camera struggled to show us the lords, ladies, priests, and so forth, properly presented in their silks and brocades, the more the production had the look of one of those Time-Life picture books about alien cultures (*Time-Life Books Visits Seventeenth-Century Japan*). Granted that it would have been less appealing to sponsors and to high-school principals if the production had translated to the screen some of the shuddery horridness of the novel: Blackthorne's sense of captivity and doom in the wilderness of Japan, with its ghastly prisoner pits, and ever present cruelty, and all those evil, slicing blades. This, of course, was itself no more than fantasy (not unlike the still present European reverie of gangsters running wild on the streets of Chicago), but it was the fantasy that Clavell had written. It was what his book was about, and what had caused so many millions to buy it and turn the pages. In its place, *Shogun* on television provided moment after moment (after moment) of solemn, beautifully composed images of inaction. And such solemnity, too! There were evidently no jokes in seventeenth-century Japan, Japanese humor and subtlety having presumably been all used up by Lady Murasaki's *Tale of Genji* in the eleventh century.

Naturally, not all the violence had vanished from the story. There was an occasional head-lopping and now and then a bit of *seppuku*. But the spirit of the violence was different: no more schoolboy *frissons*, no more stench. We were in the presence not so much of art as of Art Design. Gone, too, was the strange interior drive of Clavell's novel, for though the book was a somewhat muddled and unwieldy affair, it had at its center Blackthorne's captivity. In the novel, when Blackthorne and his crew sail through the terrible storm and virtually crash into Japan in the darkness there is no doubt in the reader's mind that the Englishman has been swept over the rim of some mysterious and alien chasm. He is not only lost in the wilderness, with its cruel and manly savages, but stuck there. In the novel, true to its captivity heritage, Blackthorne makes only token attempts to get free and sail out of there. For all its comings and goings, and marches and countermarches, the spirit of the novel is not really picaresque at all. It is preoccupied with a man stuck in a hard, dark place. But on television that feeling of being caught and stuck is quickly dissipated as Blackthorne becomes part of the ongoing costume drama. Clavell originally wanted either Albert Finney or Sean Connery for the part, according to press reports, but after settling for Richard Chamberlain found him altogether excellent. A loyal producer, one imagines, would say no less about his star—certainly not in public, on the debut of this most costly television production of the ages. It seemed to me that Chamberlain handled his role perfectly well. Admittedly, there was a bit too much Southern California in his voice, and his face (though bearded) lacked a certain weathering. Still, we are not talking about his playing Lear. If there was an askewness in Chamberlain's Blackthorne, it had less to do with Chamberlain's deficiencies as an actor, I thought, than with screenwriter Eric Bercovici's conception of the part. Bercovici is one of the better television screenwriter-adapters; his mini-series *Washington: Behind Closed Doors*, a few years back, was full of sharply drawn characters and nice details—much better as a television film than the John Ehrlichman novel it was loosely based on. But this time it seemed as if he had been overwhelmed by the pretentious, "historical" side of Clavell's book. If Blackthorne appeared to lack energy on the screen, it was because the television adapters—in the service of television culture—had turned Blackthorne's original energy as a captive into the energy of a tour guide.

Ironically, the one instance where the television team (as if it were remembering what it had given up in its adaptation) tried to shore up the almost dismantled captivity story—namely, the decision to have the Japanese characters speak only Japanese, without English subtitles—was the one aspect for which *Shogun* has been most consistently criticized. One can hardly blame the critics. There is a difference, after all, between Blackthorne's feeling alienated and isolated by the language of his captors and the viewers' feeling alienated and isolated by not knowing what is going on. Hemingwayesque pidgin translation ("Little daughter, let us drink to bravery and death, and chew us a piece of the gum of Mr. Wrigley") probably no longer works well, if it ever did, but there is surely also a general rule worth following, to the effect that anything in English works better for an audience that speaks English than anything in Japanese—and, doubtless, vice versa. Still, one can see what the television adapters were trying to do with their Japanese dialogue: to create a wilderness of language around Blackthorne; a surrounding thicket of strange, impenetrable sounds. It was not a frivolous experiment but a misguided one, for if you put a substantial element of your dramatic dialogue into a language the audience doesn't understand, you're indicating that there's nothing in that dialogue you want them to understand. In the end, I think that it was in this one crucial matter of want and wanting that *Shogun* let down its huge audience, and also the jolly and fascinating schoolboy novel that it was drawn from. It turned out that NBC's *Shogun* didn't *want* anything from us—not even an understanding of what was being said much of the time. And although the main Japanese character, Lord Toranaga, wanted to be Shogun, the story is really Blackthorne's, and he didn't *want* anything himself—at least, not very much: neither to escape, as a picaresque character might, nor to experience the terrors of the wilderness, as the hero of a captivity narrative would—neither Christian communion nor Indian marriage. Our television Blackthorne was not so much lost as a fish out of water—an English dilettante in Samurai Country. At any rate, the heart of darkness was beating somewhere else.

(1980)

THE PRESIDENTIAL SATs

So MUCH quick-cutting obtains on television—look at him, look at her, look at the telephone poles, look at the bridge, look at the truck, look at him and her, etc.—that it can be quite a startling experience to watch a scene that unfolds simply, without cuts, glimpsed through the sober, philosophic eye of a stationary camera. At any rate, this unblinking quality of perspective was but one of the unusual aspects of the Reagan–Carter debate. The two main candidates had been on the run for so long—furnishing fast-moving pieces of themselves both to the network news cameras and to their own advertising campaigns—that to finally see them whole and plain, so to speak, appeared to have something about it of a religious act. After all, one sees so few people on television whole and plain: just *there*, coexisting with us in a shared moment of time, and not simply produced, prestidigitated, for our benefit from other near or far moments of time—patchworks of rearranged gestures and emotions. Ohmigosh, it's *them*, one thought, staring straight ahead through the patient camera lens at the two men standing behind the little pulpits in the Cleveland auditorium. Candidate Jimmy! Candidate Ronald! All spring and summer and fall, they had eluded us, driving us mad with snips and snatches of themselves, wearing us thin with montage versions of their candidacy, wearing us down like a wind that blows and blows and blows, so that one began thinking: At least be definite; blow the house down! They must have felt something of the religious possibilities of the moment themselves, for each candidate was clearly terrified. Granted, they both wanted the Presidency and only one of them could have it; that sort of wanting doubtless adds a little edge to a man's composure. But there was more to their terror than the shivers of mere ambition. Here, in Cleveland, immobilized like sentries, like prisoners, on the sea of bright-blue carpet (before that pale-blue curtain), both men—for the first time in months, or years—were caught fast in a dramatic situation, and yet were unprotected by the techniques of montage. Here, if the right nuance was not forthcoming, if the correct word was not spoken, if the appropriate emotion were not registered, it could not be provided later. Awareness of such naked vulnerability seemed to have scared the pants off both our prospective leaders—freezing their faces into masks, making their no longer youthful bodies as stiff and stoic as those of petitioners for doctoral degrees, congealing their minds into that special kind of television-talk-show numbness, from which no birdsong ever escapes, in which no living thought can be discerned. In front of the two examinees, separated by a distance that seemed to widen as the debate wore on, sat the five representatives of the press, the examining board: the faculty gets to sit; the students stand, trying to remember not to fidget, not to stand on one foot, not to chew gum, not to stare at the floor, not to roll one's eyes at the ceiling, not to be smart-alecky, not to be too shy, not to stand there with one's shirt half out and one's Woolworth necktie all askew and one's hair uncombed and shoes unpolished—and with nothing at all to say. Even if they ask you for the tertiary causes of the War of the Spanish Succession, at least say *some-*

thing. Candidate Jimmy spoke of the burdens of the Oval Office, of sacrifice, of economic revitalization, of working with our allies, of the mainstream of American life. Candidate Ronald spoke of a strong America, of a consistent foreign policy, of balancing the budget, and of our defense posture. The evening, alas, did not turn out to be a religious one, except perhaps in a cinematic sense—in that, if you have been manipulated by quick-cutting for a long while, so that you seem to live and breathe and think and feel in a world composed of montage images, then sometimes the appearance of an altogether higher reality, even of a mystical and profound reality, can be produced by a steady and immobile perspective. It's not, perhaps, that one notices more that way but that one participates more. At any rate, what one noticed in the end at Cleveland was the sadness and loneliness of the event. For some reason, the press panelists (whose print and TV colleagues had spent the last nine months like children running down the road after a traveling circus) now chose to take a stern, parental tone with both candidates—our once and future Free World leaders, bomb proliferators, energy boomers, minority hirers—and thus froze them further into the strange though moving isolation that has characterized much of this great electronic campaign. For some reason, the candidates were so careful, so industrious, in removing all marks of personality, signs of passion, indications of idiosyncrasy from their on-camera performances that the beautiful, unfolding, nearly profound sincerity of the evening was largely wasted. So, it was only you again, one thought as the spectacle drew to a close: both men with such nice manners, so fluent with their answers, so properly dressed, not a button off, not a stain or a smudge anywhere. There was something close to pain—for them and us, I suspect—in seeing them so plain and whole, so empty, so unedited. Now, of course, we can look forward to another four years of quick-cuts and montage.

(1980)

SURPRISED IN IOWA, SURPRISED IN NAM

FOR SOME TIME NOW, a variety of voices have been trying to speak to us about the Vietnam War. First, long ago, beginning at the time it started to unfold, there were the daily reports from the working press: the newspaper, wire-service, and TV correspondents whose preoccupation with the details and surfaces of the operation often seemed strangely similar to the obsessions of the military. After all, the PIO colonels furnished the body counts, but who passed them on? These on-the-scene reporters, one felt, risked their lives (and sometimes lost them) covering pieces of a mosaic whose entirety turned out to be a larger tableau that the media generals in New York, no less than the Pentagon generals in Washington, seemed unwilling to reveal to the national audience that confusedly followed the day-by-day activities. Then came the analytic journalists, working usually for magazines (one thinks of David Halberstam, Frances Fitz-Gerald, Robert Shaplen, among others), who looked beyond the details for information, seeking it not merely from the military but in political Washington and historical Vietnam, and began to put together their own versions of the wider story. After the journalists came the imaginative writers. These novelists and playwrights were usually young men who had also been there, often on military service (for example, Winston Groom, David Rabe, Tim O'Brien), who now attempted to make sense of what had happened in terms of emotions, passions, and individual experience. Later still, well after the war, came the Hollywood filmmakers, often educated in their newfound Vietnam perspectives by the earlier work of journalists, often borrowing or appropriating the hard-won private visions of the imaginative writers in order to create what has become for the filmgoing public their received idea of what the war was like and what it meant. And, finally, with ABC's recent presentation of *Friendly Fire*, the war returned, so to speak, to television: to that mass audience in whose living rooms ten years ago America first glimpsed the trouble in Vietnam.

I liked and admired C. D. B. Bryan's *Friendly Fire* when it first appeared in *The New Yorker*, and then (in a somewhat expanded version) as a book, which was well received by critics and also widely read. It seemed to me to represent the better sort of journalism which was possible in this country. That is, it was a careful and feeling work, with an emphasis on both those words, neither exploiting nor parasitically living off the actual material of life, but treating its subjects with the ultimate respect of honestly noticing them; of paying attention. It was also a work of great restraint, of necessary restraint, and as I watched the "big sell" ad campaign that preceded the TV showing I wondered if the television version would be able to preserve the level of restraint that had made the literary version succeed so well. But it turned out that there was no need to worry. *Friendly Fire* on television was first-rate, and much of the credit must surely go to Fay Kanin, the screenwriter (and co-producer), who knew just what to do with Bryan's book about Gene and Peg Mullen, of La Porte City, Iowa, and what happened to them after their son was killed by "friendly fire" in Vietnam. What she didn't do, to begin with, was what so many other film or TV people do when they buy a literary property. She didn't entomb it with reverence and she didn't rip it off with hype. Bryan's book, for example, is quite long, and even wordy in places; Kanin's screenplay was uncommonly spare and yet seemed exactly true to the sense of the story. Most important, Kanin and the director, David Greene, seemed to have enough trust in the material not to feel that they had to mess around with it by throwing in extraneous and attention-grabbing visual effects. There was a blessed absence of those phony, energizing bits of visual punctuation or vocabulary which film people are so fond of using, rather as some writers use supercharged phrases when they don't have anything much to say. Kanin's script obviously had some problems to solve: for example, how to make a visually interesting story out of situations that mostly involved exchanges of conversation. But she did it the only way she could have, while remaining true to the material: by trusting the actors and the sincerity of the characterizations, and by not letting on too visibly that she was trying to solve problems. In other words, you hardly ever felt manipulated by the camera: pulled in or out of the house, for instance, because the director now wanted to "open things up," now wanted to get back to the story.

As Gene Mullen, Ned Beatty was excellent. Charles Durning might also have done well in the role, but Durning's face has become almost too ripe with pain. Beatty's face belongs to a slightly simpler man who is still waiting for pain to occupy it. There is a ruddy, fleshy smoothness to his cheeks that connotes a certain innocence as well as a certain impermeability to disaster. Carol Burnett played the more complicated role of Peg Mullen, and it seemed to me that she handled the part with distinction, and with none of that forced quality of impersonation that sometimes shows up when a comic actor or actress is asked to play a serious character. Peg's role is difficult to bring off, I should imagine, because two different strands of personality run through her: on the one hand, she is supposed to be simple and homespun, a farmer's wife; on the other hand, she is required to be politically alert and active, an anti-war protester. Burnett fused both strands in her portrayal by never failing to present Mrs. Mullen as a substantial person: a figure of ambivalences but ultimately of great force of personality.

In fact, if I have one question about *Friendly Fire* it has to do with Bryan's original conception of Peg Mullen's character. For though Peg is obviously a real person, and Bryan, in the spirit of a careful journalist, was faithful to observable details, all the same a journalist is in some respects not unlike a novelist in that, in the end, he sees whatever his eyes tell him to see. In Bryan's case, it seems to me that what he first must have seen in Peg Mullen was an Iowa farmer's wife whose son had been killed in Vietnam and who was starting to protest the war. In due course, he came to understand the clues in her background which helped to explain this decision to become a war protester, and he tried as a responsible journalist to indicate in his book some of the complexity in her nature that he had gradually uncovered. But I wonder if his instinctive and most powerful sense of Peg Mullen was not his first one: the simple farmer's wife. And I wonder if this character isn't the one on which the book, and thus the TV version, is really based.

The question is, then: Who was Peg Mullen? Of course, she *was* a farmer's wife. Gene Mullen owned some farm acreage in Iowa, though he mainly worked at a nearby John Deere plant, and Peg was certainly his wife. But, as Bryan tries to inform us early in his book, she was some other things too. For one, she was a Catholic in a predominantly Protestant town. For another, she was an active Democrat in historic Republican territory. And even before her son Michael went off to war she had become a member of a moderate protest group: Another Mother for Peace. So it is not altogether impossible to begin to see in Peg Mullen someone quite different from the simple farmer's wife whose seemingly sudden protest against the war took on a larger symbolism: the member of the conservative bedrock of society who turns against her own establishment! It's true that small-town values are no longer as parochial as they used to be, but, even so, how establishmentarian could it have been to have spent a lifetime in a small Midwestern town, not merely as a politically oriented woman, but as a member of a Catholic minority? What room could there have been in the bedrock of Republican Iowa for an active Democrat? In fact, far from ever having been entrenched at the solid center of her community, was not Peg Mullen always something of an outsider—someone whose life, even before the story of *Friendly Fire* began, already conflicted with the mainstream of the community, and sometimes, one imagines, at a fairly sharp angle? Bryan certainly didn't try to conceal these aspects of the Mullens' existence, and in various ways attempted to fit them into the narrative, as the TV version also attempted to do. But I suspect that his heart wasn't really in the refitting, since I wouldn't be surprised if his own sense of being an outsider in Iowa hadn't made it difficult, even impossible, for him to see the Mullens as outsiders there, themselves: as people whose lives had been shaped well before Vietnam along a kind of feisty, anti-establishment bias, and for whom the war, with its personal tragedy of a son's death, then became an occasion for the acting out of a lifetime of pent-up protest.

Still, despite this problem, it seems to me that *Friendly Fire* on television was an unusually humane and understanding treatment of our Vietnam experience. It was not quite as dramatically wrenching, perhaps, as the movie *Coming Home,* with its tough, poignant scenes of paraplegic veterans, but it possessed the same quiet, numbing tonalities, while fortunately doing without the film's Hollywood theatrics. Both *Friendly Fire* and *Coming Home,* in fact, have been better, juster, more successfully realized statements about what the Vietnam War meant to Americans than such flamboyantly conceived pictures as *The Deer Hunter* and *Apocalypse Now,* with their bogus mythology and production designer's fondness for the savagery of battle. It will be hard, of course, to dissuade the public from the newfound version of recent history that it has discovered in such grandiloquent epics. For some reason, the mass audience seems to have a deep yearning to believe that there was something uniquely horrible about our engagement in Vietnam: uniquely horrible in battlefield terms, in the form of unique savagery and bloodletting; and uniquely horrible in political terms, in the form of uniquely poor leadership and self-deluding strategy. That there exists no significant evidence to support this notion of the Vietnam War as unique either in its mayhem or in its misconceived policies—certainly not when considered in the context of mankind's long and bloody involvement in the annals of war—is probably beside the point, at least for the time being. History, as Napoleon is supposed to have said, is the version of past events that people have decided to agree on. Even so, if there is reason for a moviegoer with any sense of history to writhe uncomfortably at the tricks and manipulations that gave *The Deer Hunter* and *Apocalypse Now* the larger measure of their supposed power and realism, there is doubtless reason, too, to think that the substantial audiences for *Coming Home* and *Friendly Fire* indicate that the public is not altogether swayed by the flashier and more self-conscious dramas and is still making up its mind.

I have mentioned self-consciousness in connection with some of our Vietnam films because of a key ingredient that seems to exist in nearly all of them. The ingredient I've noticed might be described simply as *surprise*. Sometimes the element of surprise is right out there in the open, flatly depicted. I'm thinking, for instance, of the wounded young soldier in *The Deer Hunter* who is suffering not so much from physical shock as from a seizure of astonishment: how could this have happened to *me*? At other times, the feeling of surprise is less something to be played out on the screen than it is a pool of apparently shared emotion to be plugged into by filmmaker and audience alike. It is a given that the public itself brings to the story and that permeates the darkened theaters like tobacco or marijuana smoke. In this connection, the part of Captain Willard (Martin Sheen) in *Apocalypse Now* was repeatedly criticized by literary-minded critics, first for having been modeled after Conrad's favorite narrator, Marlow, and then for having been modeled inaccurately. Willard's saturnine coolness, it was pointed out in a lengthy critique in the Sunday *Times*, bears little resemblance to the inquisitive, moralizing, and warmhearted Marlow. Granted that Coppola and associates were doing Conrad no favor by borrowing the old man's clothes to dress up in. But one doubts that they would have done him any better favor by having worn the clothes correctly. In fact, if Captain Willard had been too closely copied after Marlow, the whole dramatic structure of the movie would have foundered. For if Willard had been morally involved, like Marlow, then it would have been up to him to respond to Coppola's continual and mechanistic parade of the horrors, absurdities, and ironies of war. He would have served as a lightning rod, grounding Coppola's fine display, thus defusing the audience's own response or making it superfluous. Instead, by rejecting Conrad's warm, involved Marlow and by choosing as narrator someone with the cool detachment of, say, Fitzgerald's Nick Carraway, Coppola was able to make Willard into the conduit of the chief emotion he was trying to play to in the audience. It was not guilt, I think, as in Conrad's great tale, or even a feeling of personal or historical tragedy, but something much closer to a national sense of surprise.

It is a curious emotion on which to base high drama, which is perhaps one of the reasons why the treatment of Vietnam in the mass media often has such a forced, unreal quality about it, which the filmmakers naturally try to pass off as "surreal." Surprise, after all, is such a weaker, younger, less noble emotion than even shock or outrage. Shock, at least, has the underpinnings of genuine trauma to give it dramatic weight, while outrage, as the word suggests, is a form of rage: rage outer-directed. At any rate, it is an emotion that comes from knowing where one is. A man who lifts up his head in outrage and curses the gods (or whoever happens to be handy) usually knows where he stands and doesn't like it one bit. But surprise is the small voice that says, "Gosh, how did I get here? How did this happen to me? Where am I anyway?" It is not, in any case, the voice of Odysseus or Aeneas or of Shakespeare's Henry or, for that matter, of Bill Mauldin's mud-spattered GIs, Willie and Joe, on the battlefields of World War II. Willie and Joe never much liked where they were but they always knew damned well how they had got there. For the time being, though, it is the voice that speaks in many of our Vietnam dramas, where the rhetoric sometimes appears to have the force of classic outrage; but when the words finally reach our ears they usually turn out to be much closer to "How come, *me*?"

Even Gene and Peg Mullen in *Friendly Fire* are not completely exempt from this enfeebling virus of self-consciousness, although their surprise, when it is finally expressed, is a somewhat more valid and outer-directed emotion than that of the current Vietnam movie hero, who usually seems to glow with the pale fire of little more than the uniqueness of his own experience. The Mullens were not really surprised by the death of their son in Vietnam, but they were very much surprised at their inability to obtain satisfactory information from the army as to where, how, and why his death had occurred. A great part of the energy of the story, in fact, comes from Gene's and Peg's astonished frustration at not being able to extract from a military bureaucracy the precise details concerning a lone soldier's death, eight thousand miles away, in jungle combat. Accordingly, their surprise might be said to be more a by-product of the Communications Age than of the general narcissism of their time. The implicit question posed wasn't the familiar "How come, us?" but a classic citizen's query of an impersonal technology: in effect, "Why did you tell us that your newfangled communications equipment worked so efficiently when it can't give us the facts about one man's death?" Granted, fifty years ago the Mullens would have been considered mad for expecting such information at their fingertips. But expect it now they did. The technocracy of the world they lived in had convinced them that they were connected to a communications system of such intricacy and omniscience that nothing could happen *anywhere* (certainly not the death of a son from a badly targeted artillery round in south Vietnam) that they couldn't ask questions about it of the system and receive clear, complete, and prompt answers. In earlier times, before people got in the habit of making inquiries of systems, one imagines that the Mullens would have asked God for answers, who then doubtless would have kept silent, as deities commonly do, thereby requiring men and women to commune with their own souls and so heal themselves. Instead, however, the Mullens took their case to the machines (our new gods), who chattered back with telex messages and telegraphed instructions and computerized pay vouchers and automated grave-registration forms and even, at the end, some personal correspondence from their son's battalion commander, all of which unfortunately represented essentially incomplete answers to the real question that had been on the lips of the poor Mullens, whose hearts were first broken by their son's untimely death, and then over and over again by the chattering of the machines they wanted so badly to be plugged into.

(1979)

FRED WISEMAN'S
KINO PRAVDA

As with the work of many serious and obstinate men,
the nonfiction films of Frederick Wiseman have a certain obsessive quality, though in his case the obsessional
note is of a rather unexpected sort: not so much a con-
centration of effect as a diffusion; not so much a sense
of drive as a seeming absence of intensity. Indeed, his
films share a tone of gray matter-of-factness (reinforced,
but not altogether produced, by the black-and-white
cinematography) that is as individual, and as deliberate
in its way, as Billy Wilder's wit or Ken Russell's baroque
artifice. Unlike a work of the entertainment cinema, however, a Wiseman film seems at virtually no point in its
unreeling to defer to—or even to acknowledge—the
frivolous impulses of the audience. Not only does it un-
wind casually and naturally, as it were, upon the screen,
unaided by music or sound effects, or even by narration,
but the theme of the picture is usually so unfocused or
unemphasized as to be almost nonexistent. In this respect,
Wiseman's nonfiction resembles certain modernist musical compositions: the work is clearly not without artful
design and interior structure, but both design and structure appear to be unfamiliar ones; the notes, of course,
are the same as always, yet here they form unusual
chords, which proceed in what seem to be eccentric pro-
gressions, not necessarily jarring but somehow unsatisfying to the untrained ear.

Thus, in Wiseman's films, though there is no lack of

brief episodes and vignettes, there are few of those little self-contained dramas that seem to turn up so conveniently before the cameras of other recorders of actuality. When Wiseman uses a conventional event as a basic framework for a film—as in his recent television release, *Manoeuvre*, which is ostensibly an account of a United States army battalion that is transported from Louisiana to West Germany for two weeks of North Atlantic Treaty Organization maneuvers—he makes almost no attempt to adapt the basic framework into a conventional story. It isn't that *Manoeuvre* consists only of disconnected or impressionistic situations (such as nowadays are often linked by the grammar of fast-cutting into a pointed, dramatic design) but that the filmmaker seems uninterested in the welding of dramatic connections, or in the forging of an attractively unified whole out of the separate elements. There is the case, for example, of a certain battalion commander, a lieutenant colonel (one knows he is a lieutenant colonel only by his insignia), who appears at several points in the film, and not randomly, either, not by happenstance, for he is clearly the man in charge of a particular (though to us vague) sector of the mock battle. We watch him give several briefings; we watch him chew out his company commanders; we watch him in conversation with other officers. His is obviously an important role, but the "story" it belongs in is only hazily defined. The lieutenant colonel is *there*, before our eyes, but he is not positioned in the flow of film in any causal way; he is a figure not without "weight" but without linkage. The same is true of a certain also nameless tank-company commander, who appears even more frequently in the film. We see this captain conferring with his sergeants, and giving instructions to some men, and observing an "enemy" assault through binoculars. We become familiar with him—with his face and with his voice—but we never "know" him. Is he a good commander or a bad commander? What does he think of defending Western Europe? Of his battalion commander? Such questions are never asked and never answered, for the captain is never *followed*, according to the accepted documentary manner; there is no "One Day in the Life of" this tank-company commander. Once again, the man is *there*, undeniably real—not at all one of those lighter-than-air characters who inhabit the made-for-TV movies—but something appears to be missing from his portrait: a touch of drama at the most; at the least, a note of personality. We watch him, as we watch much of the nonnarrative in *Manoeuvre*, and wait for things that never happen. When General Alexander Haig, the commander of NATO, has lunch with the troops on their arrival, one imagines that surely he will somehow bump into the young captain—praise him; admonish him; perhaps talk about football or baseball with him, in the way that generals do. But no such meeting takes place; at least, if there is a trigonometry that connects the lieutenant colonel, the captain, and General Haig, it is not a trigonometry observed by Wiseman's camera.

There have been times when Wiseman's avoidance of an ordinary story line has been so unyielding as to seem downright perverse. I am thinking, for example, of his three-hour film *Canal Zone* in which scenes of boats passing and lock gates opening and closing and nameless men working unidentified machines succeeded one another in a near-stupefying parade of actuality. What *is* Wiseman trying to do, I have often wondered. The by now well-worn phrase *cinéma vérité* springs to mind but is not much help. Of course, he is after truth; everyone in film is after truth of some kind. Wiseman himself has provided some modest explanations from time to time, speaking gravely in interviews of his interest in "American institutions." Perhaps *cinéma institutionnel* is what he is up to; that would account for all those locks and levers and whatnot in *Canal Zone*, but one would still be hard pressed to describe *Manoeuvre* as a report that made much sense of the institutional aspects of military life. Maybe Frederick Wiseman is just a guy with a camera and a lot of black-and-white film who likes to travel about the world making movies about things and people. Maybe so. A few afternoons ago, at any rate, I thought I would run through *Manoeuvre* once again on my Betamax and see what clues turned up. There was one sequence in particular that interested me, about two-thirds of the way through the film. Essentially, it was a scene of three or four soldiers standing in a field and talking about a certain aspect of the ongoing but largely invisible maneuvers; in due course, the group shifted, with some of the men drifting away and the others being joined by two men who appeared to be military observers and who began talking about some quite different, though equally routine, military matter. There was little that was notable about this footage; indeed, what had struck me originally was its seemingly total lack of notability. When I watched the film for the first time, I had assumed at the outset of the group discussion that the men were telling us something significant or, at least, relevant about the maneuvers; but this didn't seem to be the case, for the situation was unexplained, and the terminology was mainly technical, and none of it was ever made any clearer. Then I had imagined that the soldiers themselves must have some causal bearing on the rest of the film, that they fitted into it in ways that would soon be apparent: one of the soldiers would move one of the tanks as a result of the discussion, or the observers would inform the tank commander that the latest segment of the exercises had gone well or badly. But none of these things happened. As with a lot of Wiseman's footage, the logic of it was perplexing. It was not *without* logic; so much was clear. Wiseman's films are neither artless nor unedited. His technique, if somewhat more informal than, say, Cecil B. De Mille's, is not as random as that of a blind man throwing darts. But what had been the point of this scene? I ran it through once again: American men in combat fatigues and steel helmets standing in a West German field and talking perfunctorily about such matters as fields of fire and weapon ranges. The discussion rather droned; the men seemed rooted to the spot; the camera also seemed rooted to the spot, patiently giving us a close-up of now one man, now another man, now part of the group, now the whole group. I felt myself becoming bored, impatient. Perhaps the point was to show the American troops in relation to Europe, to the European countryside, but Europe and its countryside were not really visible: some faraway gray fields and gray trees, but they might have been anywhere. I played the scene again. For the third time, the plainspoken Americans reappeared, speaking their same casual military-technical words about events and processes that had not been referred to before and were not to be referred to again. Was this merely the flotsam of *vérité* filmmaking? One knew that this discussion had actually occurred, but had it *merely* occurred? As I watched the patient close-ups, I began writing down the dialogue, partly for something to do, partly in a final attempt to find the dim logic of the scene; and as I scribbled the words while watching the faces on the screen I found myself suddenly less conscious of the words—the droning, strangely textured discussion— and more mindful of the faces: ordinary American faces. Was this the point? To show the ordinariness of faces? I looked harder, for there seemed to be something behind the ordinariness of the faces. And then I saw it, for it was so simple, really, so plainly there to be seen; in fact, I had been making such an effort not to see it! What Wiseman's camera had been giving us was not so much a glimpse of "ordinary men" (as are now seen cinematically virtually everywhere: in movies, in television entertainments, and maybe especially in television commercials) as a look at *men without masks*. The soldiers in the field, after all, were not actors contriving cleverly to appear to be soldiers, to have the "look" of soldiers. Nor were they real soldiers who gave any evidence that they were presenting themselves, even unconsciously, for the camera; at least, given Wiseman's methods, it seemed unlikely that his subjects had been in any way nudged with tactful requests to "be soldierly," or even to "be themselves"—indeed, to "be" anything. (One should acknowledge here that a criticism that was originally directed against a certain loosely made and self-important style of *vérité* filmmaking— namely, that the camera's presence has a tendency to distort the "truth" of particular scenes—has lately become rather gratuitously expanded into an all-embracing cliché to the effect that *any* camera inevitably distorts, and thus renders "untrue," *any* human environment it appears in. Sometimes even Heisenberg's rigorous uncertainty principle has been put forward in expert support of this opinion, as if subatomic particles and human beings brushed their teeth in the same way. A more reasonable view, one imagines, would be that a camera held by a cameraman is not all that unlike—in intrusive social effect—a notebook held by a reporter. That is, in both instances, provided there is care, patience, self-effacement, and a willingness to be bored to death, a record of actuality may be obtained whose distortions, as a result of even unconscious "acting," will prove to be negligible.) At any rate, it seemed a measure of Wiseman's dogged logic that one's sophisticated, entertainment-prone contemporary eye should be so eager to resist him. For what Wiseman had clearly done was to take these soldiers—and all the other soldiers, all his other subjects—and deliberately try to strip them of the masks and reference points and self-conscious attitudes that men and women continually and almost implacably present to the world; and my instinctive response had been to attempt to resupply (in my own mind, at least) what he had taken away. Conditioned not merely by most fiction films but by non-fiction films, too, even by so-called *vérité* filmmaking, to expect narrative, drama, incidents that always lead somewhere, information that is always directed to some useful or striking point, I had searched Wiseman's film in vain for purpose and dramatic focus, for unity and narrative cohesion, and finding them wanting—possibly mislaid—I had become restless and bored, in the manner of an impatient child raised on sweetened, fizzy drinks who is suddenly asked to drink clear mountain water and finds it tasteless.

Granted, my "discovery" about Wiseman's work is a personal response, and one of no great subtlety. Of course, one realizes, he is trying to show us without our masks—we who are almost all of us actors (governed by a President-actor; thrilling to the exploits of athlete-actors; receiving information through newsmen-actors, etc.), living in our self-conscious, theatrical era of easily manufactured identities and appearances. Still, it has given me renewed respect for his films. No, it is more than respect, for I have never begrudged Fred Wiseman admiration. In film after film, beginning with *Titicut Follies*, in 1967, and continuing with *High School, Law and Order, Hospital*, etc. (with each new release being presented by WNET/13, in the stouthearted manner of an old-fashioned publisher who publishes his author's oeuvre, volume by volume, no matter the commercial ups and downs), he has clearly been doing something important, something altogether untrivial, something surely admirable. Even in the case of the overlong and repetitive *Canal Zone*, it was hard not to feel respect, if sometimes only for the single-minded obstinacy of the attempt. Perseverance and seriousness were everywhere in evidence. Only emotion seemed sometimes in short supply: the emotional tones and colors in which our popular fiction filmmakers, and even some of our nonfiction filmmakers, bathe their subjects (as on a stage set) in order to make them more appealing and accessible. But where obstinacy lurks it is likely that not merely emotion but passion will be close behind; it is bound to be there somewhere. And it is this passion of Wiseman's not just for being quiet and playing the faithful recorder but for stripping bare and building anew—for disassembling our conventional musical scale and fashioning a new music out of the same notes—that appears to be finally making itself plain.

There is, in fact (or so it seems to me), some of the same obdurate, against-the-grain, though ultimately passionate quality in Wiseman's films that may be found in the work of the pioneer Soviet realist Dziga Vertov. It would not be entirely a coincidence that this were so, for Vertov was properly the founder-theoretician of the cinematic-reality movement that came to be known as *cinéma vérité*. That is, before the French avant-garde gave a French translation to the slogan "film truth," it had already been codified and practiced by Dziga Vertov in the early nineteen-twenties as *kino pravda*, also "film truth." (In homage to Vertov, the screen credits on Jean-Luc Godard's late-sixties films listed them as being produced by the Groupe Dziga Vertov.) Vertov was clearly a remarkable man, although infinitely different from Wiseman in background and the surfaces of personality. Vertov comes through to us today (by means of a few surviving films and a few surviving notebooks) as above all a child of the great 1917 Revolution; himself so youthful and enthusiastic, though already with a certain manic quality to his temperament; one of those children who wanted not merely to destroy their fathers but to make things new again: to become, instantaneously, their own fathers. This much is known. He was born in 1896 in Russian Poland. Before he changed his name to Dziga Vertov, it was Denis Arkadievich Kaufman. (The first thing one destroys is the father's name.) As a youth, he seems to have been hyperactive, and had literary ambitions. In his notebooks, he reported simply, "I began early." He wrote "various fantastic novels," as well as sketches, epigrams, and satirical

verse. At the time of these activities he was still what
we now call a teenager. For a while, he experimented
with sounds and language, attempting to reproduce in
words and letters "the sound of a waterfall, the noise
of a sawmill." By the coming of the Revolution, he
appears to have found his way into film work with the
recently established Moscow newsreel bureau, on
Gnezdnikovsky Street. He was twenty-one years old then
and worked under the celebrated editor and director
Lev Kuleshov, who was nineteen. Years afterward, Vertov wrote in his notebooks, "Nineteen-eighteen. I moved
to Gnezdnikovsky #7. Did a risky jump for a slow-
motion camera. Didn't recognize my face on the screen.
My thoughts were revealed on my face—irresolution,
vacillation, and firmness (a struggle within myself),
and again the joy of victory. First thought of the *kino*
eye (camera eye) as a world perceived without a mask,
as a world of naked truth (truth cannot be hidden)."
During the period of civil war that followed the Revolution, Vertov traveled the countryside with a "war photo-
graphic unit," turning out a series of forty-three
newsreels and such combat documentaries as *Battle at
Tsaritsyn, The Trial of Miranov*, and a twelve-reel *Anniversary of the Revolution*. By 1922, having made a
thirteen-reel *History of the Civil War*, and now head of
the All-Russian Central Executive Committee's Cinema
Department, Vertov entered the period of his most fer-
tile and innovative work: a second newsreel-documentary
series, called by him *Kino Pravda*, in which he began
in earnest to try to introduce his ideas about cinematic
truth and the "camera eye" into what was already an
established orthodoxy of the newsreel film.

Vertov was not exactly what one would call a conciliator: a proponent of smooth transitions, an accommodator to the past. "I would just like to establish that all we have been doing in cinematography up till now was a 100% muddle and diametrically opposed to what we should have been doing," he once wrote. Another time, he declared in a manifesto to Soviet cinematographers: "The organism of cinematography is poisoned by the frightful venom of habit. We demand being given an opportunity to experiment with this dying organism, with an objective of finding an antitoxin." Vertov's antitoxin was the *kino* eye—"the utilization of the camera as a cinema eye." But the point was not simply to have the camera mimic the human eye. "To this day we raped the movie camera and forced it to copy the work of our eye," he wrote. "And the better the copy, the better the shot was considered. As of today we will unshackle the camera and will make it work in the opposite direction, further from copying." Only the eye, he believed, "enters life simply," but the human eye is tricked and distracted by false perceptions, impressions, movements. When the eye "obeys the will of the camera," however, there is a new possibility created, "of a fresh perception of the world." There was no telling, in Vertov's opinion, what a liberating and invigorating sense of life—what "unusual freshness"—might result from the truth-telling resources of this "*kino* eye." It would be, he wrote, "a 'candid camera,' not for its own sake but to show people without their makeup on; to catch them through the camera's eye at some moment when they are not acting; to capture their thoughts by means of the camera." As he saw it, the *kino* eye was "a means of making the invisible, the obscure clear, the hidden obvious, the disguised exposed, and acting not acting. But it is not enough," he added, "to show bits of truth on the screen, separate frames of truth. These frames must be thematically organized so that the whole is also truth. This is an even more difficult task."

It is hard today to imagine Vertov. There are the few notebooks that have been translated into English. There are a very few surviving films. There is a glimpse of Vertov himself in one of his extraordinary later films, *The Man with the Movie Camera*: a youthful, angular, Slavic face, with quick, intelligent eyes and a broad forehead partly concealed beneath a jaunty cloth cap, such as even Soviet filmmakers appear to have worn in 1929. Unfortunately, the twenty-three "editions" of *Kino Pravda* seem no longer to exist—at least, anywhere in the West. Lenin, who set the pace, as it were, in making things new, is reported to have once said, "For us the cinema is the most important of the arts." Another time, he issued a directive—so Vertov mentions in one of his notebooks—which "pointed out the necessity of changing (i.e., raising) the proportion of fact-films on film programmes." In the heyday of *Kino Pravda*, Vertov spread a network of documentary camera crews across the Soviet Union. Mobile processing labs were established wherever work was being done. Afterward, special propaganda trains carrying the *Kino Pravda* newsreels traveled across Russia, stopping to show them wherever audiences might gather. How to conceive of such an audience, and of such a *cinéma vérité* train, stopped of an evening in the smoky provincial station of the township of K——, not far from the city of N——? Alas, Vertov's days of glory—or, at least, of official acceptance—did not last

long. Doubtless his aversion to propaganda, coupled with
Stalin's probably never very great enthusiasm for fact
films, served to diminish Vertov's popularity in Soviet
film circles. At any rate, by the middle of the nineteen-
thirties he was being officially accused of "Formalism,"
and, in what might be described as the original instance
of movie blacklisting, was deprived of creative filmmaking functions. He passed roughly two decades in
near-anonymity, editing Soviet newsreels, and died in
Moscow in 1954.

Luckily, however, what may well be his masterpiece
survives: *The Man with the Movie Camera,* one of whose
original prints is in the tender care of the Film Study
Center in the Museum of Modern Art. By contemporary
production standards, it appears somewhat crude and
amateurish, and even a bit odd: a black-and-white film,
without sound, without sets, without plot, without narrative structure, without progression. Technically, it is in
fact a virtuoso performance, a 1929 compendium of
cinematic technique: long shots; close-ups; fast-cutting;
speeded and slow motion; overhead shots; low-angle
shots; montages and multiple exposures; fades and dissolves; split-screen effects; and so on. But what makes it
so vital and eloquent, even today, is its remarkable feeling of exuberance about the most commonplace details
of life. For once, the Soviet Union is shown devoid of
the rosy tint of self-glorification as well as of the deep
hues of the National Epic. Instead, the film is partici-
patory, almost lighthearted, and above all forthright.
That is, it is neither unsubtle nor uncomplex (and not
at all sentimentally lyrical, in the *Family of Man* tradition), yet it has the overall effect of great simplicity

and penetration. It is certainly one of the first and finest films about the Camera Age, for not only does Vertov's Man with the Movie Camera (actually Vertov's younger brother, the cinematographer Mikhail Kaufman) go *everywhere* with his sturdy, tripod-mounted camera—crowded city streets; a factory; a room where a girl is dressing; a coal mine; a bathing beach; a sidewalk where children are watching a magician—but it is clearly the camera itself that is the main actor. Indeed, two of the most telling scenes are a wonderfully playful and carefree moment when the movie camera, with its spindly tripod legs, is shown positioning itself in a kind of dance, and even walking about, unaided by human hands; and then a more ominous sequence when a long shot of a strangely quiet and distanced city street suddenly reveals in a corner of the frame the silent, almost eerie presence of the same camera—swiveling, peering, looking, all-seeing. Thus, in 1929, did Dziga Vertov foretell our media era in both its key aspects—on the one hand, the brash, self-confident energy of the camera: Look at me! Aren't I great?; on the other hand, its unsettling nonhuman, sometimes threatening quality: What *does* the camera eye see?

I don't know if Wiseman ever studied Vertov. On the whole, I would rather doubt it, for Wiseman, who was born the year after *The Man with the Movie Camera* was made, and who trained as a lawyer, and even taught at Boston University Law School for two years, seems to have come into filmmaking with his own kind of freshness—walking in off the street, so to speak, and not from film school. And Wiseman, of course, employs none of Vertov's technical flashiness. Wiseman's technique is very good, very sure, but it is quieter, less self-conscious; some of those battles have been won, after all. But in the special kind of passion that each man has brought to nonfiction filmmaking, I suspect a close and sympathetic bond exists between the work of these two realists—these two unlikely cinematic kinsmen. For, despite Wiseman's sincere self-explications of his interest in "American institutions," what he has been doing all along is to dare to show us ourselves without masks; to let the camera strip us bare, so that the camera may build us anew. In short, he has been working with the *kino* eye. What an adventure it must be! And what obstinacy must be required to pursue it! A British film director, Thorold Dickinson, once described Vertov as "probably the most obstinate film personality of all time," and told of how, when Vertov attended the presentation of his first sound film, *Enthusiasm*, in London in 1931, "he insisted on controlling the sound projection. During the rehearsal, he kept it at a normal level, but at the performance he raised the volume of the climaxes to an earsplitting level. Begged to desist, he refused, and finished the performance fighting for possession of the instrument of control, while the building seemed to tremble with the flood of noise coming from behind the screen." Frederick Wiseman's passion, one imagines, is of a less manic and obdurate variety, but maybe it will prove to be more durable. He hangs in there, at any rate, not so much looking at us as letting his camera look at us, and neither "coldly" nor "hotly"—in other words, not confusing the human eye with the camera eye—but letting the camera see whatever it sees. Perhaps he is *our* Man with the Movie Camera. It is not an altogether easy job or a widely popular one, this stripping bare, this

rearranging of the old scale in order that we may hear
a new music, but, as Dziga Vertov showed a while ago,
it is a way of relating to life that is simple in the noblest
sense, and brave, and by no means without love.

(1980)

THE OPENING OF THE BASEBALL SEASON

I'M TELLING YOU, instability is going to be the finish of this country. The end. Finis. The Republic down the drain. Nothing left of the plains and the Rockies and the sun belt and the snow belt and the corn belt and the coal belt after too much instability gets loose in the land. By gosh, but there is a beauty, a real American beauty, in the state of things standing in their place. Washington. Niagara Falls. The Houston Space Center. Everything right where it should be. After all, how much instability can a nation take, especially a nervous and visionary nation such as this one, which has only lately realized that it is not actually nailed to the floor of the earth but is in fact floating rather randomly about on tectonic plates? What are the *limits* of instability? A change in the NFL schedule? An interruption of regular programming? A nuclear catastrophe? I'm telling you, there was a moment of instability out there last week. I hate to say it. Everybody was doing what he or she could to keep things even-keel. But sometimes instability just sort of creeps into the situation, if you know what I mean. No matter how hard people try to hold things level and stable, instability sometimes just kind of seeps in, through the keyhole, maybe, or through the chinks in the window frame where one tries to remember to wedge Mortite before winter. And then it's gone. Vanished. Oh, but people are glad to see it go. Do you remember the incident at the Three Mile Island nuclear plant a couple of weeks ago? Most people call it an incident, though nuclear folk, I think, call it an "event." Of course you remember. There was a malfunction in one of the pumps. Or something broke in a valve. There was not enough coolant. Or too much steam. The utility people were doing what they could. Some of the younger TV guys hung around the busted plant at Three Mile Island, offering us distant camera views of those four strange cooling towers, trying to make the best of the fudgy information they were getting from inside the plant, and doubtless hoping that the confident tone of the utility's press releases had more basis in fact than everyone supposed it did. The whole thing started so slowly, didn't it? There was something wrong down there in Pennsylvania. One sort of paid attention, but lots of things go wrong in lots of places, don't they? Automobiles sometimes don't work quite right. Airplanes have equipment failures. Space capsules catch fire. The difficulty in Pennsylvania seemed to have something to do with radiation, which is, naturally, a serious problem, though since it is also a serious, mainly invisible problem, most people appear to place it in the category of other serious, mainly invisible problems, such as tight money and original sin, and so never really manage to think about it quite as vigorously as they would like to. There was talk of fuel rods and primary reactor-cooling systems and quench tanks and coolant-flow pumps. The utility officials were pompous and evasive. The TV people were matter-of-fact and levelheaded. Whatever might be going on inside the damaged reactor—and stories varied as to whether things were getting better or were getting worse —outside there was at least a stability of language. "The valve on a pressurizer opened as planned," a newsman

explained, "and excess water flowed into a quench tank."
Another correspondent reported: "An emergency cooling
system has been activated, injecting water into the loop."
There was an interview with a representative of a nuclear
power plant in Florida. "We will see how the problem
relates to our own plant," he said, "and if it relates we
will implement our procedures." An engineer from a
nuclear plant in the Midwest said: "As an engineer, I
can't say nothing will never happen." The Governor of
Pennsylvania said: "There is no reason to disrupt your
daily routine." One of the officials at the Three Mile
Island plant said: "We see no indications of an emergency at this time." One would have to say that the
forces of national equilibrium were working strenuously
from within our television sets for the common good.

By then, it was the evening of Friday, March 30; time
for the network news. Earlier in the day, there had been
rumors and radio reports to the effect that "puffs" of
radioactive gas or steam had been escaping from the
stricken nuclear plant. Now, from his customary desk
in the CBS newsroom, at the center of the earth, the normally imperturbable face of Walter Cronkite hove into
view. "Good evening," said Cronkite, speaking with
unmistakable gravity. "The world has never known a day
quite like today. It faced the considerable uncertainties
and dangers of the worst nuclear-power-plant accident of
the atomic age. And the horror tonight is that it could
get much worse." As one watched the familiar countenance and listened to the familiar voice (whose easygoing mellowness now seemed dry with tension), one
suddenly had a feeling of being part of one of those
small, deceptively simple moments when time itself
seems to shift into some other gear, bearing us along

with it, though whether at a faster or slower rate than before was not yet clear. "It is not an atomic explosion that is feared," Cronkite continued. "The experts say that is impossible. But the specter was raised of perhaps the next most serious kind of nuclear catastrophe—a massive release of radioactivity. The Nuclear Regulatory Commission cited that possibility with an announcement that, while it is not likely, the potential is there for the ultimate risk of a meltdown at the Three Mile Island atomic power plant outside Harrisburg, Pennsylvania." Was it possible that Walter Cronkite had just released— albeit contained within the containment chamber of his own sturdy personality—his own cleansing puff of instability into our atmosphere? For a number of years, I have admired Cronkite's avuncular humanity and gen- ial newsmanship, while sometimes feeling skeptical of the contrived neutrality of the anchorman's role, which often serves to put a veil or barrier between the anchor- man (however humane and genial) and his audience. But, just then, I thought Cronkite had broken through the barrier and for a tiny moment dared us to see the real terror of the times we live in, through the eyes of a most decent man who could not, and perhaps would not, keep the fear and despair and anger out of his voice in the service of the higher stability. And so for a brief while afterward, and as the evening news ran its course, with accounts of a newfound gas bubble in the reactor core, and of the release of radioactive gas into the air above Middletown, Pennsylvania, and of the evacuation of pregnant women and small children from nearby areas, one had the sense (so rare and frightening to a modern citizen) that *nothing* was in its place, or might ever be in its place again. On our behalf, Old Merlin had peered, not so much into the future as into the present, and it seemed that we were now adrift, free-falling, spinning helplessly in a maelstrom of possibilities that perhaps nobody might be able to check.

And then, of course, as things must, the level of instability decreased and stability returned—was hauled back in. On the mechanical side, over the weekend a way had been found to lower dangerous gas levels in the containment chamber. On the TV news, a more matter-of-fact tone swiftly returned to the reports from Three Mile Island. From Washington, it was announced that President Carter had promised a "thorough inquiry" into the disaster. A different kind of problem was soon being discussed. "As many as three thousand dairy farms could be contaminated, which would mean a loss of millions to Pennsylvania dairymen," said one correspondent. Another remarked, "Any radiation or contamination would destroy the tourist industry." When Secretary of Energy James Schlesinger was questioned about the future of nuclear power, he declared, "What we have seen here is the case of an error made in operations. I think that all of us should withhold judgment until we have had the opportunity to look at this incident in the light of total experience." Walter Cronkite was back on his regular beat. "The tone is optimistic," he said; "however, the convalescence promises to be dangerous, long, and costly." Ten minutes later, in his staunch, well-modulated voice, he told us of twenty-five persons who had died in a fire "in what was described as a clean, well-kept boarding house in Farmington, Missouri." We were back home, safe. Everything was in its place. A sports announcer spoke about the opening games of the new baseball season. The Yankees were going to play the Brewers. Instability had been banished once again. But what of that brief, sudden, freezing wind that had blown through the house only a short while ago—so chill that it had made even Walter Cronkite shiver? Had it ever happened? Was it only an embarrassment, as moments of instability usually are? Had Walter Cronkite really shivered? Yes, he had.

(1979)

JIM PECK'S CABARET

THE FACT IS, I'd never have been watching *3's a Crowd* if I didn't hate to jog. I don't much like to row, either—or whatever it is that one does on a rowing machine—but a rowing machine is what I bought a little while ago to avoid jogging, setting it down first in the room of an absent child, where I used it once (a thirty-minute experience of such deep, such nearly sublime, boredom that I would have betrayed my whole regiment not to repeat it) and then didn't look at it again for several weeks, until one day, for reasons doubtless as subtle and inspirational as those that compelled Archimedes to keep an eye on his bathwater levels, I removed the sleek and stupefying rowing contraption from the absent child's room and set it down in front of my television set. Soon, in the time-honored fashion (or so I like to think) of elegant, brawny undergraduates sculling along the dank and murky waters of the Charles or the Schuylkill or the Housatonic, I was rowing my way each day through a veritable scenic vista of television programs. Some programs, I can say, are definitely better for rowing through than other programs. A Cowboys–Steelers game, for example, might seem like a good row, but it is actually too exciting, and also too infrequent; a man who waited for a Cowboys–Steelers game before hunching into position over his oars would soon find his muscles and so forth deteriorating to Jell-O. The *Today* show, on the other hand, is desirably frequent and is not a bad row, especially when Tom Brokaw is being a little tight and snappish, but you have to pick the right part of the show; too much weather news from the Mountain States or an overchatty interview with a visiting heart specialist can sink one's entire craft into the carpet. Similarly, *Good Morning America*, though it would doubtless be very enjoyable if one were seated properly at the breakfast table, drinking a cup of coffee and staring into the middle distance, is hard to really focus on after the halfmile mark; on the whole, I would imagine that *Good Morning America* is probably a better show to dance to than to row to, but that is only a guess. For a while, I rowed quite happily to reruns of *Ironside* in the afternoons on Channel 9. There's enough action on-screen to sustain a fairly steady thirty-stroke beat to the first commercial break, and then to warrant raising it—in tiny, gallant bursts—to thirty-five as the first victim gets rubbed out; then you can more or less hand the whole thing over to Ironside himself after the second commercial break. But the drawback to *Ironside* is that midafternoon isn't really a practical time of day for rowing. An oarsman, it seems to me, needs the vigor of the morning air for his best efforts, and that—to make a long story short—is how I've come to be watching a game show called *3's a Crowd*, which is shown at nine-thirty in the morning on CBS, every single, blessed day of the week.

Ostensibly, as I said, *3's a Crowd* is a game show, or quiz show. Basically, I guess you could call it a sort of sex show, though perhaps that gives the wrong impression, implying that wonderfully delicious activities are taking place on Channel 2 at nine-thirty in the morning, when in fact, as is the case with most game or quiz shows, very little activity of any kind seems to take place at all. Maybe it would be better to call it a sexy type of show, though that isn't quite right, either; sexiness, according to the current definition, seems to involve not only what is sometimes described as ample displays of flesh but also a whole contemporary hammer-and-tongs approach to eroticism, and there's really very little of either flesh or eroticism that gets revealed on *3's a Crowd*. In any case, what does take place is very simple, even classical in its unities, and very swift-paced—not a beat lost, not a second wasted—and follows a pattern that varies little, or not at all, from day to day. First, there is the usual musical fanfare, with sounds of applause from an invisible audience, and then the appearance of the host, Jim Peck. Peck is a clever choice for the role: a curly-haired fellow of boyish charm and sprightly manner. In real life, he might be a junior ad-agency executive in Chicago, or one of those actor/model types who once essayed the Joel Grey part in a summer-stock version of *Cabaret*. Peck, in fact, has something of his own cabaret ringmaster's manner, but it is an act modeled more on Johnny Carson than on Joel Grey; the Grey character had seen it all and didn't really want to look anymore, while Carson—our American media Candide —still has his eye to the keyhole.

Then the first phase of the game unfolds. On the bare studio stage are now seen three men, each one seated on a little game-show podium (on chairs that somehow seem a half size too small). Sometimes, the men are youthful, in their twenties, but for the most part they are older—family men; in fact, husbands and businessmen. The threesome is quickly introduced, in semijocose fashion. Thus, "Husband No. 1 is a lawyer who wears his own briefs. Say hello to Lamar Taylor," or "Husband No. 2 is a physical-education director who runs

around a lot. Say hello to Dave Norris," and so forth.
Then Jim explains that we're about to find out "who
really knows each husband best, his wife or his secretary," and that whichever woman, secretary or wife,
matches most of the husband's replies to the game's
forthcoming questions will win "a cash prize of one
thousand dollars." And we're off.

On an average day, things might start off as follows.
First question: "How many days a week are you in a
sexy mood?" Each husband writes his answer down on
a card, which he holds up to the audience—or, at any
rate, to the camera—in the spirit of a show-and-tell
exercise. Two husbands write "Seven," for which they
are roundly applauded by the invisible audience; one
writes "Five," for which he is also applauded. Next
question: "Between what hours of the day or night is
your best sex life?" One husband answers "9 p.m. to
midnight"; another, "10 p.m. to midnight"; the third,
"6 p.m. to 2 a.m." Third question: "How would you
complete the blank in this sentence? 'Lately, my wife's
sex drive has been ————.' " One husband writes "On
automatic pilot"; another writes "Terrible"; the third
writes "Delayed." Fourth question: "How would you
complete the blank in this sentence? 'My wife's ————
is droopy.' " One husband answers "Chin"; another
answers "Ears"; the third answers "Chest." Fifth question: "What is the strangest or funniest thing you ever
asked your secretary to do with you?" One husband
writes "Go to the beach"; another writes "Going naked
in the Jacuzzi"; the third writes "Skinny-dipping."

After the first commercial break, when the camera
returns to the studio, three couples are now seen onstage;
the husbands have been joined by three women, with each

couple now seated cozily together on the little podiums in the accepted fashion of husband-and-wife contestant teams. Here, however, the couples are not husband and wife but employer and secretary. The secretaries are also briskly and humorously introduced and are asked to answer the same questions. Thus, "How many days a week is he in a sexy mood?" is answered by the first secretary with "None." Jim Peck asks her to elaborate. "Well, he comes in like such a grouch, as if he hadn't thought about sex for months." The second secretary smiles shyly and says, "I'd like to say *nine*, but I guess I'd better not go into that." The third secretary says, "He's really not like that. He never thinks about things like that." Second question: "Between what hours of the day or night do you think his best sex life would be?" One secretary says, "Between 9 p.m. and 10 p.m." Another says, "Well, it sure couldn't be any other time. He comes in at dawn and he stays there most of the evening. I'd have to say between twelve and twelve-thirty." Third question: "How would you complete the blank in this sentence? 'Lately, his wife's sex drive has been ————.' " The first secretary says, "Low. I mean, like I said, he's always such a grouch." The second secretary says, "I can't believe it's very high." The third one says, "I don't know; she's always got the kids and all. She's young, though, so I'd say medium." Fourth question: "How would you complete the blank in this sentence? 'His wife's ———— is droopy.' " The secretary to the husband who answered "Chin" says matter-of-factly "Boobs." The secretary to the husband who answered "Ears" says "Drawers." The secretary to the husband who answered "Chest" says, "I'd definitely have to say she's missing something up *here*. You know, her boobs. I mean, she even has a nickname." Jim Peck says, "What's the nickname?" The secretary says "Pancake." Jim Peck then asks the husband, "Is that right?" The husband smiles, and says, "I guess so." Fifth question: "What is the strangest or funniest thing he ever asked you to do with him?" The first secretary says, "Well, there's this beach where people swim in the nude." Jim Peck says, "So *that*'s the beach?" The secretary says, "No, no, we were going to wear flesh-colored bathing suits and just *watch*." The second secretary says, "Well, he asked if he could use my Jacuzzi." Jim Peck says, "*Your* Jacuzzi?" The secretary says, "Yes, my apartment came with a Jacuzzi; it's really very relaxing." The third secretary pauses a moment and then says, "Well, he and his wife once asked me to go to this club with them." Jim Peck asks, "What kind of a club?" The secretary says, "Well, it was an unusual kind of club. I guess I really don't want to go into that." Jim Peck persists: "A country club? A golf club?" The secretary says, "No, a pretty unusual kind of club—you know, with nude swimming and all. I really don't want to go into that."

After the second commercial break, the wives make their appearance—each seated on the other side of her husband, so that each little pair is now a trio. The wives are introduced and are asked the same set of questions. As to the frequency of her husband's sexy moods, one wife says, "Not during the week. I'll have to try to remember." Another says, "Maybe Saturdays. He's definitely Mr. Tired these days." Jim Peck says, "Well, let's see what your husband answered. Seven days a week!" The wife laughs, and says, "He's got to be kidding." As to the hours when their best sex life occurs, two wives answer "Between 10 and 11 p.m.," while the wife whose husband answered "Between 6 p.m. and 2 a.m." says "Between 9 and 10 p.m." When she is told of his answer, she looks at him and laughs good-naturedly. "I usually fall asleep at ten," she says, "so I can't vouch for what happens afterward." As to the status of their own sex drives, the first wife says, "Well, he better have said tremendous or out goes the water bed." The second wife says, "I think it's been pretty good. I mean, for us." When she is told of her husband's answer ("Terrible"), she digs him playfully in the ribs and says, "I guess he's not crazy about those big curlers I wear." The third wife says, "Frankly, we've been having a problem about that, but I don't think it has much to do with my sex drive. It's more that he couldn't—you know, carry it out." As to which part of her is droopy, the wife whose husband answered "Chin" and whose husband's secretary answered "Boobs" says, "My face. I drink too many milkshakes." When Jim tells her of the secretary's answer, she says, "My boobs? How can you say that? I can't believe you actually said that!" The wife whose husband answered "Ears" and whose husband's secretary answered "Drawers" says "Behind." Jim tells her of the other answers. "Ears?" She giggles. "I have cute ears." The wife whose husband as well as husband's secretary answered "Chest" also says "Chest." When she is told that both husband and secretary said the same thing, so that both women scored big points on the same question, she embraces her husband and pats the secretary on the knee. Finally, as to the strangest or funniest thing that either she or her husband might have asked the secretary to do, the first wife says, "Drive the children to music school." The second wife says, "Swim nude in the Jacuzzi." The third wife says, "Well, I once asked Roberta to go out on a date with us." Jim says, "To the club?" The wife says, "Oh, you heard about the club? Well, I thought she'd enjoy it. Some really nice people." The secretary says, "Well, I wouldn't have."

And, suddenly, there ends another performance of *3's a Crowd*, with the camera zooming back from the nine contestants (who seem, as a result, to be receding into a galactic void of studio drapery), and with Jim Peck, now close up and smiling boyishly, telling prospective contestants what number to phone to get on the show, and with the invisible audience surrendering one final burst of applause, and, as often happens, with no mention of who has won the "cash prize of one thousand dollars"—a victory that by then must surely seem almost beside the point even to the competitors.

What is one to make of such a show—such an event? Is it good? Bad? Funny? Tasteless? Or maybe all those things? My guess is that the only prudent reply to such a question is a sort of makeshift Delphic shrug: Who knows? Besides, as is the case with most other successful artifacts of popular culture, one imagines that *3's a Crowd* not only is impervious to most ordinary analysis but also probably has the last laugh, both on those who would put it down for lack of taste and on those who might feel drawn to celebrate it too patronizingly for its vulgarity. In the end, though, I think it reminds me of nothing so much as the raunchy penny postcards that George Orwell wrote about in his essay "The Art of Donald McGill." Mind you, those postcards (which were popular in the shadier British stationery stores in the thirties and forties, and doubtless right up to the removal of sexual censorship in our own time) weren't the really "dirty," or "French," variety, later called "hard-core."

They were a much jollier, cheaper, and less sophisticated kind of thing: "A genre of their own," as Orwell wrote, "specialising in very 'low' humour," displaying an "endless succession of fat women in tight bathing-dresses," or "a sort of sub-world of smacked bottoms and scrawny mothers-in-law." More than half, perhaps three-quarters, of the jokes were sex jokes, Orwell wrote, "ranging from the harmless to the all but unprintable," and focusing on such perennial subjects as newlyweds, illegitimate babies, old maids, and nude statues, also policemen and babies' diapers, also chamber pots and public lavatories (both of which "are *ipso facto* funny"), but not actual infidelity ("very seldom exploited") or homosexuality (which is "never mentioned").

Orwell's upper-middle-class, Etonian sensibility struggled mightily in this essay (perhaps our first pop-culture critique) with the unbuttoned McGill's artistic preoccupations ("A recurrent, almost dominant motif . . . is the woman with the stuck-out behind") before concluding that, despite the "crude drawing and unbearable colours" (with designs "full of heavy lines and empty spaces . . . the faces grinning and vacuous, the women monstrously parodied"), McGill's postcards affirmed the virtues of English working-class marriage and humor. Granted that Orwell's representations of working-class marriage and humor, to say nothing of the working class itself, need some updating, it seems to me that his perspective on the subject is not a bad guide to *3's a Crowd* —or, in fact, to most of our popular television game shows. In other words, while the superficial conventions of marriage and sex and so forth have certainly changed since Orwell's time, the underlying messages from the participants in *3's a Crowd* seem really not very different from the messages of McGill's postcards, or from most folklore. Husbands talk a big game but rarely deliver; Mr. Hyde, the Jacuzzi flirt, is actually Dr. Jekyll, or Mr. Tired. Wives get older and seem to be fighting a rearguard action, but then, like the Russian troops retreating before Napoleon, they still have Mother Russia to fall back on. The secretary, of course, is the classic temptress, the serpent in the Garden of Eden, although, as so often occurs, Adam and Eve have long grown apple-shaped and apple-souled from eating all the apples off the Tree of Knowledge, which only she has never tasted. In brief, marriage is something that only clever, erotic, and thin people ever succeed in escaping. I include "thin" because the other evening I overheard a remarkably elegant and thin woman commenting to a remarkably elegant and thin man on "how thin" everybody was getting these days. The next morning, dawdling more than usual over my oars, I couldn't help noticing that most of the participants in that day's *3's a Crowd*— men as well as women, but on the whole, wives and secretaries more than men—were definitely *not thin*. Indeed, there was no great notion or spirit of thinness anywhere in the air; no sense anywhere, say, of thinness having been attempted and not achieved. On the contrary, in short order a secretary could be observed on-screen attempting to answer a question about "what kind of fruit or vegetable" she most resembled. "I'd have to say mango," she said solemnly. "Because they're hard to get?" asked Jim Peck. "No, because I've got a good figure. Also, I peel easily." Jim then asked the employer-husband to repeat his answer. "Grapefruit," he said. "Only *one* grapefruit?" the secretary asked. "*Two* grapefruit," he said. The secretary beamed. "I'm glad you didn't say carrot or something." There was a furious burst of studio laughter, and then Jim Peck said, "Now for our fourth question. Has your boss ever given you a ham, a turkey, or a goose for Christmas?"

Come to think of it, the only strange thing about *3's a Crowd* is who watches it. I don't mean the invisible people who do all the laughing. I mean the actual viewers— a group that in earlier times one might have assumed to be composed largely of women. From all the labor statistics that are constantly being published, however, it is clear that women have so inundated the job market that there can scarcely be a dozen left at home at nine-thirty in the morning to idle away the hours watching raunchy game shows. That presumably leaves very old people relaxing in miniature-golf clubhouses, tiny children languishing in day-care centers, off-duty policemen, and, of course, oarsmen: an eccentric audience, if you will, but doubtless a faithful one.

(1980)

PRUFROCK ALOFT; PRUFROCK BEFORE THE TELEVISION SET

A FEW DAYS AGO, while seated snugly in an airplane seat on my way back to New York from Chicago, with a drink in front of me, last week's copy of *Sports Illustrated* on my lap, the soothing hum of the engines washing over my ears, and with the memory of the hectic taxi ride to the airport and wretched traffic jams and ticket-counter chaos already receding in my brain, it occurred to me that a rather striking similarity existed between the situation I found myself in then, flying in a modern airliner, and what I've often felt as I watch television. To begin with, both experiences are largely passive, or at any rate they have been transformed into passive experiences. But this shared passivity is itself more complicated than it seems, for though it produces in both cases an obvious condition of quiet and inactivity, it also demands from the passenger or viewer a very definite emotional commitment. One might call it a commitment to specifically nonaggressive and uninvolved behavior.

Consider the airplane journey, for example. In many ways, the level of ordinary comfort for passengers has been decreasing since the days of the old Pan American Clippers, with their well-appointed dining rooms and sleeping quarters. Even so, there is undoubted pleasure of a sort to be had in a routine jetliner trip of reasonable length, at least without squalling babies or hyperactive grandparents in one's vicinity. As an extreme instance of this, I mention the experience of a friend who, being harried to exhaustion by a project in New York, determined suddenly to fly to California for a few days by the sea. No sooner was he airborne on the way out than he began to relax. Five hours later in California, however, once on the ground and dealing with baggage and car rentals and freeways and his overcrowded motel-by-the-sea, he began again to unravel. The same evening, he drove back to the airport, took a return flight to New York, and, after five more hours of airplane massage, was in a suitable condition for resuming work.

People still talk of the romance of travel, and perhaps it is still romance for cruise-ship passengers or fashionable visitors to Ethiopian ruins. But where travel was formerly an active and difficult undertaking, with the pleasure to be gained from it consisting largely in the mastery of the event (or of the unexpected sequence of events), nowadays the point is not so much in surmounting the chance encounter as in never having one. The goal of modern travel, in fact, is to have "experience" (as on a photo-safari to Kenya), but without experiences: without involvement. Indeed, involvement and aggressive behavior are actively discouraged, as anyone has discovered, for example, who ever tried to open a dialogue with an airline employee as to *what* the maintenance crew were doing to a certain engine (and *why*) that required a departure delay of three and a half hours.

Once aboard the shiny, experienceless airplane, however, our passenger lumpishly settles into his narrow seat, usually disheveled in mind or spirit from the hurly-burly of the outside world, often still quivering from the hazards of actually getting to the airplane. If he is a business traveler, flying first-class at company expense, the stewardess has already relieved him of his coat and briefcase: his downtown symbols. Wifelike, too, she will give him an initial reward for having reached her: a Bloody Mary. Perhaps also a smile, a bit of chat, depending on how severe the pressures of the airplane-household have been. Prufrock, in effect, has arrived home: to *his* seat, with a number on it that matches the number on his boarding pass so that no one may take it from him. Now he need do nothing more, except buckle himself into it, and follow modest instructions "for his own safety and comfort," and continue to act unaggressively. For doing so, he will be rewarded throughout the voyage: by forward progress through the air; by the loan of a magazine; by the outright gift of the airline's own magazine ("Yours to keep after deplaning"); by more drinks; by the larger hospitality of a meal; by preselected music for his ears; even by the appurtenances of an overnight guest: a pillow and a blanket. Indeed, a veritable shower of benefits is rained upon the passenger by the authorities of the airplane (including periodic descriptions of the unseen ground being traversed, which are delivered over loudspeaker by the unseen captain), who ask in return only that the passenger continue to do nothing, stay quiet, keep still. Bathroom privileges are formally tendered, but can be suddenly revoked. Primary addictive substances, such as cigarettes, are permitted the passengers more rapidly after takeoff than secondary substances, such as alcohol, which (except in first class) might cause unrest or even spill. When all the right conditions are met, determined by the chief authority in the cockpit, moderate mobility is allowed, but since there is usually no place to walk to, except the bathroom, it is a pleasure seldom accepted. Besides, as the captain announces, even when the seat-belt sign has been turned off one would do well to keep buckled and stay put.

Passivity, in short, holds sway in the modern airliner. And when aggression reappears, it is sternly chastised. Right after the plane has landed, for example, but before it has arrived at the gate, several passengers—doubtless summoned once more to their former aggressive ways by the imminence of the outside world—will leap to their feet and begin reaching for coats and bags like children who have been held too long in school. At this point, the formerly benign stewardess becomes severe and quickly reprimands the unruly passengers for their aggression. If these passengers, she suggests, do not abandon their aggressive behavior and return to the domicile of their seats, they will be deprived of the one thing they still lack: further forward motion toward the gate. Thereupon, the misbehaving passengers feign non-aggressive behavior, making the pretense of returning to their seats, though rarely quite doing so, until the second the plane has docked at the gate and they have been released from the spell of docility. Immediately, aggression floods back into the veins, and now all the passengers crowd the aisle, then push past each other down the airport corridor, and once again resume their conflicts over baggage, taxis, buses, or parking space.

It seems to me that the experience of watching most commercial television involves a similar passivity, and even a similar sense of the experienceless voyage. Here, of course, the seat belts are figurative rather than actual, though there appears to be a variety of television lounge chair on the market whose chief function seems to be to safely enclose the viewer during his nightly journey as if he were on a space flight. Also, it is probably no more than a coincidence that the TV dinner and the standard airline meal are made the same way, with the same technology, often the same ingredients, and generally the same results. Of course, with television, the forward motion is through time, not space, but the effect is somewhat the same, since in today's world final destinations rarely exist. That is to say: the end of each day's program schedule, like O'Hare Airport, is as much a beginning as a terminus.

In any case, rewards for good (i.e., uninvolving, non-aggressive) behavior flow similarly throughout the TV voyage as on the airplane trip. First, there is the vague sense of progress or forward motion induced by the seemingly linear progression of the evening's programs. We have seen Show A and are now starting on Show B, which is a step forward, at least in time. But where are we then? Show C, and then Show D and E, and then bed. And then the new day's shows. Thus, the present program contains the next one, and so forth; each new satisfaction breeds another. Second, there are the messages of the commercial sponsors, which act on the viewer in two different ways, both of them "beneficial." On a symbolic level, as is well known, they sing to him of a better, finer life: of a new car to make him feel rich; of a new hair spray to make him feel virile; of a laxative to make him feel "regular." But on a more immediate, less dreamlike level, the commercial interruption is also a release: permission, as it were, from the authority of the network or station to make a trip to the bathroom or to get another bottle of beer from the refrigerator. The instant gratification that comes from the beer or the bathroom (while the commercials are supposedly being ignored) is in fact a stand-in for the larger, more abstract rewards they promise. And throughout this period of time travel via television, aggressive or involving behavior is once again discouraged, though not so much by steely Clairol stewardesses as by the form and content of the programs themselves.

These nightly, factory-made entertainments are sometimes dismissed as soporific, and sometimes extolled as fascinating, gripping, *fun*, but the fact is that though they are sometimes each of these things, for the most part they are none of them. They are, instead, permeable: constructed in such a way that life can seep through them. A book, for example, is not permeable; even a trashy book is hard to read with any enjoyment while one is paying bills or talking on the telephone. And plays and movies are just as opaque in this way, though increasingly the TV-trained audience tries to engage in casual domestic chitchat while seated in darkened theaters, staring at the actors on the stage or giant screen. But television programs not only coexist with routine household transactions; they seem to present a kind of porous substance to the audience that almost invites an uninvolved, quiescent response. Who has not, for example, observed a family living room (one's own!) where somebody's "favorite program" is on the air, while the somebody in question carries on a desultory conversation with another party, and somebody else (also watching) gossips on the telephone with Clara, and somebody else (naturally also watching) doodles with her history homework? Do the TV programs create our uninvolved response to them? Or does the uninvolved nature of the modern family somehow evoke the TV programs? Whatever the answer, there seems to be a kind of subliminal understanding in effect, a new form of social compact. In any case, if fear of flying has played some part in creating the ceremonial ritual of the seat belt and the stewardess, then fear of another kind has presumably helped to shape the quite unusually uninvolving nature of our television entertainments. Is it fear of the future or of impersonal, uncontrolled technology, as is periodically suggested? Or, once again, just fear of ourselves? At any rate, one can know this much: that the passengers who angrily jam the airplane aisles and rush pell-mell down airport corridors for taxis are the same people who, moments before, sat meekly buckled in by seat belts. As it is, the TV viewers who chat and read and pay the bills and even have sex while looking at and through their "favorite programs" could probably only engage in one activity that doesn't blend easily with the soft messages of the TV set: they could really *notice* one another. One imagines that most of them would do so if they could.

(1976)

BARETTA'S T-SHIRT

LIKE MUCH of the country, television is obsessed with youth, and especially with adolescence. Of course, there are still plenty of "old people's" programs around, such as game shows and the news, though game shows are said to cut across age lines and even the news is gradually being made to seem more youthful. On the whole, mass-oriented commercial television is a "young people's" network, while the less popular public television is more of an "old people's" network. That is, public television responds to youth primarily in an institutional way, which means that by and large it keeps youth out, or carefully under control. Granted, there are exceptions: for instance, probably nowhere in broadcasting has youth been better served than by the Children's Television Workshop's *Sesame Street* and *The Electric Company*. Here the institution took thought of its duty to the young—albeit, originally, of its duty to the underprivileged or disadvantaged young—and spared no expense in bringing alms of literacy to its needy clients. In keeping with the latest instructional style, the children were not preached at, scolded, lectured; instead, they were entertained. Efforts, generally successful, were made not to condescend, not to talk down, not to be boring. Modern psychology was employed. Show-business celebrities, like successful high-school alumni, were invited to participate—not to boast and so make their young audience feel unworthy but, rather, to tactfully radiate success and so invite a desire for emulation and achievement. What ragamuffin, after all, might not learn to spell "ragamuffin" correctly with Bill Cosby himself portraying each letter by means of somersaults? All in all, public television has served its young clients honorably, though nearly always from a fundamentally parental point of view, somewhat in the manner of a great lady who, remembering that time long ago when she herself was a child, organizes amusing educational events for the town children. Thus, even when the point is entertainment, usually a higher purpose exists so as to dignify or elevate it. In short, on public television, as with most adult institutions, a tone of adult responsibility generally prevails, even where "fun" is involved. As, for instance, in the new historical-drama series *The Best of Families*, where "entertainment values" have been doggedly introduced, as befits an expensive and supposedly entertaining production, but have been kept decidedly in the background to serve the higher cause of painstaking (and overabundant) historical authenticity. Public television, then, more often than not responds to youth in the manner of the school, and not so much of the actual classroom (which now contains all kinds of Communications Era training aids) as of the institution of the school, with its built-in tendencies for expressing first of all the paramount virtues of the parent generation and then for ceaselessly attempting, parentlike, to protect the young from sin, temptation, and often new experience—for their own good.

Meanwhile, the larger and dominant arm of broadcasting—commercial television—has been approaching youth in the altogether simpler, tackier, more easygoing fashion of the marketplace. Here there are few claims to higher purpose, except when absolutely necessary. Here, too, the young are frankly welcome, not merely as somebody's children but on their own. Commercial television doesn't exactly love kids, either, but it's more fun. Of course, it wants to sell them something; it wants a transaction. But at least it wants them.

Granted, commercial television isn't above donning an ill-fitting institutional manner on certain occasions: for awards ceremonies, for instance, or when it is trying to con some branch of the government, or when it is actually forced to deal with parental institutions on the subject of kids. Some years ago, when early parent groups, such as Action for Children's Television, began to complain about the quantities of cheery, mindless twaddle which were being beamed at children, especially on Saturday mornings, the first response of the networks was to huffily refuse to listen or else to claim that the kids loved the programs (which was partly true; some kids would gladly watch test signals on Saturday morning). Their second response was to put on their institutional clothes and try to deal with the parents on an institutional basis. Thus, many strange-sounding pronouncements were made by network executives about their overpowering concern for the future of the race, and eventually some minor reforms were introduced into Saturday-morning program practices, such as the addition of "educational consultants" to the staffs of several of the cartoon shows. In effect, what had happened was that parents had institutionalized themselves in order to "protect" their kids, and the television programmers had made a show of institutionalizing *themselves* in order to deal with the parents. Then, a few years later, it was noticed that most of the kids in the country seemed to have grown up to the point where they were no longer watching just kiddie shows; they were watching regular prime-time entertainment. Therefore, the parent groups reinstitutionalized themselves and called for a diminution of sex and violence in network evening programming—especially of violence, since there was virtually no sex. And the networks responded by putting on their most sobersided and sanctimonious institutional manner and decreeing a new, institutionalized "philosophy of programming" known as the Family Hour, whereby adult programs (i.e., those with sex or violence) would be shown only after 10 p.m., by which time, it was institutionally reasoned, most young viewers would be in bed, or at least saying their prayers.

Fortunately, at least for a commercial society, commercial television has a life and logic of its own; and so the attempts of well-meaning American parents to perform their time-honored ritual of protecting the young from impure thoughts by creating an adult-conceived structure for them to play in hasn't really brought anything but cosmetic changes to the hurly-burly of the television marketplace. The parents now have their educational consultants and a modest decline in the amount of gunfire per evening. The kids, however, still have their transactions. In fact, if anything, youth-oriented programs have gradually come to dominate the marketplace, as though the strongest—or, at least, most popular— value systems in America right now were those of young people, and especially of adolescents.

Consider, for example, how many of the more successful network entertainment programs play and replay a continuous drama whose primary virtues appear to be those that are associated with the sensibilities of the modern adolescent: a certain surface coolness that conceals a passionate and usually misunderstood nature, and an alienation from the adult world ("the system") which often takes the form of outright rebellion. Adolescent rebelliousness actually seems to be the most common single virtue currently possessed by heroes in commercial-TV series, although, unlike the rebelliousness of real adolescence, which rises and wanes throughout the day—often with no great conviction—it has been elevated on television to something of an art form. There it exists, for instance, regardless of age or race, in such recent heroic characters as the Mexican-American Chico in *Chico and the Man*, and in the elderly black Mr. Sanford in *Sanford & Son*, and in the Italian-American Fonzie in *Happy Days*. In *Welcome Back, Kotter*, an entire classroom of adolescents appears to be in rebellion against the teacher, Mr. Kotter, but this is only a token rebellion; the real rebellion is Kotter's against the school system. In *MASH*, the funny doctors are in perpetual schoolboyish rebellion against the military system. On detective shows, such as *Starsky & Hutch*, the good-guy cops are now nearly always mavericks, misunderstood and hamstrung by the "grownups."

Think of *Baretta*, the popular tough-guy-detective show that stars Robert Blake. Blake is a good actor, who puts a lot of grit and energy into his work, and the success of the program derives from a support base far wider than that of the adolescent audience. Even so, its values are mainly adolescent. That is, though Baretta's social politics seem to be abstractly descended from earlier tough-guy-detective models (such as Sam Spade, whose fight-for-the-underdog sympathies were rooted in the leftist movement of the nineteen-thirties), his emotions and life style appear to be those of the contemporary teenager. For instance, he doesn't wear grownup clothes—not even grownup street clothes—for his undercover work; instead, he shuffles or sprints along in a tight pair of trousers and an old T-shirt. His hair is long, though not too long. His apartment is genially scruffy, the kind of happy-go-lucky mess that a mother would always be tidying up. He has the appearance of a toughie, too; when he is going about his dangerous business, he can be real cool or hard as nails —if he has to. But just beneath the surface, like a teenager, he is all heart and soul; he passionately *cares*. Of course, he can't stand phonies. Grownup, downtown sophistication doesn't fool him or impress him. But what he really hates is badness, truly evil people, like those in a recent episode who were mean to kids. Here the baddest guy was a creepy old downtown lawyer—in reality, he appeared to be no more than middle-aged—who looked weak and wicked and obviously corrupt. Indeed, he *was* obviously corrupt, for he had bought the services of a boy prostitute and then had beaten him to death. Baretta briskly took on the problem and did his usual thing; that is, he talked and acted tough on the surface but let you know that, deep down (or even not all that deep down), he was a really feeling guy. Never mind the bad grammar. Never mind the clothes all over the floor of the apartment. Baretta *cares*. In other words, he is like everybody's fifteen-year-old kid, which is more than you could say for Sam Spade or Hercule Poirot, or even old Lieutenant Kojak.

Consider another extremely popular program, *Charlie's Angels*. This also appeals to "all ages," but what is it, really, except a mild adventure format—a very mild adventure format—that is plugged into classic adolescent sexual fantasies? Thus, the three pretty, teasy Angels speak to the adolescent boy's *Playboy*-type musings, and also to the adolescent girl's perhaps less physical sense of romance; they provide her with an electronic "crush" on three beautiful and accomplished older girls. Accordingly, there is nothing too definite about the Angels, which might disrupt the dream. They are vaguely, chastely sexual, because they're pretty and because men make passes at them; but they don't seem to "do it," or to want to very much. Nor are they too maidenly, for they are well trained in karate and can chop a fat old person to the greensward faster than you can say "Amelia Earhart." Nor for that matter are they too emphatically feminist, except on what might gruffly be called a rather immature level; that is, they consider it their right to wear seductive (or, as some might say, manipulative) clothes, and are not averse to a little wink or a giggle, but they also expect to be taken seriously as "persons." Generally, however, their approach to life and its problems is one of friendliness and good grooming. They are as neatly, trimly dressed for each adventure as a high-school girl is for each day of classes. Why does a Charlie's Angel turn herself out immaculately before setting off to pursue an armed and homicidal drug pusher? Why do so many teenage girls spend two hours washing their hair and choosing the right ensemble before heading off to take a quiz in algebra or study canal and waterway construction in the eighteen-thirties? In short, the serious matters of life are given their proper place in *Charlie's Angels*, and nobody comes onscreen to hammer on the bathroom door and say, "What are you doing in there? Trying to look cheap again?" Charlie's Angels don't drag around in curlers and don't look cheap. Also, they're conveniently chaperoned by an uncle figure—or perhaps a capon figure—John Bosley, who doesn't follow them so closely that they couldn't have fun or mess around a bit if they wanted to, but who sees to it that they don't get into any really serious trouble. In short, it's a teenager's dream of how terrific teenage life would be if you could only extend it up through time and out into the real and dreary grownup world. *Baretta* is the real world reduced to adolescent terms. The Angels are a dream of teenage life aggrandized and expanded beyond the classroom and the drive-in. Thus, kids can have their crushes on the nifty girls (and on themselves), and the parents can plug into the program with their fantasies, too: maybe *our* kids will grow up and be like *them*: clean, friendly, and employed.

Further examples of the adolescent subculture on television are all around this year. For instance, there is *Saturday Night Live*, which plays to a slightly older crowd as well, but which definitely plugs into a basic adolescent perspective, with its parodies of TV commercials (youth against the TV "system"), pop-jazz-rock music, and insistent counterculture humor. Also, there is a rising genre of family-oriented drama series, which doubtless derive from old-fashioned sentimental domestic comedies such as *My Three Sons* or *Cheaper by the Dozen*, or even *The Waltons*, but which attempt to take family situations one or two steps further toward reality—at least, toward what conventional wisdom now tells us is going on near the psychological surface of modern American families. Not all these programs are primarily concerned with adolescents. For instance, *Eight Is Enough* and *Mulligan's Stew* both have to do with multitudinous families that contain most youthful age levels, but in a way the focusing point of view remains close to the adolescent "line"; in these cases, the adolescent's fantasy of other people's families being so warm and solid and practically perfect. In such programs, problems always (or often) beset the various TV families, but the problems can always be solved and the families thereby become stronger, more tightly knit. Family problems on television, in fact, are somewhat like a knight's quest in a chivalric romance: they exist in order to affirm the family's dreamlike strength.

All in all, it's easy to pick quarrels with commercial television's marketplace approach to youth and the family; indeed, with its current obsession with adolescence. The perspective is usually self-serving, often downright exploitative, and not without its irritations to those who are not themselves adolescents. On the other hand, I suspect that everyone has gained a little something from the current youth mania on television. As Joseph F. Kett has pointed out in his interesting book, *Rites of Passage: Adolescence in America, 1790 to the Present*, two general movements seem to be underway among the young people of the country. The more progressive of the two has often brought dismay to parental ranks, for it has been responsible for the erosion of the so-called traditional institutions and behavior patterns of American childhood: in other words, the one-hundred-year-old, adult-sponsored orthodoxy of youth organizations, societies, fraternities, sororities, church groups, scout groups, cadet groups, and so forth, which has been in a steady and quickening stage of disintegration since the nineteen-fifties. But as these old icons have been discarded, young people, fashioning their own icons, have learned to be far less immature and self-protective than they were back in the days when their roles were defined for them by the older generation. Thus, although the Boy Scouts and Girl Scouts are out of favor, with ever dwindling teenage membership, American young people today seem increasingly self-reliant and independent. Despite their noisome stereo paraphernalia and heavy footfall, young Americans travel the country or even the world on their own, initiate political action, handle sex and narcotics no worse than anyone else, and generally model their aspirations more closely after Thoreau's than Booth Tarkington's. Nowadays, parents in their jogging outfits vainly imitate the greenness of youth, while their children in certain subtler ways sometimes seem more adult. Young people, in fact, appear to be gradually emerging from the dark wood where adults of previous generations had put them (of course, for their protection!), and where they remained for so many decades, restrained by classification, by what they supposedly could or couldn't do, by what they could or couldn't be. It would be excessive to claim that television, all on its own, has piped this youthful army out of its adult-defined isolation and back into the wider possibilities of the world. All the same, it is fair to say that television—especially the hustle-bustle television of the marketplace—has played an important part in giving young people something of their own, something they can reach for themselves and not wait to have brought to them by watchful and well-intentioned grownups. Young people select their own programs in much the same way as grownups choose the things they need and want. It is no small matter, after all, for an emerging person to own a little piece of territory, even if the territory is nothing larger or more solid or "better" than a television program: *Charlie's Angels* or *Baretta* or *Welcome Back, Kotter*.

So far, so good. But if there are two movements underway, only one of them points toward greater maturity and assimilation in society. The other movement is in the reverse direction, and not only back to isolation but to a fortress isolation. In other words, it is the movement that leads to a rival, competitive, youth culture, as if youth were one nationality and age another, as if the two categories could be defined as neatly and easily as they are elsewhere: for instance, on TV. Commercial television plays on this polarization more often than not, for it speaks in easy symbols to the young. Its transactions are quick and simple. It is the voice that in the end trivializes both youth and age by isolating one from the other, by making youth self-conscious and age invisible. Fortunately, after the programs are over and the set is turned off, the audience remains: parents as well as children, young and old and in-between. Here the real power of the race resides, not in dangerous or seductive or irritating images on the screen. Here in the bosom of the family lie the classic dangers: dreams of sex and violence and Oedipal murder that no Production Code is going to have much effect on. Here, too, rests our capacity for imagining the future. Of course, sometimes the older members of the audience could use a bit of help in nurturing the younger members, though a bit of help in these matters seems invariably to lead to too much help: some more Boy Scouts or a teenage Civil War militia corps or a new "philosophy of programming." In bringing up young people, the best thing, one imagines, is to get a good night's sleep and a fast start in the morning. In any case, it's probably good to keep in mind that those contented, competent, problem-solving families are usually the ones *on* television, not looking at it.

(1977)

THE PROSECUTOR

IT'S HARD not to like *60 Minutes*, at least much of the time. The general reporting is brisk and capable, neither too trivial nor too densely detailed, as in the better tradition of the general-magazine feature. And the investigative stories, for which the program has become well honored and remarkably popular, are often hard-hitting and dramatic. The show's four correspondents, Mike Wallace, Morley Safer, Dan Rather, and Harry Reasoner, are all good interviewers, and Wallace and Rather are also uncommonly tough interviewers: combative, probing, a far remove from the once typical TV newsman whose interrogatory technique consisted mainly of proffering his microphone, like an ice-cream cone, to a public figure who would then, as often as not, make an election speech with it.

It's been good, at last, to see tough interviewing on the air—especially in an era when important persons so often try to hide behind imperturbable, on-camera pronouncements, or else behind shields of lawyers and accountants so thick that most politely mellifluous TV reporters can scarcely make a dent in them. The pugnacious *60 Minutes* musketeers unfailingly dent such shields, and sometimes penetrate them, while awards are won and ratings climb. But there's also a danger in this approach, for clearly much of what sustains the popularity of the program is the thrill of the chase: the excitement that comes from watching a quarry being pursued and brought down by aggressive questioning on the air. As a result, the program (with its large staff of producers and researchers) is bound to be on the lookout not just for newsworthy stories but for situations that will specifically provide this drama of pursuit, and for interview subjects that can be made to serve, willingly or unwillingly, as the quarry. Thus, with the *60 Minutes* newsmen being more frequently drawn into prosecutorial scenarios, it's been inevitable that some of them would begin to assume a trial lawyer's role or at least manner, with its emphasis on courtroom tactics and judgmental righteousness.

An example of this increasing tendency to have prosecutorial indignation do the work of actual investigative reporting—or do more of the work than it should—occurred recently when one of *60 Minutes*'s sternest musketeers, Dan Rather, galloped into Wyoming to uncover low- and high-level corruption in the state. To begin with, let me say that I have no doubt whatsoever that all manner of wickedness exists today in Wyoming, for it is a region of enormous mineral and petroleum wealth, much of which has only lately begun to be developed (or exploited), and it seems to be one of the givens of natural-resource capitalism that wherever there are grown men (or women) trying to make some money out of the ground there are usually all kinds of deals and payoffs and improper goings-on to be found in the offing. The challenge, then, was to find the story, and not so much to make the case, for that is presumably a matter for the law to undertake, but at least to ascertain the basic facts and present them to the audience. What seemed to interest *60 Minutes*, however, was less the story than the *appearance* of a story: the dramatic texture of televised confrontation.

The first of the two Wyoming reports (CBS News's

foray into the state was clearly no nickel-and-dime operation; two separate twenty-minute installments were
prepared, to be aired on successive Sunday evenings)
was titled "Our Town," and seemed largely devoted to
the prostitutes of Rock Springs, Wyoming: a historically
rowdy mining town of around twenty-five thousand
inhabitants, half of whom had arrived in the last five
years, as a result of the energy boom. From the start,
somewhat in the manner of a district attorney running
for office who tries to stir up the citizenry against the
local whorehouse, Rather professed to be astonished at
the presence of vice in Western mining communities:

> Tonight, *60 Minutes* looks at charges of payoff and cover-
> up in one American city where vice runs rampant and
> a handful of men run the city as they please. New York?
> Detroit? Los Angeles? Chicago? Wrong. Not this time.
> The corruption we're talking about is in a city far off in
> the hills of Wyoming.

Then he professed to be shocked at vice itself:

> When the sun goes down in Rock Springs, the town be-
> comes a Western sin city. Hookers openly work the
> streets and the bars, each of them earning a minimum of
> of a thousand dollars a week.

Then, as if his audience wasn't sufficiently writhing
in prurient disapproval, he returned to his opening
theme, which presumably had made *Winesburg, Ohio*,
so popular sixty years ago: Good people, can you believe
that they're doing it *right here* in Winesburg? Thus:

> If you're saying "So what?"—remember this is not New
> York or New Orleans or Chicago. This is Rock Springs,

with more working hookers than you can shake a wallet at. By conservative estimate, prostitution alone is a two-million-dollar-a-year business here in this little Wyoming town.

Notice that Rock Springs has changed from "one American city" to "a Western sin city" to "this little Wyoming town." Notice also the mathematics. If each prostitute earns a thousand dollars a week and all of them together earn two million dollars a year, then there must be a grand total of around forty hookers in Rock Springs. Which may be vice, but in a town of miners, oil workers, and construction hands it may not be everybody's idea of vice running rampant.

Then we got to see the sinful creatures themselves. For *60 Minutes*, sparing no expense, had brought "a special night lens," as Rather described it, which "enabled us to film it all in almost total darkness." Indistinct women varying in color and appearance drifted about in the murky Rock Springs night, as if moving through fog. Stoutish women, clearly of ill repute, shuffled along on a sidewalk. Others stood in a parking lot. There was a brief scene of a prostitute overheard engaging in a transaction with a man. She: "Well, what can you spend—thirty?" He: "Well, what kind of work for thirty?" This was surely pretty heady stuff for members of the urban audience, who would otherwise have had to drive several miles out of their way, wherever they lived, to witness similar transactions in their own cities.

But Rather wasn't only interested in bringing back U-2 photographs to show that prostitution existed in Rock Springs. He was after bigger game: official corruption. Thus he observed solemnly, "The local police will hurry to stop a fight but hardly ever to arrest for prostitution." A female undercover agent was produced on camera, who substantiated this grave charge.

"Were you hassled by the police?" Rather asked the woman.

"No, not at all," she replied. "The police—we've seen them several times on K Street in their cars. Never was any attempt ever made [at an arrest]."

A less determined prosecutor, one imagines, or a less pious reporter who had once worked a city beat, might have asked himself if police in most American cities (certainly including New York, where *60 Minutes* and Rather are based) even hurry to stop fights, let alone bother with arresting hookers and dumping them in the courts. But to admit the question, or the answer, would be to diminish the tone of moral outrage, and thus the story. As it was, having so far put forward a supposedly significant case against Rock Springs vice which consisted of (*a*) blurry views of prostitutes on a sidewalk and in a parking lot, and (*b*) his own shocked indignation, Rather next brought his courtroom talents to bear on an effort to involve the upper reaches of the state administration itself in the shady doings on K Street.

Now there were two undercover agents on camera, who sat facing Rather, all business in a trimly tailored suit, seated stiffly in a straight-backed chair and balancing a reporter's notebook on his knee, though it was unclear why he needed the notebook, since a sound recorder was clearly running along with the camera. One of the agents had just given it as his opinion that Rock Springs not only was a place where prostitution ran rampant but also was a transfer, or "pass through," point for narcotics. Rather then engaged the two agents in a trial lawyer's catechism that went as follows:

RATHER: In your personal opinion, the police chief knows about it?

AGENTS: Yes.

RATHER: Sheriff know about it?

AGENTS: Yes.

RATHER: Mayor know about it?

AGENTS: Yes.

RATHER: Members of the city council know about it?

AGENTS: Yes.

RATHER: County attorney know about it?

AGENTS: Yes.

RATHER: State attorney general know about it?

AGENTS: Yes.

RATHER: Governor know about it?

AGENTS: Yes.

On a theatrical level, this was an obviously effective performance. In the manner of a trial lawyer, Rather had presented his allegations in the form of dramatic questions—knowing, as trial lawyers do, that the questions themselves contained the power of persuasion, regardless of the answers—and so had cleverly led his jury, or audience, in the direction he wished it to take. For, starting with little more than those blurry glimpses of prostitutes, he had next asked the audience to accept an opinion that pimps and narcotics traffic existed alongside the prostitutes, which is generally a plausible supposition though not necessarily a fact; and then, by presenting, in a deliberately courtroomlike fashion, additional opinion as to who might "know about" the situation, he had involved the attorney general as well as the governor of the state in the vice in Rock Springs.

But the fact remained that, whatever the actual state of affairs in Wyoming might be, Rather's "case" before the television audience consisted almost entirely of style and texture, with little reportorial substance to back it up. After all, think of whom a reporter might *not* ensnare in a similar catechism about vice in most cities. "Sir, do not prostitutes openly parade the sidewalks of Forty-second Street?" asks the accuser sternly of his witness. "And does not the mayor know about it? Does not the police commissioner? Do not both senators? Does not the governor? Does not the archbishop? Does not the Vice-President of the United States? Does not the President himself?" In other words, if a link did exist between vice in Rock Springs and the State House in Cheyenne, it was not being shown on *60 Minutes*; it was only being implied or insinuated.

Even so, Rather, with his "special night lens," seemed on solider footing in the first week's installment, trying to press charges of sinfulness against the little Wyoming town (or "Western sin city") of Rock Springs—whose mayor, on camera, inspired no greater confidence than the mayors of most American towns, and maybe less—than he did a week later, when he attempted to expose and attack corruption at higher levels in the state. This installment was titled "High Noon in Cheyenne," and Rather began it in the briskly confident style of a successful prosecuting attorney who has already proved his point and is now going after the "big one." Thus:

> Our story last week, entitled "Our Town," looked at the little city of Rock Springs, Wyoming, steeped in prostitution, gambling, and narcotics . . . Tonight, "High Noon in Cheyenne," as we look at charges that Wyoming officials as high as the governor and the attorney general

may be involved in covering up corruption, not just in that little city of Rock Springs but in the state as a whole, with alleged links to organized crime out of state. It is accusation and confrontation and it is high noon in Cheyenne!

Soon it became clear that Rather's charges were actually those of a man named Neil Compton, who until his dismissal five months before by the governor had been head of Wyoming's criminal-investigation unit. On camera, cued by Rather, Compton was an assertive and articulate witness.

Rather asked him why he had been dismissed.

Compton said, "I was fired because I went to the governor on two separate occasions and brought to his attention that the attorney general for the State of Wyoming was a crook."

Rather then backed up his own witness. "We'll return to the specific charges in a moment," he said, "but first it's important to know that the man who makes them, Neil Compton, has a long reputation for being a superb investigator. He does not have a reputation for shooting from the hip."

However, after a brief check with members of the Wyoming press and with civic officials around the state, it turns out that Neil Compton has been at the very least a highly controversial figure on the local scene, whose authority had been frequently questioned—privately and publicly—on the very grounds that Rather had mentioned: shooting from the hip. It was a fact, for example, that Compton, in the two years before his dismissal, had been the subject of two separate meetings of Wyoming sheriffs and police chiefs, who had gathered largely to criticize his investigative methods, which had sometimes involved middle-of-the-night raids on unsuspecting households in an attempt to catch college-age youths in the possession of minor quantities of marijuana. (One citizen of Worland, Wyoming, had complained to the state attorney general's office that Compton himself had arrived at her house at two o'clock in the morning, seeking to arrest her son, then away at college, for selling an ounce of marijuana.) As the sheriff of Gillette said to me on the phone when I asked him about Compton: "I think about eighty percent of the law officers of this state questioned his judgment."

At any rate, Rather had three main charges of Compton's to present to the large and respectful *60 Minutes* audience. The first was that the state's Democratic Party chairman, Don Anselmi, had "attempted political cover-up" in order to protect an employee of a motel he co-owns "who was caught in a major drug case." Briskly, Rather interviewed Anselmi as if he had him on the witness stand:

RATHER: You know John Vase? He works for you?
ANSELMI: He's my assistant beverage manager. My partner's son.
RATHER: He's the son of Mike Vase. Right? Your partner here?
ANSELMI: Right.

Notice that Anselmi had already told Rather, in his first reply, that John Vase was his partner's son, so that Rather's second question had no point except as courtroom rhetoric—to make it sound as if the investigator were ferreting out information from a recalcitrant witness. Then Rather buttressed his charge by producing another female undercover agent, who had apparently befriended young Vase and then turned him in:

RATHER: The case stood up?

AGENT: The case then was transferred to be prosecuted in the federal government.

RATHER: The county attorney in effect got rid of it?

AGENT: Yes, sir. The attorney general got rid of it. It was taken out of his hands. And the federal government took over this case. And at this time he pled guilty. He didn't want to go to court. He pled guilty.

However, a fairly rapid check of this situation produces a somewhat different impression. In the first place, according to the easily accessible Sweetwater County records, young Vase's crime turns out to have been the delivery of "five baggies, a tie-stick [*sic*], and one branch of marijuana," which may be illegal but hardly constitutes a "major drug case." Secondly, the undercover agent seems to have got the disposition of the case upside down, for the state court hadn't "got rid of" it to the federal court. In fact, the federal government had never taken over the case at all, for the charges had originally been filed in the state court, where they had been prosecuted. And there, far from escaping justice, Vase had pleaded guilty for the reason that he was guilty, and was punished with a fine of seven hundred and fifty dollars, five years' probation, and the forfeiture of his car.

But, having disposed of the Vase case to his satisfaction, Rather went on to list other charges against the Democratic state chairman: for instance, "that Anselmi was party to a stolen-gun deal." He said: "Anselmi denies it. A federal grand jury looked into that case three years ago. A prosecutor told us political pressure stopped the investigation." Here a little checking turns up the fact that Compton's "stolen-gun deal" charges against Anselmi stemmed largely from accusations brought by a former convict, Michael Dansdill, whose release Compton was involved in, and who later retracted the charges. The possibility of "political pressure" always exists, but since the Dansdill affair was well known in Wyoming, having been amply covered in the local press, it was too bad that Rather's "prosecutor" didn't mention that aspect of the matter, or that Rather didn't pass the word along to the audience.

In any event, having further demonstrated Anselmi's shadiness, Rather went on to link the Democratic chairman to even bigger crime. Compton broached the charge:

At the time [1970], I found that there were the connections between Mr. Anselmi and Arizona . . . There was a real-estate and property buy-up in Wyoming by subjects from Arizona, Colorado, that had been a subject of organized-crime investigations in those particular states.

Rather took it up:

The Arizona connection means to Compton that Don Anselmi is doing business with the land-scandal people who have connections to mobsters, who have bilked the public out of the millions of dollars in fraudulent deals in the Southwest.

There was a brief glimpse of Anselmi flatly denying the charge. Then Compton and Rather tried to link Anselmi's "connections" with Arizona to a man called Danny O'Keefe, who, Rather said, had been indicted in Colorado on land-fraud charges. Anselmi also denied ever having talked with O'Keefe, or ever having known him.

Here it should be said that Rather had visually linked Anselmi to an "Arizona connection"—a connection as yet unproved—by showing unrelated film scenes of Arizona desert and also a brief film sequence of a man said to be Danny O'Keefe, who was seen arriving on his own at an airport. Now Rather proceeded to cast his net over the top officials in the Wyoming capital. First, he asked Compton what he thought a grand jury might concentrate on. Compton replied:

> I would ask that the grand jury look at the governor in relationship to land purchases with Don Anselmi.

Rather showed some exterior views of a ranch that had apparently been bought by Governor Ed Herschler, of Wyoming, and then took his camera to the governor himself:

> RATHER: Governor, your partner in purchasing this Yellowstone Ranch in Fremont County, nineteen hundred acres, is Mr. Don Anselmi.
> GOVERNOR: It's closer to twenty thousand acres. And leases—and federal leases. I suppose there's about a million acres involved.
> RATHER: And your partner is Mr. Anselmi?
> GOVERNOR: He's one of them, yes.

Having thus linked Governor Herschler with Anselmi, who had earlier been linked with a "connection" in Arizona and "land-scandal people who have connections to mobsters," Rather returned to Compton:

> RATHER: Source of the money [for the Yellowstone Ranch]?

COMPTON: Source of the money? It is my belief the source of money is from organized crime.

RATHER: Do you think that could be proven?

COMPTON: I believe that could be proven with subpoena power from a grand jury.

RATHER: Organized-crime connections with the governor of the state? Democratic state chairman?

COMPTON: That's correct.

In effect, the intrepid *60 Minutes* investigators had shown us some television views of the Yellowstone Ranch and of Governor Herschler saying that he was one of its purchasers, while darkly implying that if the real source of the purchase funds should ever be uncovered (an investigative operation that would require the assistance of a grand-jury subpoena!) it would be traceable to the coffers of organized crime. But, in fact—though, for all I know, the Governor of Wyoming may have been hand in glove with the Mafia or the Baader-Meinhof gang in other areas—in the matter of the purchase of the Yellowstone Ranch, a couple of modestly investigative phone calls produced the somewhat less exciting information that this particular deal was consummated through Lowham Associates, a well-known Wyoming firm specializing in ranch properties; that a major portion of the purchase price of $1,800,000 was financed by loans from the Federal Land Bank Association of Wyoming and the First National Bank of Casper; that a lesser part of the purchase price was financed through a second mortgage to the sellers, Mr. William McIntosh and his niece Jennifer McIntosh; and that the relatively minor sum of $25,000 in cash was paid by each of the four partners.

The subject of Rather's final charge against the Wyoming administration was not without foundation, and had already been extensively covered in the regional press, though, once again, Rather seemed more interested in prosecuting it than in reporting it. A case that involved charges that public officials were stealing from a state home for the elderly was first archly described by Rather as "a seemingly minor scandal, perhaps no bigger than that 'third-rate burglary' at Watergate," and then, more grimly, in the statement "It may become a Democratic Prairiegate here in Wyoming!" According to numerous earlier newspaper accounts, the mess in question had to do with allegations that two officials involved with the administration of Wyoming's old-age homes (both of them, in fact, *Republican* appointees from a previous state administration) between them had ripped off the Pioneer Home in Thermopolis, Wyoming, taking several thousand dollars' worth of goods presumably intended for the elderly pioneers: a half dozen or so TV sets; several stereo units; some bath towels; and generous supplies of nuts and candy. It was Compton's and Rather's accusation that Governor Herschler and his attorney general, Frank Mendicino, had engaged in a cover-up when the latter "refused to prosecute." But, once again, the facts, though they hardly spoke well for the attorney general's political savvy, were decidedly more ambiguous than they were made to appear on the air. For one of the two men, Kenneth Brighton, though he had not actually been brought to trial, had indeed been charged in a state court on eleven felony counts and was awaiting trial when he died, as a result of complications from heart surgery. It is true that Mendicino was laggard in prosecuting the second man, Lloyd Hovee, but his explanation (which was repeated in several press stories) was that he needed Brighton's testimony in order to build a strong case against Hovee, and was plea bargaining with Brighton when he died. Perhaps there was more than carelessness in Mendicino's delay in bringing the second Pioneer bandit to trial, but it is troubling that Rather, in his eagerness to produce a "Democratic Prairiegate," neglected to mention the charges already brought against Brighton, or the eleven counts that the state was prosecuting him on, or any of the background information (for example, that the culprits were Republican appointees anyway) that might have put the attorney general's behavior in a less sinister light.

At any rate, there rested the *60 Minutes* investigation of corruption in Wyoming: not exactly a legal prosecution, for there had been no indictment, no jury chosen, no counsel (at least for the defense), and no judge to guide the proceedings; on the other hand, not strictly speaking a reporting job, for there were few facts, and those facts that were referred to often turned out to be inaccurate or incompletely presented or ambiguous. A couple of conclusions seem worth drawing from this sorry affair. One is that since for some years now newsmen have been protected by the Supreme Court decision in the case of New York Times Co. v. Sullivan to the extent that "actual malice" must be proved before a public figure can be awarded damages in a libel action, it might be in the self-interest of the press—given the reporters' Sullivanian immunity—to act with less careless belligerence in its pursuit of investigative quarries. Investigative reporters, as has been observed elsewhere, are the guard dogs of society, but the trouble with guard dogs is that they sometimes attack with equal fervor the midnight burglar and the midday mailman.

The second conclusion relates more directly to television news and its conflicting attitudes toward the still different worlds of print journalism and entertainment. On the one hand, *60 Minutes* appears to imitate the surface conventions of the city room or magazine office, with its correspondents nearly always properly attired in white shirt, necktie, and suit (in the fashion of a 1950s *Time* reporter), and brandishing their little spiral notebooks as they ask the old-fashioned newsman's tough questions. On the other hand, the form in which *60 Minutes* presents its investigations has little to do with the conventions of print journalism. It's not better or worse, but it's different; a television news story is first of all part of the television process, and whatever it borrows from other media is bound to be secondary. In a standard print investigative report, although the reporter may have experienced a variety of difficulties and surmounted numerous obstacles before bringing in the story, what is finally published usually relates directly only to the subject of the investigation; essentially, it is a relatively distanced account that depends for heat and accessibility on the stylistic flourishes of the reporter. But with *60 Minutes*, the news-gathering process itself has become part of the story—sometimes a key part, with the TV newsman first shown outside, trying to get in; then inside, facing down an uncooperative or hostile subject, who in turn is shown in close-up on the screen (as were the generally cooperative Wyoming politicians), often caught by the camera in a carefully edited grimace or expression of seemingly revealed truth which later may turn out not to have been truth at all—or truth of a quite different sort. One obvious result of this cinematic dramatization of the news interview is that the public is all too likely to follow the seductive flow of the news-gathering drama without paying very close attention to its content. An additional hazard is that when on-camera newsmen assume the mantle of prosecutors, in a quasi-trial context where they control the cameras and the editing machines and where there is no counsel for the defense, then the reports that these methods produce can sometimes drift fairly far from that orderly or reporterly presentation of information that the Founding Fathers probably had in mind when they invoked their crucial safeguards for our press. At any rate, now that *60 Minutes* has made its mark as an enterprising and interesting news program, perhaps Dan Rather and some of his colleagues will consider giving up their trial robes and courthouse righteousness and return to the kind of solid, forthright reporting they've often done so well in the past. And maybe they'll even revisit Wyoming. They don't seem to have quite got the story right the first time around.

(1977)

Postscript

A couple of notes seem worth adding to this essay, whose original appearance in *The New Yorker* evoked a surprisingly thin-skinned and belligerent response from the normally cool executives of CBS News. Over a period of several weeks after publication, a series of meticulously typed, single-spaced, quasi-legal communications (often of immoderate length as well as temper) arrived at my office, in several instances hand-carried from the elegant CBS building six blocks to the north, though not presumably by the correspondents themselves. These letters generally fell into two categories. First, there were those that sought to impugn the credibility of my observations on the grounds that I was a parochial Easterner, whose surely limited acquaintance with the state of Wyoming was obviously no match for the "special familiarity" of newsman Dan Rather, who, I was briskly informed, had visited the state "no less than fourteen times." Then, when it became known that, in fact, I had actually spent quite a bit of time in Wyoming (although mostly as a summer resident, staring at the sagebrush and watching my children fall off horses), a second flurry of mail arrived, which now questioned both my candor and my motives, by suggesting that since I was reportedly a Wyoming landowner (alas, not true), I had acted doubtless "in collusion" with Wyoming "special interests" and might even have an ax to grind on behalf of the state's Democratic administration. Though I felt briefly flattered to be thought of, even inaccurately, as a power to be reckoned with in the state, it seemed to me that this latter inference was a curiously unprofessional one for a television news organization to be making in regard to a television critic going about his job, especially one who had gone to some pains to make it clear in the same essay that, far from advocating the spotless purity of Wyoming politics of either party, a person would have to be some kind of born fool to think that an energy boom might be taking place in this fine Rocky Mountain state and no one was cutting any corners there. The focus of my criticism, however, had been the particulars of the

60 Minutes report, and this was not a focus that my distinguished correspondents seemed much interested in replying to. Indeed, when now and then some elaborately titled executive got around to considering the questions of fact that had been raised, it was invariably to state, in an alternately sanctimonious and bullying tone, that inasmuch as these matters were currently in the hands of a Wyoming grand jury it would not be "appropriate" to make a public reply to them "at this time." I might add that one of the few *60 Minutes* luminaries who did not engage in any of this solemn tantruming was Dan Rather himself, who possibly did not have access to meticulous, single-spaced, quasi-legal typing, or else had better things to do.

Fortunately, the Wyoming grand jury has since been disbanded. This was the second such grand jury empaneled in Wyoming's history and it is still referred to in the state, in varying tones of voice, as the *60 Minutes* grand jury. In 1977 an official investigation had been loudly sought by Neil Compton, who was nationally seconded by Dan Rather and *60 Minutes*. The jury was empaneled by Governor Herschler in November 1977, and met for a little over one year. One hundred and fifty-five witnesses were heard. Three hundred thousand dollars of taxpayers' money was spent. The results of these labors were roughly as follows. No evidence was found that warranted naming Governor Herschler (of the so-called ranch-purchase scandal) in an indictment. No evidence was found that warranted naming former Democratic Party chairman Don Anselmi (of the so-called Arizona land-grab scandal) in an indictment. Former Attorney General Frank Mendicino was named in an indictment but the indictment was dismissed in district court. None of the Rock Springs officials, including Mayor Wataha, was named in an indictment. (The grand jury criticized the Rock Springs group for having been too tolerant of prostitution and gambling in their community.) A few minor malefactors were successfully indicted, such as Lloyd Hovee, the sixty-four-year-old Republican appointee who had been accused of playing fast and loose with the Pioneer Home's television sets and candy supplies. Hovee was sentenced to sixty days in jail but received a pardon on the grounds of ill health. In the aftermath of the grand-jury investigation, Governor Herschler was reelected to the governorship by a comfortable majority. Don Anselmi resigned his party chairmanship as a result of the *60 Minutes* publicity and is no longer active in public life. Frank Mendicino also resigned and now practices law in Cheyenne. Neil Compton left Wyoming, first for Colorado, where he held police jobs in Greeley and Fort Collins and ran unsuccessfully for sheriff in Larimer County; then he moved to California, where he reportedly has a "security job" in a Los Angeles suburb. Dan Rather, of course, was named to replace Walter Cronkite on the CBS Evening News.

An additional comment might be made here, though not with specific reference to the Wyoming programs. At the time of writing "The Prosecutor," I had suggested in my concluding remarks that newsmen, who then didn't seem to be at all badly protected by the New York Times Co. v. Sullivan decision, could probably stand to be a little more equanimous in their investigations, at least to the extent of not so determinedly playing the time-honored role of underdog newshound while at the same time laying about with telegenic accusations of persons who were handicapped by the need to prove "actual malice" in order legally to protect themselves. Even as I wrote, however, other forces were evidently at work to upset the already delicate balance between the press's right to report the news and the citizen's right to privacy —some of them, in fact, having been set in motion by an earlier *60 Minutes* program which contained a dramatically prosecutorial interview by correspondent Mike Wallace with Lieutenant Colonel Anthony B. Herbert, a well-known critic of military policy in the Vietnam War. Indeed, ten months later, came the Herbert v. Lando decision (Barry Lando had been the producer of the Wallace interview with Lt. Col. Herbert), in which the Supreme Court, by a six-to-three margin, reversed the decision of a lower court and held that journalists henceforth could *not* use First Amendment protection to avoid answering questions about their "state of mind" when they became targets of libel suits brought by public figures. The Herbert v. Lando decision did not replace New York Times Co. v. Sullivan, but it effectively changed the balance of power between journalists and their subjects. Reporters are not exactly underdogs again, but they are less free to go about their business now than they were under New York Times Co. v. Sullivan, and I don't believe it would be excessive to say that to some degree it was the reporters themselves whose immodesty, as it were, coupled with the power of television journalism, brought about the unfortunate change. Clearly, Herbert v. Lando is a terrible decision: murkily abstract, dangerously illiberal, and radically hostile to the obvious intentions of the Constitution. But, just as clearly, it is a decision that was somehow squeezed from a divided and morally uncertain court by the pressures of new behavior and new news-gathering techniques. One might go so far as to say that although fairness in reporting has been deemed in recent years to be unexciting, insufficiently dramatic, and lacking in viewer appeal, the price of prime-time advocacy journalism may turn out to have been fairly steep. Luckily, the issues involved are all continuing ones and are not likely to be decided overnight.

ODE TO THANKSGIVING

IT IS TIME, at last, to speak the truth about Thanksgiving, and the truth is this. Thanksgiving is really not such a terrific holiday. Consider the traditional symbols of the event: Dried cornhusks hanging on the door! Terrible wine! Cranberry jelly in little bowls of extremely doubtful provenance which everyone is required to handle with the greatest of care! Consider the participants, the merrymakers: men and women (also children) who have survived passably well throughout the years, mainly as a result of living at considerable distances from their dear parents and beloved siblings, who on this feast of feasts must apparently forgather (as if beckoned by an aberrant Fairy Godmother), usually by circuitous routes, through heavy traffic, at a common meeting place, where the very moods, distempers, and obtrusive personal habits that have kept them all happily apart since adulthood are then and there encouraged to slowly ferment beneath the cornhusks, and gradually rise with the aid of the terrible wine, and finally burst forth out of control under the stimulus of the cranberry jelly! No, it is a mockery of a holiday. For instance: *Thank you, O Lord, for what we are about to receive.* This is surely not a gala concept. There are no presents, unless one counts Aunt Bertha's sweet rolls a present, which no one does. There is precious little in the way of costumery: miniature plastic turkeys and those witless Pilgrim hats. There is no sex. Indeed, Thanksgiving is the one day of the year (a fact known to everybody) when all thoughts of sex completely vanish, evaporating from apartments, houses, condominiums, and mobile homes like steam from a bathroom mirror.

Consider also the nowhereness of the time of year: the last week or so in November. It is obviously not yet winter: winter, with its death-dealing blizzards and its girls in tiny skirts pirouetting on the ice. On the other hand, it is certainly not much use to anyone as fall: no golden leaves or Oktoberfests, and so forth. Instead, it is a no-man's-land between the seasons. In the cold and sobersides northern half of the country, it is a vaguely unsettling interregnum of long, mournful walks beneath leafless trees: the long, mournful walks following the midday repast with the dread inevitability of pie following turkey, and the leafless trees looming or standing about like eyesores, and the ground either as hard as iron or slightly mushy, and the light snow always beginning to fall when one is halfway to the old green gate— flecks of cold, watery stuff plopping between neck and collar, for the reason that, it being not yet winter, one has forgotten or not chosen to bring along a muffler. It is a corollary to the long, mournful Thanksgiving walk that the absence of this muffler is quickly noticed and that four weeks or so later, at Christmastime, instead of the Sony Betamax one had secretly hoped the children might have chipped in to purchase, one receives another muffler: by then the thirty-third. Thirty-three mufflers! Some walk! Of course, things are more fun in the warm and loony southern part of the country. No snow there of any kind. No need of mufflers. Also, no long, mournful walks, because in the warm and loony southern part of the country everybody drives. So everybody drives over to Uncle Jasper's house to watch the Cougars play the Gators, a not entirely unimportant conflict which will determine whether the Gators get a Bowl bid or must take another post-season exhibition tour of North Korea. But no sooner do the Cougars kick off (an astonishing end-over-end squiggly thing that floats lazily above the arena before plummeting down toward K. C. McCoy and catching him on the helmet) than Auntie Em starts hustling turkey. Soon Cousin May is slamming around the bowls and platters, and Cousin Bernice is oohing and ahing about "all the fixin's," and Uncle Bob is making low, insincere sounds of appreciation: "Yummy, yummy, Auntie Em, I'll have me some more of these delicious yams!" Delicious yams? Uncle Bob's eyes roll wildly in his head. Billy Joe Quaglino throws his long bomb in the middle of Grandpa Morris saying grace, Grandpa Morris speaking so low nobody can hear him, which is just as well, since he is reciting what he can remember of his last union contract. And then, just as J. B. (Speedy) Snood begins his ninety-two-yard punt return, Auntie Em starts dealing everyone second helpings of her famous stuffing, as if she were pushing a controlled substance, which it well might be, since there are no easily recognizable ingredients visible to the naked eye.

Consider for a moment the Thanksgiving meal itself. It has become a sort of refuge for endangered species of starch: cauliflower, turnips, pumpkin, mince (whatever "mince" is), those blessed yams. Bowls of luridly colored yams, with no taste at all, lying torpid under a lava flow of marshmallow! And then the sacred turkey. One might as well try to construct a holiday repast around a fish—say, a nice piece of boiled haddock. After all, turkey tastes very similar to haddock: same consistency, same quite remarkable absence of flavor. But then, if the Thanksgiving *pièce de résistance* were a nice piece of boiled haddock instead of turkey, there wouldn't be all that fun for Dad when Mom hands him the sterling-silver, bone-handled carving set (a wedding present from her parents and not sharpened since) and then everyone sits around pretending not to watch while he saws and tears away at the bird as if he were trying to burrow his way into or out of some grotesque, fowl-like prison.

What of the good side to Thanksgiving, you ask. There is always a good side to everything. Not to Thanksgiving. There is only a bad side and then a worse side. For instance, Grandmother's best linen tablecloth is a bad side: the fact that it is produced each year, in the manner of a red flag being produced before a bull, and then is always spilled upon by whichever child is doing poorest at school that term and so is in need of greatest reassurance. Thus: "Oh, my God, *Veronica*, you just spilled grape juice [or plum wine or tar] on Grandmother's best linen tablecloth!" But now comes worse. For at this point Cousin Bill, the one who lost all Cousin Edwina's money on the car dealership three years ago and has apparently been drinking steadily since Halloween, bizarrely chooses to say: "Seems to me those old glasses are always falling over." To which Auntie Meg is heard to add: "Somehow I don't remember receivin' any of those old glasses." To which Uncle Fred replies: "That's because you and George decided to go on vacation to Hawaii the summer Grandpa Sam was dying." Now Grandmother is sobbing, though not so uncontrollably that she can refrain from murmuring: "I think that volcano painting I threw away by mistake got sent me from Hawaii, heaven knows why." But the gods are merciful, even the Pilgrim-hatted god of cornhusks and soggy stuffing, and there is an end to everything, even to Thanksgiving. Indeed, there is a grandeur to the feelings of finality and doom which usually settle on a house after the Thanksgiving celebration is over, for with the completion of Thanksgiving Day the year itself has been properly terminated: shot through the cranium with a high-velocity candied yam. At this calendrical nadir, all energy on the planet has gone, all fun has fled, all the terrible wine has been drunk.

But then, overnight, life once again begins to stir, emerging, even by the next morning, in the form of Japanese window displays and Taiwanese Christmas lighting, from the primeval ooze of the nation's department stores. Thus, a new year dawns, bringing with it immediate and cheering possibilities of extended consumer debt, office-party flirtations, good—or, at least, mediocre—wine, and visions of Supersaver excursion fares to Montego Bay. It is worth noting, perhaps, that this true new year always starts with the same mute, powerful mythic ceremony: the surreptitious tossing out, in the early morning, of all those horrid aluminum-foil packages of yams and cauliflower and stuffing and red, gummy cranberry substance which have been squeezed into the refrigerator as if a reenactment of the siege of Paris were shortly expected. Soon afterward, the phoenix of Christmas can be observed as it slowly rises, beating its drumsticks, once again goggle-eyed with hope and unrealistic expectations.

(1978)

THE TYRANNY OF THE VISUAL

I DON'T THINK that anyone needs reminding that we are well along in that blessed era when a single picture (sometimes any picture; certainly, any motion picture) is said to be the equal of a thousand words. Of course, words themselves are no longer manufactured or treated with much care, and so the comparison grows more plausible as time goes on. Even so, there have been moments lately when I have had the feeling that—so great has been the spread of visual culture in this century, and so overwhelming its impact on the tender verbal sensibilities of recent generations—what was not so long ago the liberating, sense-expanding dynamic of a new medium of perception now seems in danger of becoming a new kind of aesthetic tyranny: the tyranny of visual storytelling.

In movies, this tyranny commonly takes the superficially modest form of surface or design effects. This is a fashion of presenting a scene or character which relates not so much to the director's feeling for the scene or character as to his feeling for visual technique. For instance, at the beginning of the 1977 movie *Bobby Deerfield* there occurred a typically striking visual sequence, in which the camera first revealed—sparely and carefully framed—the blacktop surface of a road. Then a man (though only his shoes and trousered legs were visible) walked slowly down the road toward the camera. He stopped, turned around, and with equal deliberation retraced a few steps. Then suddenly and dramatically he bent down and picked up an object from the surface of the blacktop: a key. With key in hand, he now walked briskly back up the road to where a sports car was parked; he climbed into it, started the engine, and sped off. Thus, one assumed that Al Pacino (for he was the man on the road) was driving into an adventure story, whose narrative was already underway and whose substance would soon reveal itself. For example, what was all that business with the key? Was it Pacino's car key? Had it been stolen or mislaid? How stolen, why mislaid? More important, what did his having lost or mislaid and then found the key have to do with the next step in the narrative? Was it the missing clue to a burglary, or even the reason for a missed appointment? In other words, what did the visually striking incident of the key on the road actually mean? Alas, the subsequent action of the movie provided no answer to any of these questions. Indeed, from that moment on, the film seemed totally uninterested in the matter of the key, as if it couldn't really remember having posed any questions with it in the first place. The scene had clearly been a kind of game, a visual non sequitur, though one that had been designed quite deliberately to appeal to our traditional literary orientation through the detective-story ballet of the "search," the "clue," and the "getaway." As such, there had been nothing artistic or even playfully inventive about the sequence, as in a director's or a creative cinematographer's happy conceit. What it had been was merely another example of the disconnected visual effect: a scene invested with the look of narrative importance but which related neither to the character nor the story, only to the filmmakers' apparent wish to persuade the audience that it was watching a stylish and important film. Or to put it less kindly: a minor form of visual bullying.

In numerous recent movies, this tendency to exploit visual language has become increasingly pronounced; and, as in the case of verbal language, what one notices are not so much the always abundant examples of cheap, routine visual effects as the increasing instances of "artistic" fakery and commercialism. Consider the Russian-roulette sequences in *The Deer Hunter*. Here the problem is not disconnected gesture, nor is it a simple question of the screenwriter's or director's right to make up detail and incident. The problem in *The Deer Hunter*, it seems to me, has to do with a film that is not so much composed of sequential parts (one part being set in a small town in Pennsylvania, the other in Vietnam) as rendered on two different, and largely unmixable, levels of imagination. Thus, the small-town American scenes are handled with great naturalism and affection; every effort seems to have been made to show us *how things were*. In other words, even if the energy behind these naturalistic and nostalgic details is the energy of dream, it is clearly a dream that was honestly dreamed. In contrast, the Vietnam scenes aren't just dreamlike in their unreality and contrivance (in their absence of naturalism) but are the dream, one guesses, of a professional dream-maker—a Vietnam fantasist— who has invested his story neither with honest memory nor honest imagination but with the pseudo-energy of visual effects. Part of the movie, then, is "real" (or is at least the product of a real dream), and this reality attempts unsuccessfully to nourish the "unreal" Vietnam part, with its slick, manipulative Russian-roulette sequences. Of course, we hold our breath and wince when a man takes a partly loaded revolver and puts it to his temple. But what has been gained by these automated responses, save for the further dehumanization of a war that was already bad enough without these glib but "powerful" filmmaker's touches?

"But *The Deer Hunter* didn't have to be true to facts. It showed the poetic truth of the war," a young friend said to me as I was making these complaints the other day.

"How do you know, since you weren't there?" I asked.

"Well, I know because of the movie," he said.

It seems self-evident that visual creativity, be it in fine art or in cinematography, might be expected to follow different laws of technique and dynamics from, say, literary or musical creativity. But it seems strange, though perhaps in keeping with a certain defensive self-consciousness about visual matters, that our new visually-oriented crafts should be assumed to possess a morality of their own: a morality that often seems to speak less to the wider, untidy, unframed, undesigned world of men and women (where most morality is forged) than self-servingly back to the smaller, self-isolated province of visual technique as an end in itself.

Of course, there is nowhere that visual manipulation seems more apparent than in television commercials, but I think the role here of visual technique is deceptive. Superficially (and especially if it has been done well, with no expense spared, and so forth), the television commercial appears to be a kind of game: something playful, a thirty-second play period replete with visual tricks such as cars floating in the air, or knights in armor in the laundry room, or talking cats. The television commercial seems to be a classic example of technique for its own sake; though actually, as should be obvious, the technique serves a very definite and forceful master: the selling of a certain product, or of the emotions that are thought to surround that product. As a member of the audience, one may not much care for the product in question, or may find the sales message distasteful, or the interruption irritating, but the fact is that the visual transaction taking place is a fairly straightforward one. Whatever the intricacy or trickiness of the visual effects, the technique in a television commercial rarely speaks only to itself, unless it is a bad commercial, but follows a very clear, other-directed, even at times humanely logical (if not always ennobling) morality of commerce. On the other hand, without this stern logic to guide it, and without art, or pretensions to art, to whet its ambitions, regular television programming seems to flounder happily in a generally harmless morass of what used to be called B-movie special effects. On entertainment TV, nobody seems to have the time, money, or inclination for lighting or for framing shots. Now and then, an adventurous director will borrow a snappy trick or two from a movie or a commercial, but for the most part television cinematography is too caught up with the day-by-day demands of getting through the shooting script to worry about trying anything fancy. Week after week, detectives stalk criminals along catwalks, bodies float in swimming pools, cars spin around intersections and leap across drawbridges: the visual vocabulary of most television dramas is as skimpy as that of a pulp novel.

All the same, video is perhaps the visual language of the future, even more than film, and there is an area where television has started to abuse not so much its skimpy visual skills as its basic visual power. Ironically, it is public television—that relentless bluestocking of broadcasting—that seems to have been leading the way here, by throwing its weight behind a rather different sort of visual tyranny: what might be described as the reconstituting or transforming or overwhelming of works of literature into sequences of moving images, as, for example, in the recent four-part adaptation of Nathaniel Hawthorne's *The Scarlet Letter*. Now, right away, there is a danger of getting tangled up in one of those ancient arguments having to do with the merits or demerits of transposing books into films, so first let me try to make clear what I am *not* talking about here. I am not, for example, talking about the inviolability of printed matter or suggesting that a story that has been fashioned in one form—be it novel or stage play or Holinshed's *Chronicles* —should always remain in its original form. I am not claiming the inherent or automatic superiority of one form over another: books as "high art" versus film as "low art," as has sometimes been claimed (at least by book people) in the past. After all, the evidence of five or more decades is that some of the most appealing and satisfying movies (perhaps most of the most appealing and satisfying movies) have been adapted from novels or short stories that were often inferior to the filmed version. Indeed, a large proportion of the so-called literary properties that are bought by filmmakers and turned into movies are books of the most routine nature: spy stories or detective stories or the type of popular blockbuster novel that appears to have been written from a movie-oriented perspective, employing "characters" based either on figures in the daily papers or on the personae of movie stars, and, in fact, that is literary only in having made its original appearance as a book.

So what am I talking about? For one thing: *The Scarlet Letter* itself. Worthy Hawthorne! Such a nice-looking writer chap, who married one of those Peabody sisters and worked for years with great effort on his short stories, for which he received a certain regional respect but very little cash. He wrote *The Scarlet Letter* fairly quickly, and as soon as his publisher, Mr. Fields, saw the manuscript he knew that it was going to be a big seller, although, being a publisher, he printed a first edition of only two thousand copies, which sold out in ten days. The second edition, of three thousand copies, sold well too, and subsequent editions and printings have kept on selling. (Perhaps there should be some kind of federal law, however, to prevent schoolchildren from being required to read it—or *The House of the Seven Gables* or Melville's *Moby Dick*—at a stage in life when many of them can barely respond to the literary texture of *Car & Driver*.) For *The Scarlet Letter* is not only a marvelous book, surely one of the very great American novels ever written, but also an extraordinarily, profoundly *literary* work. It is actually quite short, and its brevity imparts a feeling of compression. There is scant incident or action in the narrative. Indeed, the "story" is deliberately unrealistic (almost surreal), for Hawthorne was writing two hundred years after the supposed events, and what he was attempting to portray often has the flow and density of a dream. Fitzgerald's *The Great Gatsby* is a very different kind of book, but it shares with *The Scarlet Letter*, I think, this same dreamlike energy, as well as a marked absence of action and realistic event. At any rate, Haw-

thorne's novel is not merely a great work of the imagination but one that owes its strength and presence to
the "music" of the soul's interior. So rich is this interior
music, in fact, that the reader scarcely notices—or, at
least, is not unduly troubled by—some of the more
conventional aspects of storytelling which Hawthorne
has either not much bothered himself with or simply
left out. Not only is there a scarcity of realistic event,
but a number of the important characters have surprisingly simplistic surfaces. Dreadful Roger Chillingworth,
for instance, is a villain without shading, without re-
deeming feature. Hester Prynne's child, little Pearl, is
hardly believable on any remotely realistic terms—this
"lovely and immortal flower" who was "worthy to have
been brought forth in Eden; worthy to have been left
there, to be the plaything of angels." There is also the
matter of the author's deliberately contrived employment of natural background and coloring; or, rather,
his failure to employ it. For *The Scarlet Letter* is in the
main—and, it is clear, purposely—a novel without
colors. There are periodic symbolic appearances of the
color red, as in a fire and a red rose, and certainly
in Hester's scarlet letter, and there are similarly pointed
appearances of the color black, as in the prison iron-
work and in the mythic "Black Man" of the forest.
But with the exception of Hester's own embroidery on
little Pearl's dresses, there is an obviously intentional
omission by the author of color, the colors of life, certainly the colors of the New England countryside. Indeed, the countryside itself is noticeably absent from
the narrative, save for occasional, equally symbolic
allusions to the dark and abstract wilderness that exists
on the periphery of the story, and which is made vivid

only toward the end of the novel in the important scene that finally brings together Hester, Dimmesdale, little Pearl, and Chillingworth in the forest.

Public television's version of *The Scarlet Letter* wasn't altogether terrible. It had a couple of effective moments, especially in the third episode, when Meg Foster seemed to catch for at least a few seconds some of the transfigured bitterness in Hester Prynne. But it certainly wasn't much good. In theatrical terms, both Foster and John Heard, as Dimmesdale, seemed impossibly burdened by a kind of American high-school stage radiance, while Kevin Conway, as Chillingworth, floundered about in a part that probably only a very bad or a very good actor could have made work. And Rick Hauser's ponderous, "classical" direction propelled Hawthorne's brief and compact narrative forward with the stately lethargy of a becalmed galleon. For the most part, it seemed a misbegotten undertaking, perpetrated by people on the creative or producing end who, if they had read the book at all—at least for the purpose of blocking scenes—couldn't have had much feeling for what they'd read. Indeed, as I watched the series trudge its dutiful and cumbersome course through four consecutive evenings, I thought back to some of those foolish Hollywood recreations of the "classics" and rather missed them—their foolishness as well as their energy: Mickey Rooney in *A Midsummer Night's Dream*; Gregory Peck as Captain Ahab! At least there had been a sort of loopy fun in these portrayals: a Classics Comics approach to serious literature in which serious literature somehow never really got involved; in which the soul of the original work was left where it was, unreached and undabbled with.

But these new, solemn practitioners of visual story-telling are soul devourers. They're *not* foolish or loopy, inviting us to have a good time and to leave our highfalutin literary notions outside in the coatroom. These are serious and dutiful fellows, bound not merely by a responsibility to "art" but also, in the case of public television, by a responsibility to trustees and educators and government committees and so forth. For example, was poor Hawthorne, scribbling at his desk in the eighteen-forties and trying to work out the novel's formal symbolism, so impeded by a lack of proper archives and research materials that he ignorantly costumed most of the characters in *The Scarlet Letter* in dark colors instead of putting them in the generally colorful robes of the era? Well, then, the research facilities and academic consultants of public television were able to correct Hawthorne's deficiency in this regard by costuming the television performers of his novel in the more historically accurate, colored finery of the period. And did poor Hawthorne, lacking a camera and the creative resources of film with which to tell his tale, give his written version of the story a certain closed-in and claustrophobic atmosphere? Well, then, television's cameras "opened up" the narrative by taking us on little scenic excursions outside the town. There are moody glimpses of the sea breaking on the shore, and cheery views of open meadows and fields of wheat. In fact, by the time the significant scene in the forest finally takes place we feel that we have been in the middle of New England's wild landscape all along. Also, even though this adaptation is by television and for television, it must not be forgotten that the original creator of the literary property was Nathaniel Hawthorne, a celebrated writer, and so the television people have found time to pay respects to Hawthorne's prose. Snatches of Hawthorne's exposition are periodically intoned as scene-setting devices by a generally offscreen actor (playing Hawthorne himself!), while additional bits and pieces of the Master's prose pop up now and then as dialogue, often spliced in with the already "adapted" dialogue. Thus, sometimes the dialogue is genuine Hawthorne and sometimes it is genuine television, but more often than not it is a strange composite of the two, which must have struck the twenty-five consultants who worked on the project as a statesmanly way of solving the problem.

"But let it pass! It is of yonder miserable man that I would speak," says Hawthorne's Hester Prynne, whereas television's Hester says, "I'm here not to talk of myself but of him." Does the difference matter? Does it matter that certain details and points of character have been rearranged, or that information provided by the author in a later chapter of the book turns up as dialogue in an early moment of the television version? Does it matter that childish camera tricks are borrowed from old movies to indicate dreamlike effects or the workings of consciousness, most of them as simple-minded as dissolves on logs blazing in a fireplace? In a certain sense, one would be hard put to say—certainly in a dominantly visual society—what great wrong there was in any of this. One mustn't be too linear or too retentive about such things! But it seems to me, in the end, that all these details do matter, though not necessarily detail by detail (as if we were discussing a blueprint that did or did not match the original specifications), but, instead, in that what is at issue—perhaps carelessly rather than intentionally, in the fashion of our time—is a fundamental question of respect. *The Scarlet Letter* is valuable to us and, indeed, to the literate world, for what it is in essence: a work of literature. It may contain a describable "story"; it may contain historical information, right or wrong; it may contain opportunities for costuming and parts for players. But a great novel is not an engineering model, with interchangeable parts, any more than a great painting (say, a Cézanne still-life) is an accumulation of "graphic information" about nineteenth-century French produce (to be improved, perhaps, by the substitution of a pineapple for a plum), or any more than a great film is an accretion of describable film images. Today nobody, I think, tries to rearrange or restructure a great painting (though sometimes great paintings don't get reproduced very well), and nobody, I think, has plans for putting Chaplin's *City Lights* into book form so that a new audience can get a richer feel for the material. But the abuse of the essence of literature occurs with greater and greater frequency, as the new visual forms attempt to feed their commercial or self-serving appetites for new "artistic" material. And always (to hear the adapters tell it) it is *youth* that is being served. Think of how many young people who have never read *The Scarlet Letter* (or who ran away from school when somebody asked them to read it) will now know about Hester Prynne! Know *what*? is one question. Another question, equally unanswerable, might be: How many of those who saw *The Scarlet Letter* on television will now read the book, and read it as Hawthorne wrote it, communing through his language to the soul of the work, and not merely checking off the incidents as they relate to what they saw, perhaps more vividly, on the screen?

The present time is said not to be a happy one for literature. Good poets are largely unnoticed, few serious novels are read, and the audience for the music of words seems to be drifting away, as if mesmerized by painting, prints, photographs, moving pictures, videotape—by the new power of visual imagery. Perhaps the music of words will never reassert its ancient hold on the popular imagination. Perhaps, as some have suggested, the grip of words had become too strong, too tight, thereby unbalancing the ancient, preliterary equilibrium of the human brain. At any rate, for the moment, one has the impression that the mass media, which are largely visual, are in the process of trying to perpetuate an illusion: the illusion being that culture is somehow neutral as to form and can therefore best be communicated and recommunicated by means of the most popular forms of the day. Thus, some of the great literary spirits of our civilization have been made unwitting participants in a curious sort of visual vs. literary Capture the Flag contest, in which the visual team lately appears to have the upper hand, drawing bigger crowds and winning fatter purses. Will the visual team continue to forge ahead, chewing up Homer and Dante and the Oxford English Dictionary and spitting them out in ten-part installments, each verified for historical accuracy by a battery of academics and scripted so as to be easily comprehensible to a ninth-grade audience? One will have to wait for the twenty-first century to find out. Meanwhile, the crucial issue remains in doubt: respect for man and his art. Will the new communication forms advance this respect, as they sometimes seem to be trying to do? Or will they keep on fudging it, waffling, ducking the serious questions, but talking always of freedom—the new freedoms—and of the splendid gifts they bring us?

(1979)

WHAT WE DO IN THE DARK

I THOUGHT that the most interesting thing about the new movie *Network* was the response of the audience I watched it with—an ordinary New York movie audience, whatever that may mean. The film itself could be described as either a satire or melodrama about the television industry, and especially about network news operations and their supposedly manic concern for ratings and show-business values. As entertainment, it's probably fair to say that *Network* is lively, slick, and highly professional, and combines that attention to background detail and avoidance of interior complexity which more or less define the show-business ethos it was attempting to criticize. As satire or as serious comment, the movie seemed oddly pious and heavy-handed. In other words, it was another typically overmounted, modishly topical, overobvious popular entertainment; good for a few laughs, and something to do after dinner.

But the audience around me in the theater clearly felt something different. I wouldn't go so far as to say that it loved the movie, for there wasn't much love in evidence that evening, either on the screen or inside the theater. In fact, in the fashion of much modern satire, the movie purported to hate television while at the same time being inextricably dependent upon both its values and its overwhelming presence. Members of the audience apparently shared this ambivalent and fashionable love-hatred, but it seemed to me that they also went far beyond it, expressing reactions to the generally routine developments that were taking place on-screen as if something profound and intimate were being touched on. Rarely in a movie theater have I heard such continual eruptions of discordant laughter: angry laughter, nervous laughter, laughter in the wrong places. At one point, when the supposedly tragic figure of the broken-down, half-mad anchorman (played by Peter Finch, in a variety of Anglo-American accents) collapsed on the set, either dead or in a faint, the audience roared and raged with laughter, as if its nerves were already so on edge that no other civilized response was possible. Another time, when the much-troubled anchorman declared ponderously and on camera that the news he had been announcing was only "bullshit," I heard people around me yelling back "Right on!" and "You tell 'em!" In short, the audience seemed to be wholly and deeply involved with the movie, but on a level far beyond the more routine reactions of, say, cheering the crazy-but-pure hero and hissing the wicked network executives: parables that have been conventional entertainment staples since the end of the Second World War, with a long parade of gray-flannel-suit heroes struggling to affirm their integrity against the evil pressures of the advertising or movie business, or just big business, or even, more recently, the espionage business. Granted the moral conflicts in *Network* were scarcely different from those that have been exploited for decades in popular novels and films, to the point of banality. What, then, accounted for the strange nature of this audience's involvement? Why, for instance, did a woman near me, whose face I had periodically glimpsed during the movie as she leaned forward in her seat, with her eyes unusually intent upon the screen and her mouth almost fiercely grinning—why did she remark to her husband or companion afterward, putting on her coat in the relighted theater, that she had been "bored"?

I have no specific or original answer to this question, but I suspect that, as with a number of other seemingly unrelated matters, a lot of it has to do with sexuality. For what I think *Network* speaks to more than anything else—certainly more than the audience's appetite for pious, overworked fables of corporate integrity—is our guilty recognition of the sexual connotations of watching television. What is this activity, after all? And what other activity, if any, does it resemble? Consider that it is done just about every day, virtually everywhere in the country. It cuts across lines of class, education, color, creed, and so forth. Moreover, while we warily admit to it as an activity, we claim that it is mainly a group activity, when in fact most of us engage in it primarily on our own. Indeed, it is something that many persons simply cannot refrain from, try as they might, knowing as they do that it is in some way not quite good for them. Authorities, for example, such as parents and educators, suggest that it may cause vague harm, even physical harm, certainly if engaged in to excess, though generally speaking there are rarely any visible signs of ill effects. Thus, young and old, we continue to do it. Often, we set up a special, private room at home to do it in, for above all it is a private act, an act that we perform by ourselves and with ourselves, even though other people may sometimes share the room and engage in it themselves. What it resembles most, I think, is masturbation. And though, of course, there are differences, many differences, between the two activities, before one dismisses the notion altogether as being too farfetched or "psychological," consider also for a moment that the growth of television viewing in this country has roughly paralleled a similar rise in the acceptance of "getting oneself off," not merely as a time-honored rite of youth but now (so it would seem from the prevailing imagery of *Playboy*, *Penthouse*, and even *Vogue*) as a conventional, perhaps prevailing, form of adult sexual expression.

At any rate, in keeping with the guilty aura of the whole business, it is easier to notice these resemblances in others than in oneself. For instance, only the other evening, I happened to pass by the little side room where we keep our TV set, and in it (as he often is), bathed in the gray, flickering darkness, I spied the sprawled, glazed-eyed figure of one of our children. I walked right on by without comment, or thought I did, conscious that if I asked him if he had done his homework he would say yes, conscious that he is now old enough to manage his own school assignments, conscious that there is something about him in that darkened TV room that irritates me beyond measure, and so forth. But my wife had apparently caught something in my expression as I passed down the corridor, and now remarked: "What on earth was going on in there? You looked as if you'd just come across somebody 'in the act.' " No, no, I quickly protested. Not a bit of it. Just Billy watching a TV show. But methinks I maybe protested too much. I had seen something, after all—something that had put that look on my face. And one of the reasons I hadn't spoken to Billy, I knew, was that if I'd done so, or made my presence felt, I would have had to see that guilty look on *his* face, too.

The fact is that I've understood for years, somewhere in me, that my ritual parental mutterings on the subject of kids watching television—about their having to do their homework first, or not watching junky shows, or only watching an hour at night, or only watching an hour and a half at night—have been only partially related to what's been bothering me. In terms of moral principles or child raising, I don't actually find TV in moderate doses harmful or offensive, especially since I watch it in immoderate doses myself. I don't mind the shows that the kids watch. I don't want to watch them, too, but I don't mind their watching. Of course, a lot of them are trash, but the kids work hard at school and a little trash is not such a bad thing in its way. In my heart of hearts, do I really want or expect them to be reading the *Principia Mathematica* when they've finished with their history homework, and done their chores, and practiced their pianos and trombones or whatever? The answer is no. So, why do I fuss at them about the TV, why do I vaguely patrol the TV room without acknowledging that I'm patrolling it? What is the electricity that seems to surround this apparently so ordinary, domestic activity, television viewing, and that makes even me (let me admit it) feel some shadow of guilt when I have been communing dreamily with the Cowboys and the Steelers for an afternoon and my wife walks into the room? Do I feel guilty about *football*? I suspect not. I think we all share a secret in our house, as happens in many if not most houses, and do the best with it we can.

Admittedly, the TV set is certainly not our first or only sexual artifact. For much of the century, the automobile reigned supreme as sexual symbol. Each fall, the "new season" was a pageant of cars, not television shows: cars with their tail fins, grilles, and bogus, phallic aerodynamics, with their overstated engines (their "horse" power), their hairy-chested show of speed, and their incessant, inevitable accidents. No doubt, these glorious, tinny, supposedly liberating machines (whose "freeing" qualities have brought us traffic jams, the oil crisis, and the three-car pileup) were the last erotic metaphor, the final fling, so to speak, of the romantic, overextended, dangerous European male. These days there are surface signs that, sexually, we are on gentler ground, with our harsh, historical role differences breaking down all around us, dissolving, disappearing, and re-forming themselves (so it would sometimes seem) into a soft, quiet, hermaphroditic smile. At any rate, with what remains of our fierce male sexuality lumpishly buried in giant underground silos in the West or else hidden out of sight (and out of mind) aboard dark, gliding submarines beneath the sea, we now sit before our new symbol-machines (indeed, our auto-immobiles), neither really asleep nor really awake, neither dreaming nor experiencing. Sometimes we try to talk about what we do in our dimly lit, flickering rooms, but it always comes out that we were actually doing something else: watching a show, a football game, our "favorite program." The novelty of *Network*, as a critic wrote in the Sunday *Times*, was its "no-holds-barred, behind-the-scenes look at the TV industry." Maybe so, but my guess is that what "bored" the woman near me in the movie theater was what used to "bore" many people on seeing so-called dirty movies. Is *this* what people do in the dark? Is *this* what we do, too?

(1976)

ON THE TRAIL OF A "FINE CARELESS RAPTURE"

In 1937, the great Scots documentary filmmaker John Grierson (friend of Eisenstein and patron of Robert Flaherty; he had himself coined the word "documentary" in a review of Flaherty's *Moana* in 1926) looked back toward the dawn of the cinema age at the end of the last century and noted that when Louis Lumière, the French film pioneer, first put the new technology of his Cinématographe to use, in 1895, he had done so in the service not of art or artifice but of a simple, straight-forward reality. "The new moving camera was still, for him, a camera and an instrument to focus on the life about him," Grierson wrote. "He shot his own work-men filing out of the factory and this first film"—*Lunch Break at the Lumière Factory*, the first film made and shown anywhere—"was a 'documentary.' He went on as naturally to shoot the Lumière family, child complete. The cinema, it seemed for a moment, was about to fulfill its natural destiny of discovering mankind. It had every-thing for the task. It could get about, it could view reality with a new intimacy; and what more natural than that the recording of the real world should become its prin-cipal inspiration?"

When Grierson wrote those words, the battle for real-ity in film seemed in an especially parlous state. Long vanished was the "fine careless rapture," as Grierson described it, of Lumière's attempts at a "fresh new art of observation and reality"—overwhelmed at an early stage by the artifice of such as Georges Méliès, with his cinematic excursions to the fantasy landscapes of the moon and Hades. Vanished, too, for the most part, was the later school, or ambience, of "fresh air and real people," which had begun to appear tentatively in the pre-1914 English and Danish cinema and more definitely in the early American slapsticks and Westerns (notably in *The Great Train Robbery*, whose "engineers and telegraph men," Grierson observed, "were contacts with the real thing, and unimportant as they now seem, it was a long time before they cropped up again"), swept aside, or, rather, into the studio, by the imperatives of the growing studio system, with its institutionalization of artifice and its dependence on celebrity actors, often in historical costume. Moreover, in the world of "actuality films" things seemed no better. On the one hand, there were the newsreels: "dim records," in Grierson's stern view, "of only the evanescent and the essentially unreal," which were of interest mainly to curiosity seekers who might wish to see "the Kaiser at maneuvers and the Czar at play." On the other hand, there was the work of a few serious realists, such as Robert Flaherty, who in *Nanook of the North*, as Grierson wrote, "had the idea of making a story about people he knew—not foisting, studio fashion, a preconceived story on a background for the decorative quality it added, but taking his story from within. The blizzards were real and the gestures of human exhaustion came from the life." But the superlative *Nanook* had to be financed by a fur company, Revillon Frères (thus our present-day programming grants from oil companies seem to be part of an ancient, if ambivalent, tradition), and "was turned down by every renter on Broadway," while some of Flaherty's subsequent films, such as *White Shadows in the South Seas, Tabu,* and *Elephant Boy,* could be made and distributed only on the condition that Flaherty agree, in effect, to co-opt himself, either by allowing a Hollywood-designated director to accompany his film crew or by shooting part of *Elephant Boy,* at Vincent Korda's insistence, in a transparently studio setting. Indeed, it was Flaherty's untenable situation in America that led Grierson to find a place for the great American documentarist on the British marketing board's film unit, which he then headed. Even so, forty years ago the realist situation was not altogether bleak. In addition to Flaherty, Grierson listed Ruttmann in Germany, Eisenstein and Pudovkin in Russia, Cavalcanti in France, and himself in Britain as inheritors of the cinema's great mission of discovering mankind, and added, "Our realist showing, if secondary to the main growth of cinema, has assumed a certain bravery." Moreover, there were signs of new developments appearing in Hollywood, where, "however diffidently the more difficult [contemporary] problems may be handled, they are not altogether avoided," Grierson wrote at the time. "Prison life, the plague of gangsterdom, the new police, unemployment, lynching and the secret societies, the New Deal, finance, and Hollywood itself are inspiring writer and director alike." And in the area of actuality films Grierson was much impressed by the arrival of *The March of Time,* which, he said, "does what the other [cinema] news records have failed to do. It gets behind the news, observes the factors of influence, and gives a perspective to events. Not the parade of armies so much as the race in armaments; not the ceremonial opening of a dam but the full story of Roosevelt's experiment in the Tennessee Valley . . . In no deep sense conscious of the higher cinematic qualities, it has yet carried over from journalism into cinema, after thirty-eight years, something of that bright and easy tradition of freeborn comment which the newspaper has won and the cinema has been too abject even to ask for."

I have quoted Grierson at such length because it is hard not to admire the old Scotsman (he died in 1972, after a long and distinguished career that included not only helping to edit Eisenstein's *Potemkin* but also being named the first commissioner of Canada's remarkable National Film Board) and because the battle for a greater realism in film continues to be fought in our day, with the same sense of shifting battle lines, although, I suspect, with a frequently different sense of purpose. Grierson got into difficulties in the late nineteen-forties, especially in America, for his leftist views and involvements, but it is clear from his writings that all along he remained an unreconstructed liberal, possessed of a hard-headed Jeffersonian sense of the need for intelligent, informed discourse in a democratic society. In discussing the origins of the documentary movement, he wrote, "Many of us after 1918 (and particularly in the United States) were impressed by the pessimism that had settled on Liberal theory. We noted the conclusion of such men as Walter Lippmann, that because the citizen, under modern conditions, could not know everything about everything all the time, democratic citizenship was therefore impossible. We set to thinking how a dramatic apprehension of the modern scene might solve the problem, and we turned to the new wide-reaching instruments of radio and cinema as necessary instruments in both the practice of government and the enjoyment of citizenship." It strikes me that as one casts about among the creations of the modern cinema and modern television for depictions of reality—at any rate, of the "modern scene"—one finds a surprising abundance of it, but often not where one might have been led to expect it, and often in forms that have little to do with such old-fashioned notions as "the enjoyment of citizenship."

In television news programs, for example, where one might have expected a surge of creativity to have begun making itself felt in the film-oriented nineteen-sixties, there still exist today the same sort of limitations that obtained forty years ago, when Grierson was commenting on the newsreel that it "has gone dithering on, mistaking the phenomenon for the thing itself, and ignoring everything that gave it the trouble of conscience and penetration and thought." Certainly, there have been advances, but most of them appear to be mainly technical: "feeds" and minicams and satellite relays, all of which tend to reinforce the relevance of Thoreau's remark on being informed of the first transcontinental telegraph link between Maine and Texas: "But what if Maine and Texas have nothing to communicate?" Meanwhile, the old limitations remain solidly in place, largely as a result of the still defensive nature of broadcast news, which in its efforts to acquire a printlike respectability often transmits an officious, bureaucratic news composed mainly of the doings and sayings of "newsmakers." Then, too, there are the distracted borrowings by the news departments of not merely the techniques but the values of entertainment programming. Thus, in addition to the already stylized figure of the buttoned-up and suited network newsman, with his pompous report on what the Senator just said to the Ambassador about the Secretary of State's announcement, there has begun to appear in growing numbers an equally theatrical newsroom figure: the newsman as genial talk-show host, as good-time guy, or—as in the case of CBS's Charles Kuralt—as Will Rogers. The new informal type of TV newsman is in some ways a refreshing change from the stage-set conservatism of the old-fashioned anchor booth, but the new man's message is often just as irrelevant and unreal as his predecessor's. The conservative, officious newsman spoke of a world whose forces—and thus whose possibilities—were largely defined by *institutions*. The friendly, chatty, personal fellows like Kuralt, however, speak of a world that, no matter how complex its underlying problems may be, is largely defined by beaming, smiling, ever talking *individuals*. There is reason to believe that both perspectives are somewhat wide of the mark. Also, in recent years a newer, different kind of limitation has intruded into television news's already uncertain methods of reporting about real life. I call it a limitation though many, I know, think of it as a step forward. It is not too visible yet in the regular network news programs but it is increasingly noticeable in some of the flashier network documentaries. The limitation comes, I think, from a misappropriation of visual freedom. In other words, though the news cameras have been increasingly released by new technology from the confinements of a narrow, print-oriented coverage, they have not apparently been released into a truly free space, where the parties involved might think seriously about the new freedoms and how these might best be employed to communicate reality. Instead, the obedient cameras have been marched off in the service of another master. In a way, one can hardly blame them, for the new master is a powerful one and rules over a large and growing visual empire. How might one describe this attractive and despotic presence? Sometimes an awkward phrase is better than no phrase at all, so let us call it the realism of artifice: Artificial Realism.

I don't think it's much of an exaggeration to say that the Artificial Realism of the American fiction film is now the most powerful force in the contemporary film world. Consider, after all, some of the ingredients that contribute to the reality of a successful film today. There is the whole matter of sound, for instance: a largely hyped and artificial sound that is so taken for granted by the audience as to be scarcely felt as an intrusion; instead, films today often come across as achievements in audio engineering. Movies such as *Star Wars* and *Apocalypse Now* rely preponderantly for their deeper effects on sound. The images catch the eye, of course, but the sound catches the emotions. In *Apocalypse Now*, for instance, the sound of the helicopters fills the ears and inhabits the head far more intimately and affectively than the images of the helicopters are experienced by the optic nerves. A large measure of the movie's so-called importance derives from the portentousness of what one hears. Increasingly, too, in films—especially in important, expensive films—the sound of the dialogue is also artificial. That is, it is produced by "looping": recording it at a later time. One might even go so far as to say that, in a modern film with a big budget, the more there is of supposedly realistic dialogue (those lifelike murmurs and whispers and overheard snatches of conversation), the more likely it is that this realistic dialogue was "looped": painstakingly recorded months after the shooting by the original actors, often with the director present to see that the intonations come out right, and then synchronized with the proper frames. The role of sound in films—indeed, in mass communications—is worth a whole essay in itself, but this is probably not the place for it, except to note that TV advertisers with their songs and jingles have long been aware of the emotional receptivity of the human ear; also, popular-film audiences understand intuitively the extent to which sound contributes to the new reality and it is no surprise that movie-theater owners, with their costly new Dolby System equipment, are rushing to provide it.

In addition to sound, then, as one of the key ingredients of the new filmic reality, there is the matter of the fiction film's "look." Once upon a time, the part played by set design and wardrobe in films was a relatively minor one, except in musicals or historical epics. Though not unimportant by any means, the sets and clothes in most realistic or naturalistic films were designed not to be unduly noticed; nor did the audience really look at them. But in the past ten years or so, a whole new subindustry has grown up consisting of highly skilled professionals—often trained originally in television commercials or in the fashion industry—who, as production designers, now create the "look" of important movies. Indeed, the production designers are not far behind the film editors in their claim to a share in the *auteur*ship of recent movies, and with good reason, for in many cases the "reality" of a modern realistic film—its seeming substance; the sense it imparts of being a representation of real people engaged in a real existence—is often little more (once one has subtracted the

cumulative texture of its artificial sound) than its artificial "look": the "look," for example, of an advertising
man's life in New York, or of a Depression family's
shanty in the nineteen-thirties. All theatricality involves
artifice, but in our new realistic movies the artifice is
not only hyped but lacquered over with "art." The Depression shanty is not only "real" (as it might have been
in less insistent times) but "artistically real." Look at
that old zinc tub with the hog-bristle scouring brush—a
touch borrowed from a Walker Evans photograph! Look
at the old boots, and the dust on the boots, brought in
plastic bags from the Appalachian foothills! It is no
longer the "reality" of the ancient crafts of set design
and wardrobe—where the audience, nudged and
prompted by the props and costumes, could construct a
larger, truer reality in its head—but, rather, a new,
assertive, almost grandiloquent reality, born not merely
of artifice but of Art Design, where the audience is virtually compelled to notice every object, every "touch,"
and, while supposedly being gratified in its senses, is in
fact being controlled much too rigorously to be able to
think or imagine for itself.

Even so, it is the third element of Artificial Realism
that is probably the most important, though it is also the
most difficult to pin down or to describe coherently. Call
it, perhaps, the Screenplay Factor. For beneath the
artificial sound that, as it were, animates the movie, and
beneath the artful production values that give it its
"look," there is the more fundamental reality that is
asked for in the screenplay. Where does this screenplay
reality come from? In some rare movies nowadays,
such as Peter Yates and Steve Tesich's *Breaking Away*,
it comes from carefully observed and personally felt

experience. In a few other cases, such as John Huston and Benedict Fitzgerald's *Wise Blood*, a strong literary model may exist for a movie; this doesn't mean that it has to be filmed in literary terms but that it usually can't be filmed successfully without somehow leaving intact, or at least respecting, the original spinal cord of theme and character. In most instances, however, screenplays increasingly seem to be little more than strategies for getting movies filmed; battle plans, as it were, with the principal energies of the authors being expended on a kind of cinema logistics: on structure; on organization; on moving Character A from X to Y, maybe with the wife but not the dog, or with the dog but not the wife, or with both wife and dog but not the heart attack. Individuality of character becomes a secondary substance, which arrives, if at all, ready-made with the persona of the star. Meanwhile, the thematic core of the screenplay—not merely the relationships between the characters but the source of the energy that brings them all into conflict— appears to derive, more frequently than not, either from earlier, role-model films or from the popular novels or detective stories that gave birth to those films: from a pool of "collective consciousness" that is in fact not consciousness at all but a floating library of narrow- gauge, subliterary (which is not to say *non*literary) forms that can be fitted on to this or that situation. The truth is that the core of the modern screenplay is in many cases a core of quasi-engineering details, and that the center of the actual story is either left to the last or at- tended to in a shorthand that is largely based on the reality of other movies. For example, the mode of the detective film, which derives from the subliterary detec- tive novel (which in turn derives more commonly from observed literature than from observed life), has been allowed to inhabit a whole variety of supposedly realistic films whose "reality," modeled on such thirdhand sources, then becomes pretty much stillborn. Besides, not only the charming or sinister protagonists from these prototypical detective films but their tones, attitudes, and minor gestures are endlessly copied (even in non-detective films), thus providing a ready-made, real-life veneer which displaces the need for greater authenticity.

The influence of the fiction film on television is hard to chart with exactitude, but it is clearly present. (Television has also influenced fiction films, but mainly through commercials.) Fiction films, after all, are the great mythmaking models of our age. Where once the literate public sought to be swirled up in the literary worlds of the great poets, dramatists, and novelists, in the past half century a much larger visually oriented public seeks to be touched and sanctified by the filmic worlds of the great directors and movie stars. In the area that might at first glance be taken to represent television's reality view—namely, television news—the influence of these films seems not yet pronounced; nonetheless, it definitely exists, and I suspect that it is being felt more strongly all the time. Take what might seem an unlikely place to find any fiction-film reality at all: *60 Minutes*. Here is a conservatively mounted, news-oriented program, whose essence is the dramatic interview, backed up by solid television camera work. But look more closely. At those moments when *60 Minutes* is most on target, is most clearly in focus, is most being itself—when Mike Wallace, say, is going after some crooked manufacturer of defective wheelchairs— what reality is being conveyed, what thematic reality underlies the ostensible reality of the reporter and his interview? It is not, after all, a reality modeled on actual journalism (though now, since life imitates art, TV reporters try to place themselves in *60 Minutes* situations) but a reality modeled on a mixture of detective and courtroom movies of a generation ago. Think of the strangely conservative and old-fashioned persona of the *60 Minutes* correspondent, sometimes glimpsed by the camera as he strides manfully into the dens of corruption (in the manner, perhaps, of *Mr. Deeds Goes to Town*), sometimes carefully framed as he sits on a simple chair, dressed in an unpretentious but definitely respectable suit, a plain shirt, and a plain tie (in the manner, perhaps, of Ralph Bellamy), interviewing some miscreant, and nearly always with a little spiral-bound notebook on his lap. The content of the interview may be real, but the dramaturgy of the interview is realistic mainly in a film sense. Its reality is the reality neither of present-day investigative reporters nor of present-day prosecutors but of a nineteen-fifties movie.

Granted, the influence of fiction-film reality on *60 Minutes* isn't very pronounced, though it is more pronounced there than on the documentary program that it has not so much supplanted as pushed to the side: *CBS Reports*. *CBS Reports* still exists, and continues to do some fine work in the conventional television-documentary format (for example, its documentary on South Africa last season, which stays in the mind as a model of clarity and accessible, informative reporting), but there seems to be a general feeling, not least among certain network executives, that something is somehow missing from its format. One hears it said that the once venerated program now lacks "pace." That is, has lost a certain *élan vital*. I imagine that what it strikes some people as having lost is what ABC's new documentary series, *Close-up*, appears to have gained: namely, the look and reality of the fiction film. I have seen six of the recent *Close-up* documentaries and on a superficial level I found them definitely appealing—fast-moving, fluid, visual. The images were sometimes close to being movie clichés, but the overall effect was one of energy—movie energy. The editing gave most of the documentaries a movielike pace, and the sound track (usually loud and youthful) provided a movielike background. One was drawn along as a viewer in a sort of visual-sonic glide, building and letting down, building and letting down, with the scenes and images flowing by (I'm thinking even of what might have been a fairly straitlaced report on arson), with the music banging out, and with the smooth, quick narrative interrupted every now and then by little jolts of sudden excitement—as in a high-powered, big-budget fiction film. In fact, one might have been seeing such a film, or had one? By that, I don't mean to renew the controversy that for a while surrounded one of the *Close-up* documentaries (on youth gangs), in which some questions were raised about the staging of certain scenes. Even assuming that all the events actually took place, whose reality in the end was being displayed on the television screen? The reporter's reality? The camera's reality? The film editor's reality? In any case, could it have been a reality uninfluenced by the augmented, false reality of most popular fiction films? For the time being, these are open questions, awaiting unambiguous answers.

Still, it seems fair to say that the present condition of the reality film (be it fiction or nonfiction) in this country is generally better than it is in most other countries, though it falls far short of a healthy democratic ideal. That is, if Walter Lippmann was speaking soundly, though a bit pessimistically, when he remarked on the impossibility of maintaining a true democracy in a world where there was so much to be known, and if John Grierson was also speaking soundly, though a bit optimistically, when he wrote about the importance of shaping a true democratic citizenship through a communication of the real world to its citizens, then the current situation, which provides a powerful, filmed reality—however abundant and various—that is heavily weighted and distorted by the artificial reality of the modern fiction film, is likely to be of great service neither to the citizen-audience nor to any meaningful ideal of honest art.

Fortunately, there are signs of hope, though they can be glimpsed mostly on the outskirts of the network news organizations. Right now, the chief cause for optimism lies in the tenacity and growing skills of the independent nonfiction filmmakers: filmmakers who have been willing to sustain a sometimes difficult independence, and to struggle—if not always in garrets, then at least through the subworld of grants and funding by which our corporate and governmental establishments seek to keep unknown quantities in their place—in the service of a more personally involved form of film journalism than the networks usually permit. At present, though their names are not yet legion, there appear to be at least several hundred men and women, many young, many not so young, who practice the craft of nonfiction filmmaking at various levels of talent and acceptance. Among the better-known names in this group—though it is hardly a group, as such—are Jack Willis (*Paul Jacobs and the Nuclear Gang*), Richard Cohen (*Deadly Force*), Lynne Littman (*Once a Daughter*), Errol Morris (*Gates of Heaven*), Jon Alpert and Keiko Tsuno (*Vietnam: Picking Up the Pieces*), and Alan and Susan Raymond (*The Police Tapes*), all of whom have worked under the auspices of WNET/13's enterprising department, the Television Laboratory.

It is unwise to generalize about an array of young talent as diverse as this, whose imperfections are sometimes as noticeable as their skills, although there is clearly much to be said for the passion for making things known which seems to exist among them all. The truth is that passion has been sadly lacking in nonfiction reality films for a long time, one might even say since the days of Flaherty and Grierson. Of course, there have been exceptions, though usually outside the networks: such nineteen-sixties documentarists as Richard Leacock, Donn Pennebaker, and the Maysles brothers, who continue to do fine work, though all of them have been compelled to branch into other fields—teaching, distribution, and television commercials. There is Harry Rasky, the Canadian, and Michael Rubbo, from Australia. There is the remarkable Frederick Wiseman, who is remarkable in his pursuit not only of a documentary style but of a moral technique for showing the filmic truth of a situation, and remarkable, too, for his inability sometimes to stop himself from pushing both style and technique into inaccessibility.

In the main, however, nonfiction filmmaking in the television era has been primarily a function of the television networks, and although these well-meaning films —which, more often than not, are deliberately buried by the network brass in some late-evening time slot—have done their duty, so to speak, in the matter of informing the audience about certain broad and usually distant issues, there has rarely been much more to the transaction than that: a sincere, dutiful, and passionless communication from the schoolroom. Even the noble Edward R. Murrow, whose radio broadcasts from England touched so many emotions in the early stages of the Second World War, seemed confined to solemn lecturing in his documentaries for *CBS Reports*. It would be unfair to blame Murrow or his producer, Fred Friendly, for the network constraints that surrounded and inhibited their work for CBS News. Still, when I rewatched *Harvest of Shame* (the noted David Lowe documentary about migrant farm workers) a few months ago, it seemed, after the passage of twenty years, a worthy piece of journalism, and in some places a fine piece of journalism, but on the whole a strangely distanced work. Such passion as the documentary contained appeared to reside mainly in Ed Murrow's voice, which was heard, for the most part, in stately, resonant narration. In contrast, the actual scenes and images (in short, the essence of the film) were dry, conventional, and quite remote, as in a well-made sociological study. At any rate, the point of the observation is not to disparage Murrow or those early *CBS Reports* programs (which were generally in advance of any comparable television journalism being shown in America) but to suggest that commercial and political factors already built into the network system have so curtailed the role of passion and personality in communicating actuality as to render most network documentaries intrinsically no more communicative, and no less alienating, than lectures from a distant and uninvolved authority. At the beginning of the class, the teacher is *there*, and we are *here*, and the subject is *over there*, scrawled on the blackboard in easy-to-read letters, and at no time during the next hour do any of those positions or relationships change. The participants remain fixed in their respective places. We are communicated at but not involved.

For years, under the heading of news or documentary, the networks have been broadcasting a noninvolved reality, often with skill, even with occasional bursts of moral courage, such as has resulted lately in some well-publicized coverage of once unacceptable subjects. But then the problem was never one of conservatism in the choice of subject matter. For, despite the stern Puritan spirit that is so close to the center of the documentary form, the truth is that an audience might gain at least as much from a great nonfiction film about, say, the Colorado River as from conventionally filmed journalism about minority hiring or industrial pollution. The problem is the noninvolvement of the communication. Consider, too, that in the last decade there has been a considerable rise in the number of regionally oriented documentaries produced by local stations. This is all to the good, in that most of them at least relate to genuine local problems and interests, and are generally a step forward from the old days, when the TV station in, for instance, a lumber-company town would suddenly come forth with a "documentary" filmed on the lumber company's land and mostly showing the lumber-company president discoursing on the virtues of tree harvesting. But here, again, what seems to have happened (at least, in the several dozen local documentaries I watched last year) is that the local documentary-makers have set out to imitate not only their big-city colleagues' puritanical choice of subject matter but their unemotional, distanced methods as well. Instead of personal, accessible, humane, even sometimes (perish the thought!) humorous stories of America and American life, the local stations seem bent on producing their own punishing provincial sagas on minority hiring and industrial pollution, as if these obviously newsworthy flaws in our society were the only things that mattered in American life; indeed, as if societal sin were the single divinely decreed subject for the nonfiction film.

And so one looks beyond the networks to the new movement of documentarists. They tend to be film-makers first, and not converted print journalists with cameras in their hands. Also, their passion to communicate runs high—this passion which scarcely anyone can do without in trying to communicate the real things, which the public often has so many defenses raised against. But we are not yet home free with the independents. To begin with, most of them are still out there, often in a depressing economic limbo, scurrying around for grants, worrying about the cost of film, and being alternately starved and bored to death by funding committees. Then, too, many of them seem to be as ambivalent about the practice of journalism as in fact are some of their more casual colleagues in the world of print. That is, they would like to deal with nonfiction subjects, because those are often the most interesting, but they would like—some of them, some of the time—to deal with them by employing, as the phrase goes, "fictional techniques," because those are often the most appealing. This ambivalence lurks as a troubling quality, for example, in the otherwise admirable documentary *The Police*

Tapes, by Alan and Susan Raymond, about the activities in the combat zone surrounding a South Bronx police precinct. Here the point of view is never inhibited or distanced. The camera is intimate, jumpy, nosy, scurrying along, always involved. The level of communication is much above that of mere duty, much above the schoolroom. So far so good. We have been starved for nonfiction reality, and here it is. But there is something else, too, though it is hard to pin down: a mode, let's call it, or a modeling, that blurs the images of *The Police Tapes* with those of a dozen fiction films, TV series, and the like. One is "real," of course, and the others are "made up," but what is that bridge between the two, and how did it get there? And what other traffic—what appealing, blurred mixtures of fact and fiction—may be presumed to have shuffled back and forth across it? The Raymonds, it should be noted, have recently taken a step upward from the garret, having been adopted, as it were, by ABC's documentary unit. One wishes them luck in the heady, fast-paced, filmic atmosphere of *Close-up,* because they are young and serious and good. One also wishes that, as nonfiction filmmakers, they won't try to be what they shouldn't be, because it is mere foolishness for a nonfiction craftsman to take the current trendy talk about "fictional techniques" too seriously. The "techniques" that are usually referred to are the property neither of fiction nor of nonfiction but are simply techniques for filmmaking or writing, as the case may be; in a sense, anyone who wishes to may use them. The stumbling block is the particular craft that one practices. If one practices fiction, then one's goal is the reorganization of experience (an artistic reorganization, even a falsifying, of experience). But if one practices nonfiction, then one's goal might be said to be *careful-ness*: a careful, loving fidelity to the real. Fancy foot-work, dazzling movement, dramatic confrontations, by all means! But if there is no careful, loving fidelity to the real at the center of the work, then it isn't nonfiction, and it probably isn't fiction. What it may be is yet another fashionable, ambitious space probe, floating in the commercial void.

Meanwhile, as we await the millennium, at which time the networks will be flooded with passion and personal-ity, and the young filmmakers will be suffused with nonfictional carefulness, and the whole nation will be bathed in such a glorious glow of information as to make Walter Lippmann spin nervously in his grave, there is probably, even now, more workaday *reality* being communicated by such relatively quiet, well-constructed television fiction series as *Lou Grant, The White Shadow,* and *Skag* than by most of our flashy, "realistic" fiction movies, as well as by most network public-affairs programs stacked end to end. An im-perfect reality, to be sure; an unassertive reality, with room to breathe in. Nonetheless, these television enter-tainments provide a depiction of certain aspects and areas of American life which is accessible and involving and generally realistic, and is clearly none the worse for being unassisted by important sound effects and un-graced by Scandinavian cinematography. Indeed, there is something about the prosaic, small-screen, acoustically undernourished home television set that may well make it (as long as it stays that way) the greatest communi-cator of realistic life that the world has seen, once people understand how to use it. There is a modesty to the equipment, and a sort of petlike familiarity surrounding its domestic lodging in our homes, that seems to militate against too much artistic hype, too much fake art-designed reality. Junk, yes; the TV set has ample room for junk. But those high-gloss, quasi-artistic, falsely important film spectacles that arouse near-orgiastic responses in darkened movie theaters appear only to make the nineteen-inch picture tube uncomfortable. Alas, I saw in the morning paper that *Skag*—that fine program not so much about steelworkers as about an American family—was having rating trouble and might be canceled. Too bad. Sooner or later, people will get the hang of such shows, for they have a powerful logic behind them. In contrast to the trendy fiction films that play on our alienations, or the public-affairs programs that preach to us like children—sinful children in a classroom—these solid, humane, carefully done reality fictions help make us a community. I imagine that old John Grierson would have been pleased by them, too. Like all good men, he loved the reality of the world, and like most great men, he was none too awe-struck by hyperbole or Art Design.

(1980)

THE PRISONER OF THE GOLDEN DREAM

Ever since Alex Haley's best-selling documentary novel (or "faction," as he described it) *Roots* first appeared, in 1974, and then reappeared, on television, in 1977, still as *Roots* (or *Roots I*), before an audience of roughly a hundred and thirty million, and then reappeared once again as *Roots: The Next Generations* (or *Roots II*), before an audience of roughly a hundred and ten million, the story of Mr. Haley's efforts to retrace his lineage to its African beginnings has been talked about in terms of power. To *Roots* in its various forms, though perhaps especially to its television dramatizations, have been attributed the power to uplift the pride of American blacks, the power to raise the racial consciousness of American whites, the power to affect the emotions of all races through its epic narrative, and the power to teach.

There is obviously no denying the power of a popular story that persistently attracts such huge audiences, although, considering the several weaknesses, dramatic and otherwise, of *Roots II*, it is worth speculating about where the real power of the overall drama resides. For example, it surely does not lie in an enormous respect for historical accuracy, since, despite Haley's much-touted labors of research, the dimensions of the several plagiarism lawsuits brought against him, and of at least one settlement, indicate that there was at times some more than modest confusion in his mind about his sources. Also, a 1977 challenge by a reporter of the

London *Sunday Times* to the plausibility of Haley's *griot*-obtained information about his remote African ancestor Kunta Kinte has cast at least a little doubt on the factual, or detective-story, basis of his adventure. Nor has *Roots II* treated its parent, the original *Roots*, with all-embracing fidelity, being content, perhaps, to subject the sacred text to the same poetic process that the author sometimes employed upon his earlier research. To mention only one of the numerous liberties taken in *Roots II* with the already fairly liberated material, there is a scene in the final episode in which Haley's father, who has been shown to have consistently disapproved of his son's writing career, comes to the airport to see Alex off to Africa, and while both men are at a newsstand the father spies a paperback copy of a book Haley has written (or collaborated on), *The Autobiography of Malcolm X*, which Haley buys and then inscribes: "To my dad—I no longer need his approval but I will always need his love." It is a touching scene of reconciliation, nicely acted by James Earl Jones as Haley and by Dorian Harewood as Haley's father, but, alas, in Haley's book there is no indication that his father ever saw him off at the airport or anywhere else, so one must assume that the scene whose actuality we were asked to be touched by never took place.

On the one hand, this seems more like tricky manipulation than powerful dramatization; on the other hand, if this sort of thing doesn't bother Haley, perhaps it shouldn't bother us. But there are some more substantial problems concerning *Roots II*. Chief among these, I suppose, is the extraordinarily lopsided nature of Haley's story—a lopsidedness that existed in Haley's book and has only been magnified in both television versions—wherein the black characters are almost uniformly depicted in terms of dignity and moral courage, while the white characters are generally portrayed as loutish and mean-spirited when poor, or weak and corrupt when rich. Thus, in the town of Henning, Tennessee, where most of the first half of *Roots* takes place (and which was reconstructed at the usual great expense by the television producers), one gets not so much a sense of real drama or interplay between the blacks and the whites—of the two peoples being really involved with one another—as a sort of old-fashioned, static morality play, reminiscent in part of *Uncle Tom's Cabin* and also, in some ways, of those movies about life in the trenches in the First World War, where Allied soldiers are shown in one set of trenches and the Germans are shown in another set of trenches, and the point of the drama seems to be to wait for some off-stage captain's whistle which periodically signals a skirmish between the two. In *Roots I*, the propaganda element was rarely absent, although, perhaps because of the more eventful pattern of the story, the racial messages seemed less obtrusive. In *Roots II*, there are extended periods when propaganda seems to have been substituted for story, as in the Henning episodes, in which the drama seems to come to life only at those carefully structured intervals when the coarse and violent whites are sent off to brutalize the stoic and philosophic blacks.

The men in *Roots II* are for the most part close to racial caricature; the women are not much better. Black women in *Roots II* tend to be wise, sexual, philosophic, and invariably in touch with basic human emotions. White women are usually shallow and unsexual—or, if sexual, slightly whorish. But there are a couple of exceptions to the general rule of caricature; at least, there are attempts at exceptions. For instance, Colonel Frederick Warner (played by Henry Fonda, with what seems to be an eccentric Nebraska variation of a Tennessee accent), Henning's superficially genteel but morally bankrupt aristocrat, has two sons. Andy, the older son, is drawn from the same Hollywood stewpot as the colonel himself; he's a hard-drinking wastrel, slyly ambitious. The younger son, Jim, however, is clearly intended as a sort of bridge between the races, or trenches, for he marries a black girl (naturally, a college-educated black girl of great sensitivity and good looks) and goes to live on the black side of town. But there is something off-key about the role. On the surface, Jim (played by Richard Thomas) seems to be a decent sort of white American boy, at least by *Roots II* standards, being relatively nonalcoholic, noncorrupt, and nonloutish, but he is also a kind of oddity: poetic, sensitive, literary—almost, to use an archaic word, something of a sissy. Thus, while striking a blow for brotherhood in the "plot," the underlying ambivalence of Jim's role suggests, first, that the only way for a white man to escape the inherent wickedness of his nature is by surrendering a large part of his masculinity, and, second, that the surest way to achieve goodness is for him to marry a black girl. *Roots II* also suggests a couple of other options open to a white man wishing to achieve some measure of salvation—or, at least, dignity—in Henning, Tennessee, in the late nineteenth century. One of these is to be a sound, progressive, forward-thinking, liberal-minded small businessman. Not just an ordinary businessman, mind you, for, although business is clearly an occupation that attracts a better sort of person than the white trash who commonly engage in rural activities in television depictions of the South, it nonetheless often brings out the devil in the white soul by driving such a person to drink on the job and become shiftless; as in the case of poor, weak Mr. Campbell (nonprogressive and therefore drunk all the time), whose lumberyard is taken over by Haley's sober and hardworking ancestor Will Palmer, with the financial assistance of a presumably sober white banker who has demonstrated his sound, progressive, forward-thinking, etc., qualities mostly by having been nice to Haley's kinsman. Another option for a white man aspiring to decency in television's Reconstruction-era South is to be Jewish. According to *Roots II*, there has rarely been as deep and affecting a fondness between two peoples as that which existed in Henning, Tennessee, in the eighteen-eighties and eighteen-nineties between black Americans and Jewish Americans. In fact, except for the forward-looking banker who sets up Mr. Palmer in the lumber business, just about the only decent adult white man anywhere near Henning is a cultivated gentleman called Mr. Goldstein, who runs a small dry-goods store in town. When we first see Goldstein, he is trying to be dignified and philosophic toward a member of local rural redneck society who is loutishly trying on a suit. In due course, Palmer comes in seeking a dress for his daughter, and he and Goldstein hit it off immediately, perhaps recognizing the bond that comes from being the only two grown men in Henning, Tennessee, who are neither corrupt nor violent.

Even when one wants to like *Roots II*, it seems to require some effort to peer through the curious racial propaganda, and something of a further effort to care very deeply—beyond the purely reflexive response of not wanting to see helpless people beaten up on-screen —about characters, white or black, whose personalities contain so few ambiguities, and no surprises, and who are mainly sent off, like freight cars, on their tracks of nobility (for the blacks) and meanness (for the whites) while we wait for them to collide.

There is also another fairly important weakness in the story. For, though the two *Roots* dramatizations have been repeatedly appraised in epic terms, in *Roots II* (which is supposedly based on the last section of Haley's book, together with "one thousand pages of notes" that he provided for the project) the television writers seem to have reduced the potentially epic dimensions of the story of Haley's ancestors in this country since the Civil War to a generation-by-generation series of boy-meets-girl encounters. Obviously, there's a place for romance and sexual relationships in a long family narrative, but in much of *Roots II* the problems of young love seem to be the real focus of the drama—in some cases, the only focus. At the center of the stage, girl flirts with boy, or boy flirts with girl; girl runs after boy, or boy runs after girl. Around these perpetually romancing kinfolk stand, on one side, the older generation of black men and women, persistently displaying wisdom and dignity, and, on another side, the hostile white people brandishing clubs and displaying a general air of menace. And behind them, hazily sketched on a backdrop, or sometimes only hinted at, are the larger events of the times that Haley and his ancestors lived through. It seems a strangely condescending view of black history, or of the part played in it by Haley's ancestors, as if the only moments worth rendering were youthfully romantic ones. In the later episodes, where Haley himself enters the drama, there is some attempt to set the epic in a wider historical context: for example, Haley's much-publicized interview of the American Nazi George Lincoln Rockwell (much-publicized because Marlon Brando plays Rockwell). But the interview doesn't really belong in the story of Haley's ancestral quest. It's mostly a diversion, thrown in for effect, and it comes across that way, although it also serves to affirm once again the gratuitous notion (perhaps added by the screenwriters for reasons best known to themselves) of the historical affinity or "racial bonding" between blacks and Jews.

And so, on the surface, the power of the *Roots* stories remains something of a mystery or a paradox. Their audience-drawing power is evident. If *Roots II* drew a somewhat smaller mass of viewers than *Roots I*, its appeal was still enormous, and audience size, in certain basic ways, speaks for itself. But the nature of this power is not so clear. For example, the dramas are alleged to be uplifting to blacks, and so they are, but they are also in many instances subtly and not so subtly condescending toward them. Or they are supposed to be instructive to whites, whereas in fact the instruction is often biased, implausible, and sometimes downright inaccurate. And what is especially surprising in a melodrama that has enjoyed such widespread popularity is that much of it is so unusually static, with the principal characters trapped less in tragic conflict than in the predictable patterns of stereotype, and with the possibilities for dramatic crisis being repeatedly dissolved in debating rhetoric or in the soft, bittersweet byplay of youthful romance. From *where*, one wonders in the end, does the mighty power of *Roots* proceed?

It comes, I suspect, from a simple and most familiar source: from fantasy—notably, those tribal or family fantasies, those dream memories of a golden past or golden youth, that most of us have summoned into consciousness at some time in our lives. These are the "remembrances" of happy summers in joyous places that no one else may quite remember, or remember in the same golden haze. These are the "recollections" of some moment in the otherwise dim past when the family —perhaps for a split second—seemed altogether *perfect*. In *Roots I*, the element of fantasy was only intermittently obtrusive, since the first television series was based extensively on specific events in Haley's book. Yet, even beneath Haley's stolid, journalist prose and his concretely rendered scenes of slave ships and slave whippings, etc., the softer, golden colors of his dreaming could be glimpsed. For instance, one of the most vivid sequences in the long drama were those scenes, right at the beginning, when we were shown Haley's real or imagined African ancestors: strong, handsome black warriors and fine-looking black women living harmoniously together in a sunny African Arcadia until the time inevitably came when their harmony was shattered and Arcadia destroyed by the arrival of the white man in his slave ships. Did such a graceful, happy Polynesian Arcadia actually exist in western Africa in the eighteenth century, with its poverty and its tribal wars and its predatory black slavers? Was there ever such a race of noble ancestors? There is little point in putting this sort of question to historical archives or record books—as if one might prove anything one way or the other by the answer—for, though the facts of the drama may here and there correspond with history, the "poetry" of the storytelling is in the extraordinary energy of dream. One should instead put the question to a child, or anyone who can still hazily remember that most cherished childhood vision of "the happy place," of the golden summer of long ago in which everyone's ancestors were, at least briefly, wise, noble, and benign.

If Haley's private fantasies were subterranean in *Roots I*, glowing at us from underneath the dark tales of slavery, in *Roots II* they seem to be much closer to the surface. There is one scene in particular, it seems to me, that expresses the underlying fantasy of the whole narrative. It is a pointed moment in the drama (one that was only suggested by the last section of Haley's book and so was deliberately written and rendered for the TV version), and we are clearly meant to regard it as such, for the short scene, which occurs in the final episode, was shown on all six of the preceding evenings as part of the montage at the start of each installment. What one saw in the scene was this: Haley has recently arrived in Gambia, on the coast of western Africa, in order to seek out traces of his ancestors. Earlier, he has met with some Gambians, who have directed him inland and up-river. Now Haley, holding notebook and pencil, has reached his apparent destination. The sun is shining. There are sand and palm trees. (A vision of Arcadia reappearing!) A crowd of friendly, smiling Africans approaches across the sand. Haley stands watching them, and then, with mounting excitement, begins to cry, "I've *found* you! I've *found* you! Kunta Kinte, *I've found you!*" On the television screen, it is a triumphant moment, and one that is given almost heroic dimensions by the stature and the voice of James Earl Jones. I suspect, though, that it would be an emotionally stirring scene had it been played by Haley himself or almost anyone else, for both the triumph and the emotions are mainly derived from fantasy.

Certainly it is not a fantasy unique to Haley; probably most people have indulged in it at one time or another, which, I suspect, accounts for its effect on audiences. Call it the fantasy or dream of Going Home. There are old, folkloric sayings that seem to speak to this dream, or, rather, to some hidden danger or difficulty within the dream. For instance: *"You can't go home again."* The traditional phrase implies a mysterious obstacle to Going Home, ambiguously suggests either prohibition or impossibility, though in fact the experience of increasing numbers of people—whether they are flying to Greece or Africa to discover roots or driving back to Worcester, Massachusetts, for Thanksgiving dinner—seems on the surface to demonstrate the triumphant ability of modern men and women, assisted by advanced methods of transportation and by the high motives of genealogical self-consciousness, to surmount such obstacles as lie in their way and to reach their destinations. Even so, one fancies that the spirit of the old wisdom still has the last laugh, for the mysterious difficulty in Going Home, it keeps turning out, is rarely caused by obstacles along the road but by what one experiences upon arrival. Once the returning voyager is "home again," amid his kinfolk, with the ancient doors creaking shut behind him, the danger, real or imagined, is usually to himself—to his sense of self. This is apparently one of the most secret—or, at least, most private—areas of human psychology, and surely a sort of reverse testament to the real hazards of the experience can be found in the myths and popular fables that have grown up through the centuries to reinforce the dream-like, or protective, version of what takes place. Consider the fantasies that surround most family holidays, especially when members of different generations have not seen each other often and have traveled from afar. Frequently, the "holiday" period is rent by an almost visible tide rip that exists between the fantasies of the returning voyagers and the actuality of what they find. How many people, surrounded by their real rather than their imagined relatives, have ever experienced a Norman Rockwell Thanksgiving? Or consider a prototypical modern version of the returning-voyager myth: the Irish-American senator, say, who "returns" to Ireland, and makes his way perhaps to County Cork, where his forebears came from, to a little town where a band is present to welcome him at the station, and where the mayor is on hand to greet him, so that he sets off, accompanied now by the band and the mayor and some television cameras, through the back streets of town, through the humbler quarters, until at last he comes to a dilapidated, weather-beaten little shack on whose crooked steps stands a very small and very wrinkled old man, with five days of stubble on his chin and bloodshot eyes. If a strange expression flits across the senator's countenance, it is not caught by the TV cameras. "Grandpa Groggins!" the senator cries, with apparent delight, bounding up the steps to embrace his ancient kinsman. After which he turns to the gathered crowd and declares: "It's good to be home!" *Home*? On that ghastly, mud-soaked, sour-smelling street, with that decrepit and whiskey-laden ancestor? The senator is no fool. He is not taking up residence there. In fact, he allows the mayor to push him inside the gloomy shack for no more than seven minutes, during which he sits on an old bedspring and sips from a glass that appears to contain seaweed and hot water, and then takes his leave. So where was the danger in the encounter? It was where it always is in such encounters: inside the mind, where our unspoken thoughts are spoken. For instance: "Can I really be descended from *you*?" And: "Am I, then, really like *you*?" And finally: "Grandpa Groggins, are you really *me*?" So great, apparently, is the element of fear in such transactions of recognition that folklore and popular literature have combined to place a wall around the unspoken part of the encounter, often shielding the truth from even the returning voyager's eyes and creating a protective response of sentiment and fantasy. The dark shadow or strange expression evoked by the actuality of Grandpa Groggins swiftly disappears, and once the voyager is safely back by his own hearth he develops a narrative more pleasing both to himself and to his listeners. "Children," the senator may declaim of a winter's evening, "long ago, in sunny County Cork, there was once a mighty race of warriors. Their name was Groggins." Indeed, Grandpa Groggins himself has disappeared, surrendering his perhaps charmless, though undeniably human, actuality in the service of his reincarnation as a character in the senator's dream of a nobler past; doubtless, as Grandpa Groggins's hoary ancestors had unwittingly done for others over the generations, and as the senator's grandchildren will find themselves doing decades hence.

Thus, in print and on television, and especially in *Roots II*, Haley's work seems to be only incidentally a drama of the progress and the tribulations of black people in America. This is the overlay of the story: the plot: the journalistic message that people tell themselves they are responding to. The deeper energy of the story, and its real strength in terms of audience appeal, proceeds from Haley's own fantasies about Going Home, and above all from his apparent willingness to leave the fantasies intact and unchallenged in much the same way that his audience does. One could almost say that the power of *Roots* lies in its weakness, albeit a most human weakness, for nearly all of us seem prey to fears that our ancestors were *not*—at least, at some point in the remote and golden past—mighty warriors, noble, sexual, and brave; and, worse, that if one of our kinfolk should now come before us, having traveled from a distant century or a far-off country, he would only let us down and make us look bad. "Kunta Kinte, at last I've found you, and I sure hope you make me *look good*!" Of course, if Haley had bitten the bullet and broken through the dream he was so movingly trapped in, he would have had to write a different, braver, and almost certainly a much less popular book. But then he might have given his people, and also other peoples, a truer Kunta Kinte, clothed, however dangerously, in his real humanity, and who knows but that in the long run this might have turned out to be the greater gift?

(1979)

THE STATE OF THE ART

THIS BEING a Presidential-election year, with the sounds of amateur punditry and armchair second-guessing already beginning to rise like the chattering of field mice above the land, it seemed as good a time as any to pay a call on David Haskell Sawyer, who is a member of that small and relatively new profession of political media consultants: those men and women (though in fact mostly men) who handle the media campaigns that appear to be a virtual requisite for election to local, state, or national office. Sawyer is forty-three years old, of middle height, with trim, Ivy League good looks, thinning hair, and a sincere and sometimes intense way of speaking. His office, in the West Fifties, is in the modern style, with one wall given over to elaborate sound and video equipment, and shelves on which are arrayed what seem to be at least several hundred cassettes of videotape. There is a desk, a couch, several chairs, and, in a corner of the room, a wooden stand that holds a large white display board on which is printed, in bold letters, "The Attitudinal Communications Process," and then, in smaller type, "Problem Identification," "Problem Definition," "Options Analysis," and "Goals Reanalysis."

"I think of our business here as political communication," Sawyer said. "I don't say that because it's a fancy phrase but because political advertising doesn't quite cover it. When we take on a candidate, we handle all media aspects of the campaign: print, radio, TV—the works. So far, we're going to be doing three senatorial campaigns this fall: Chris Dodd, in Connecticut; Tom

Eagleton, in Missouri; and Warren Magnuson, in Washington. We're not involved in any of the Presidential campaigns. A few months ago, we had some serious conversations with Teddy Kennedy and his people, but we backed off. It seemed to us that they wanted to approach the campaign in too fragmented a fashion. You know, with one guy handling print and another guy radio and another guy doing the TV coverage. That's the way they did things in the old days, back in '68, but it isn't really workable anymore."

I asked Sawyer in what other ways political media consulting had changed since the old days of 1968. I remembered, I said, going out to California that year in order to write a magazine piece about the kinds of political advertising employed by Eugene McCarthy and Robert Kennedy in the ill-fated Democratic primary there, and being greatly impressed by the sophisticated quality of the TV advertising produced by the Kennedy staff—especially an ad put together by John Frankenheimer and Bill Wilson that featured a speeding train and raggy banjo music and rails pointing into the distance.

"Frankly, 1968 was still the dark ages of political communication," said Sawyer. "It was a beginning, but techniques weren't very advanced. I mean, that railroad-track ad didn't really tell you much beyond the fact that Bobby was a candidate. The rest of it, if you recall, was stock footage taken from old campaign stops, except for the banjo music, which made you think of *Bonnie and Clyde* more than the primary. The real progress, I believe, has been in the area of polling. I'm very excited by polling. It's a terrific tool, because it lets you know what the voters are thinking. When it's done right, it can give you something very new in the electoral process: a two-way communication between the candidate and the voter. Of course, polling has been around for a while, but in recent years there has been a steady advance in terms of the skills involved, especially in the field of attitudinal polling; that is, not only in the matter of probing deeper but in anticipating shifts in political attitudes. Twenty years ago, Lou Harris put political polling on the map with his work for John Kennedy's Presidential campaign. Harris was the guy who figured out the extent of Kennedy's Catholic problem. Nowadays, he doesn't do polling for candidates; he mostly works on major corporate surveys. But his methods seem outdated compared with what's being done by the new group of younger, more innovative pollers—guys like Pat Caddell, Peter Hart, Bob Teeter, Bill Hamilton, Lance Tarrance. Their probing is so much more sophisticated. Now they'd tell you not only the rough extent of somebody's Catholic problem but precisely what kind of people make up this problem, and *why*—what trade-offs are involved. In other words, one voter might be adamantly against a Catholic candidate, while another might feel okay about him if there were a certain trade-off involved—if the candidate took care of him in some other area. The new polls are subtle enough to get into the whole trade-off question."

Was attitudinal polling, then, the key to a successful campaign?

"I can't imagine how you could win a modern election without the help of attitudinal polling," said Sawyer. "But the most crucial element in a campaign, it seems to me, is establishing a level of trust. That's why I always thought that Joe McGinniss's book *The Selling of the President, 1968* was so misleading. It was an entertaining and seductive story, but I think McGinniss was dead wrong in his central premise—that a bunch of clever Madison Avenue guys figured out how to hide the real Nixon and then packaged a campaign version of the candidate like a bar of soap and sold it to the public. Of course, that's what the Nixon people *tried* to do. Haldeman borrowed all those public-relations techniques for setting up artificial forums—you know, where the people were carefully preselected and the questions they were going to ask were decided in advance, and then Nixon would appear, answering questions in his best statesmanlike manner, as if he had dropped in on a little, informal New England town meeting. The Nixon people did their best to conceal their candidate. But look what happened."

"He won," I said.

"Yes, he won," said Sawyer. "But that's not the moral of the story. What happened is that Hubert Humphrey came staggering out of that terrible Democratic Convention in Chicago with a flawed nomination, with his own party divided and in shambles, with a nearly empty campaign treasury, and he did really the only thing that he could have done: he put himself on the line. Wherever there was an audience, wherever there was a microphone or a camera, he stood up and said 'Here I am; this is what I feel.' It was a classic Hubie performance—excess and rhetoric, but always feelings. And in six weeks Nixon lost fifteen and a half points! That's the real significance of the 1968 campaign. If it had lasted one more week, and if Hubie hadn't run out of media money at the end, I think Nixon would have lost the election. As it was, he won by only one half of one percent."

I asked Sawyer what he thought of Senator Edward Kennedy's media campaign so far.

"I think that Teddy's big problem, right through the Iowa caucuses, was that he just wouldn't deal with the questions that were in people's minds—questions about himself," Sawyer said. "To a great extent, I think, he was plain overbriefed. For instance, as in the disastrous Roger Mudd interview on CBS, though there were two or three other important interviews that were just as bad. You had the feeling that he'd spent six to eight hours before each interview closeted with his staff, rehearsing answers to every conceivable issue question, so that by the time he went before the cameras he was tighter than a clam. The main emotion he communicated from the screen was tightness—a feeling of somebody closed up and trying so hard not to make mistakes that people were bound to start wondering what it was he was trying not to make mistakes about. Which naturally led the audience to thoughts of Chappaquiddick—which was a negative communication, because the public's problem with Chappaquiddick wasn't so much the event itself as the atmosphere of cover-up that was allowed to surround the event. To be tight and guarded when talking about Chappaquiddick was a disaster. It perpetuated the idea of cover-up. I mean, people were thinking about it—people in Iowa, people everywhere—so when you saw this guy on television with his mouth all tight, and his face cold, and his eyes distant, and talking some nineteen-sixties language about the promise of the future, or whatever, well, you automatically wondered: What's he hiding? The same thing was true of Kennedy's responses to questions about his marriage. If only he had said, 'Look, it's been very difficult, we've had some very difficult times,' at least half the voting public would have identified with his problems. Difficult marriages are what an awful lot of people know something about. But instead he kept his mouth tight and his guard up. 'Joan and I are just fine,' he'd say. 'She's behind me on the campaign. We're working together.' People would just look at that face on the TV screen and think: Bullshit. What's he hiding?"

"What about the speech at Georgetown University?" I asked. "And those TV ads in New England where he says how sorry he is about Mary Jo Kopechne?"

"Those ads are good, because they show him beginning to be himself, beginning to talk about his feelings. They show him in a sincere mode. The Georgetown speech was the speech he ought to have made when he announced his candidacy. When Teddy announced, you had the feeling he hadn't conceptualized the campaign. He didn't seem to really know why he was running, except that he rather vaguely wanted the Presidency, or thought he ought to want it. In fact, most of what he had to say in the first phase of the campaign was little more than warmed-over rhetoric from the nineteen-sixties—you know, the future of America, concern for the elderly, the vigor of the next generation—with some hastily conceived attacks on the Shah of Iran and Carter's grain embargo thrown in for good measure. That kind of New Frontier stuff must have been very appealing to the veteran New Frontiersmen on his staff, but it doesn't really relate to what people are thinking today. And it certainly didn't relate to the main requirement of the campaign—of any modern campaign: that it be a process of enabling the public to get to know the candidate. At Georgetown, however, I think he finally put together a presentation that he can live with and build on. He finally found a message to communicate—though there's a problem in the speech, aside from its coming a little late, which is that it's essentially a strategy for winning the Democratic primaries. In other words, with Carter running strong as Commander in Chief on the international scene but vulnerable domestically, Kennedy sensibly decided to attack on the domestic front, by appealing to his own basic Democratic constituency, which is somewhat left-leaning, oriented to minorities, and so forth. The trouble here is that it puts Kennedy in severe jeopardy in terms of a general election. It gives the Republicans a very easy target to jump on, and it seems to me that not the least of Kennedy's problems has been his poor percentage comparisons with Reagan. Mind you, it's not that the country has really given up on liberalism but that liberalism—and the whole American dream, for that matter—needs to be redefined for the nineteen-eighties. And Teddy doesn't seem to have had the time, or maybe the inclination, to redefine it yet."

"When you were talking about new techniques in media campaigning, you mentioned advances in polling," I said. "What else is there?"

"We use focus groups a lot," said Sawyer. "This is a technique, borrowed from advertising, where you preselect fifteen or twenty people, on a psychodemographic basis, and get them all together in a room for a period of time and then ask them to speak their minds on a specific subject. We employ the technique differently from most advertising agencies, which are a lot more interested in persuading people to switch product loyalties, because in a political campaign it's practically impossible to persuade people who are dead set against a certain politician to vote for him. You can't advertise a politician as if he were Anacin. You know, the box and the name, the box and the name—all that repetition. People's feelings about politicians are too complex. But you can work *with* those feelings if you can find out what they are. For instance, when we started handling Kevin White's campaign for reelection as mayor of Boston in 1979, we found out from our focus groups that many people had some very definite and unfavorable responses to White's personality. White was perceived as arrogant, abrasive, and not really caring very much about people, while his opponent, Joe Timilty, was perceived much more favorably—as a nice guy, with a new face but a soft image. At the start of the campaign, White's recognition factor was very high— close to a hundred percent—but he had only forty percent of the vote, while Timilty's recognition factor was only sixty percent but he had a good thirty percent of the vote. Right away, we figured that there was no way we were going to be able to hide White. He was a tough, aggressive, arm-twisting kind of mayor, and you can't hide a guy like that. Also, it was clear that a lot of voters just didn't like him, and that if the election was going to be decided on the issue of whether Kevin White was a nice guy or not he was going to be beaten. So we decided that we wouldn't try to pretend that White was somebody he wasn't, because nobody would believe us, and that we would try to have the election decided on the issue of effectiveness, because this was where White was strong. The first phase of our campaign, then, was designed to raise the issue of our *opponent's* effectiveness."

Sawyer walked over and pulled out a cassette from the cassette library on his shelves and put it in the video-playback machine. What soon flickered onto the screen was an image of a pinball machine, very close up—a baseball pinball machine, so close up that the little figures of the baseball players seemed almost lifelike. A ball pops down the chute; the batter swings and misses. Another ball; another miss. One more swing and miss, and an off-screen voice says firmly, "In fact, of forty-one bills Joe Timilty proposed in 1978, thirty-nine times he struck out. That's a ninety-five-percent failure rate." Then the voice asks quietly, "Joe Timilty for *mayor*?"

Sawyer continued: "A lot of people were surprised that we started with a negative campaign, but the fact was that we had to work our way up to the effectiveness issue. At any rate, the negative ads did what they were supposed to. David Garth was handling the Timilty campaign—Dave is one of the best in the profession— and he had started out with a lot of positive stuff on Timilty. But when he saw that we were going negative on Timilty, he went negative on White, which is what we'd hoped he'd do, because his best bet all along was to concentrate on building up Timilty's effectiveness credibility and he couldn't do that while he was attacking White. Besides, White was hard to attack, since he wasn't hiding. So when Timilty's people went negative on White, right away we went into Phase 2. Our focus groups had told us that people tended not to like White personally, though they thought he had effectiveness credibility, so we took the tack that you don't have to like him in order to vote for him. In other words, don't vote another guy in just because you don't like this guy, with the implication of look what happened when you did that and got Jimmy Carter, because in the fall of '79 everybody was down on Jimmy Carter. What we did was to work out a series of ads that showed White as the kind of guy everybody knew he was but showing him as *mayor*."

Sawyer put in another cassette, and now on the TV

screen appeared Kevin White—white-haired, Irish, and vaguely ornery—chatting with a visitor in his office while a voice-over narrator says, "It's a tough job, but that's your job when you're the mayor"; then an ad showing White alone at his desk, while the narration describes him as "a loner in love with the city"; then an ad showing White looking out his window, while the voice-over says, "Kevin White—he seems to know which hands to hold, which arms to twist. He's a complicated man, well suited to this complex city."

Sawyer went on: "Toward the end of the campaign, while we were stressing the effectiveness issue, we went into a final focus group, and what we found there was that people kept saying, 'Look, we know about his accomplishments, we think his accomplishments are terrific. But we still don't like him, because we don't think he cares about the city.' Which meant, of course, 'We don't think he cares about *us*.' There was obviously some truth in that perception. White had been mayor for twelve years; sometimes now he acted a little bored, a little arrogant. Naturally, he wanted to win the election, but people needed to be reassured that he really wanted the job. They wanted to actually hear him say that he wanted to be *their* mayor. So we got him to say it. We made up this ad that showed White moving around the city talking to different people, and then we stopped him on one of the bridges."

Sawyer punched the forward button on the video-playback machine, and then it showed a picture of Kevin White leaning against the rail of a Boston bridge, with the city's rooftops behind him—the whole scene bathed in a kind of pinkish haze, perhaps from sunset, or smog, or both. "I like the job," says Kevin White, rapping the words out, but softly. Then he grins, "Tell you the truth, I *love* it."

Sawyer stopped the machine. "That's what I mean about connecting to what people already feel," he said. "In the end we won by ten percent of the vote."

I'd been wondering about the trend toward what advertising people call "emotionality" in commercials—all those happy, jokey, singsongy ads for beer, soft drinks, long-distance telephoning, and so forth. I asked Sawyer if it was possible to sell a politician on TV the way they sell a bottle of Coke.

"Isn't that new Coke commercial terrific?" said Sawyer. "The one with Mean Joe Greene and the little kid. That's Scott Miller's work. He's at McCann Erickson, but he's also done some things for us from time to time. Look, there's a difference between manipulation and emotionality. I think that maybe one could sell a very simple product—say, a kind of soap—by means of packaging and repetition. You know, massive time buys. But I really don't believe that the American voter can be manipulated. Take what happened in the senatorial campaign between Richard Roudebush and Vance Hartke in Indiana in 1970. Roudebush's people put out this phony ad trying to associate Hartke, who was anti-war, with a guy dressed up to represent a sinister Vietcong soldier, and the whole thing backfired. Nobody believed Roudebush afterward. His campaign went downhill, and Hartke won. Or take what happened when Richard Ottinger made all those really massive time buys in the 1970 New York senatorial race—and he lost to Jim Buckley. You have to remember that the American voter has become pretty sophisticated in media terms—in being able to evaluate media language. But emotionality is a whole different thing. Emotionality is when you speak directly to people's emotions—to emotions that are already there. That's the key: the emotions are already there. Now, here's an example of a controversial political ad that packed a whole lot of emotion." Sawyer got up and slipped in another cassette. "This is from Lyndon Johnson's campaign against Goldwater in 1964. It's not one of ours. Hell, I wasn't doing political work back then. It was done by Tony Schwartz, who's another top guy in the business."

On the screen appeared the figure of a little girl standing in a field. The little girl is plucking petals off a daisy, counting aloud in a lilting, childish voice: "One . . . two . . . three . . . four . . . five . . . six . . . seven . . . eight . . . nine . . ." The little girl remains frozen in the frame while a man's voice takes over, now counting backward in the unmistakable rhythm of a rocket launch: "Ten . . . nine . . . eight . . . seven . . . six . . . five . . . four . . . three . . . two . . . one . . . zero." There is a zoom in on the little girl, and the screen is suddenly filled with the soundless spectacle of an A-bomb explosion, and with the cloud billowing and billowing until a brief caption line appears: "Vote for President Johnson on November 3."

Sawyer stopped the machine. "That was considered very vicious back in '64," he said. "In fact, the Goldwater people complained so loudly that the ad was taken off the air. It was a rough ad, all right, but I don't think you can fault it for its emotionality. I mean, people really cared about war and peace in those days; they really worried about the bomb. Tony's ad spoke to those feelings. It's not unlike the Mean Joe Greene ad in that respect, because what is Coke selling, after all, except feelings? Think of all the Coke ads you see—those groups of people in funny kinds of situations, in smily kinds of situations. Viewers watch those ads and they get drawn into smiling, too. Mind you, the desire to smile is there .already. What the Coke ads do is that they put the viewer through the emotion, and then people identify the emotional connection with Coke. That's why they're such great ads. Of course, you can't do that sort of thing with most politicians, because politicians are complex—more complex than a bottle of Coke, anyway—and people's feelings about them are complex. When you're trying to communicate a politician, you need more than a smile or a simple emotion."

Sawyer had remarked that he wasn't working in politics back in 1964. I asked him when and how he had started.

"I guess you could say I angled into it," he said. "My first interest was the theater. I ran a drama group back at Princeton. I came to New York and studied acting and directing, but then I got turned on by film. I became an assistant editor and then an editor for Leacock and Pennebaker when they were with Drew Associates. In those days, you could just about walk in off the street and if you had any brains they made you an assistant editor. Fifteen years ago, I started my own company to make documentaries, which was fun but pretty slim pickings. Then, ten years ago, Bill Wilson, who'd been working on Bobby Kennedy's campaign in 1968, asked me to help out on Governor Frank Licht's campaign in Rhode Island. That's when I began doing politics. I've done all sorts of campaigns since then: Governor Jay Rockefeller's, in West Virginia; Governor Jim Hunt's, in North Carolina; Governor Julian Carroll's, in Kentucky; Charles Ravenel's gubernatorial campaign, in South Carolina; the presidential races in Costa Rica and Venezuela."

I said I wondered what, from a professional point of view, was the best political media campaign he had observed.

"I'd have to say Nixon's 1972 campaign. From a state-of-the-art point of view, that was perhaps the most sophisticated media campaign ever run. It wasn't just the money, though that certainly helped. It was the way they went from positive to negative—positive on the leadership issue, negative on McGovern's credibility. From the start, his people picked up on McGovern's problem of trust and credibility, and they built it right into the campaign as if it were an issue. Well, it *was* an issue! I remember they did this ad that showed a profile of McGovern's face, and then they shifted it back and forth, back and forth—like a weather vane. It was an effective method of demonstrating indecisiveness—going negative on the leadership issue—and we used the technique later on Joe Timilty in the Kevin White campaign. The Nixon 1972 campaign was probably the best I've seen, and the McGovern 1972 campaign was probably the worst. McGovern had two separate and very sizable problems that were allowed to come together, and they eventually destroyed him. First, he had a credibility problem. For example, there was the matter of the $1,000 tax rebate. He proposed it and then he took it back. Then, there was the trouble with his Vice-Presidential nominee, Eagleton. First he backed him and then he didn't. It wasn't that McGovern was dishonest but that he was perceived as lacking credibility. The second major problem he had was that he had won the Democratic primaries by appealing to a definitely left-leaning constituency. After he had won the nomination, he needed to reach a wider constituency if he was going to make any strides on a national level. But in making the transition—or in trying to make it—he came to be perceived as someone who didn't know what he stood for. The credibility issue undermined his efforts to achieve a wider constituency. I remember people used to say that McGovern was so heavily criticized because he tried to force an unwilling public to think about Vietnam. But I don't believe that his raising of the Vietnam issue was what made people so angry at him. Vietnam by then was a legitimate concern to a large number of voters. There was a lot of emotion tied up in the Vietnam issue. Charlie Guggenheim was running McGovern's media campaign, and the irony of the situation was that by the time Charlie got McGovern on the air talking about Vietnam and war-related issues, trying to broaden the base of his constituency, hardly anyone believed what he was saying about *anything*. He'd blown his credibility. Actually, Jimmy Carter had the same kind of constituency problem in 1976. He tried going national with the same kind of campaign that he'd used in the primaries—all those peanut-farmer spots—and in six weeks of national campaigning he lost thirty-two points. Gerald Ford had a very strong, very effective campaign, designed by Bailey Deardourff ('President Ford—He's Making Us Proud Again'), which went negative against Carter on the trust issue, and he nearly pulled it off. Carter won by only two percent."

I asked Sawyer whose campaign Charlie Guggenheim was handling now.

"Teddy Kennedy's," said Sawyer. "Look, Charlie is

a pro. He's a bit old-fashioned. I think he spent too much time in Iowa on those old-time question-and-answer sessions. But Teddy's moving in the right direction now. He's talking feelings. He's communicating more emotionality. A lot can happen between now and Illinois. In the end, though, there are issues and issues —really pressing issues, like inflation and national defense—but what really counts in a campaign today is trust. Or maybe I should say: a perception of trust."

(1980)

HARD NEWS, SOFT NEWS

A BIG STORY broke a few weeks ago that seemed made to order for television news. At 2:30 a.m., long after most of the nation's morning papers had gone to press, Israel's Foreign Minister, Moshe Dayan, and President Carter's press secretary, Jody Powell, at the end of hours of talks between the President and Dayan, held a press conference at the United Nations Plaza Hotel in New York and announced to the world, or to anyone who was listening, that the United States and Israel had just reached a sudden, and perhaps surprising, agreement to reconvene the Middle East peace talks in Geneva later in the year. Some hours after the event, newspapers were being delivered that carried no information about what had happened; the *Times* and the Washington *Post*, for example, had to wait one full day before they could get the story of the U.S.–Israel accord before their readers, such being the exigencies of press runs and of publication schedules. But television—purveyor of electronic journalism and the fabled techniques of fast-flow information—had clear sailing; in fact, the network news departments had a scoop on their desks about an important story that no one in print could touch until, at best, the nation's surviving afternoon papers reached the newsstands halfway through the day.

And what did they do with it? They did just about nothing. This isn't to say that the U.S.–Israel agreement went entirely unreported on the *Today* show or *Good Morning America* or the *CBS Morning News*; in a way, nothing of a factual nature and of a certain level of bureaucratic significance ever goes entirely unreported on television. But so little was made of the story on morning television that as news it scarcely existed, and as a scoop—exciting news—it existed not at all. The *Today* show ran the bare bones of the announcement, amid early-morning chitchat by the program's announcers, and then produced NBC's "State Department correspondent," Richard Valeriani, for the equivalent of a slight, hundred-word commentary that was done mostly in the new give-and-take sports-announcer style, in company with Floyd Kalber, the *Today* show's chief news reader. Thus, Kalber asked Valeriani what the "chances of success" were for a Middle East peace conference, and Valeriani replied, "I think the chances now are about sixty–forty," shortly after which Kalber thanked Valeriani "for getting up so early and coming in and talking to us—we appreciate it." While the skeletons of deceased city editors twitched frantically in their graves, doubtless remembering the number of times they had forgotten to thank reporters for getting up early and coming in to talk to them, matters were not proceeding much more satisfactorily on ABC's *Good Morning America*, where the same brief news clips of the announcement were shown, followed by the most perfunctory of commentaries, this time by ABC's "diplomatic correspondent," Barrie Dunsmore, who said that "a major rift between the U.S. and Israel had been healed."

In any case, the point to be made is not about the language level, high or low, of ABC's and NBC's handling of the peace-talk story but that, first, at no time did these electronic purveyors of fast-flow journalism indicate that a story of major proportions had fallen into their hands, and, second, no television news editor's voice appeared to have been raised, or raised loud enough, to rescue the story from the preponderant entertainment flow around it and give it significant news space of its own. As is their custom, ABC and NBC repeated the original announcement a couple of times in the course of each two-hour program, along with other noteworthy news items of the morning. But, practically speaking, on both these widely popular, once news-conscious and now "informational" shows, the bizarre and dramatic early-morning U.S.–Israel rapprochement simply disappeared into the treacle jar of already scheduled programming. Thus, *Today* devoted its news-feature space to an account, already scheduled, of the natural-gas legislation, and also provided stories about a whistling contest, paperback-book advertising, and truck-driving accidents. ABC's *Good Morning America* stayed with its interview of Billy Graham; also with Howard Cosell, a report on "New York's troubled diamond business," Rona Barrett discussing contraceptive advertising, and a sweet film about lions in Africa. On the whole, the *CBS Morning News* appeared to do best with the U.S.–Israel story (though actually it did little better than its competitors, also failing to really press the story, and providing similarly warmed-over commentary by Ed Bradley), for the simple, if negative, reason that the *CBS Morning News* is still a news program, not yet having surrendered to the growing vogue for "soft" news or for informational entertainment. Thus, its not very enterprising account was at least able to make a modest place for itself as news, and not be instantly swallowed up or merged with Howard Cosell or whistlers or those sweet lions.

It's not yet a question that hangs on everyone's lips, but still it is a question that has more currency than some might imagine: What is one to make of the news these days, especially of the news on television? To begin with, what a strangely modern question this is, for what is now usually meant is not *the news*—the problems that news reports refer to, such as might have led a concerned citizen of a generation or more ago to say he or she was "worried about the news." What is meant increasingly is the form and shape of these reports: "the news." The concerned citizen of today, in fact, has the novel opportunity of worrying, first and fleetingly, about the constant flow of crisis, catastrophe, and assorted information that pours from the news media, and then, somewhat more contemplatively, about the way this news is being presented. Is the news slanted or unslanted? Is it too elitist or too populist? Do anchormen carry too much authority? Do correspondents in the field stage-manage the stories they report? Not just the news executive but the casual newspaper or magazine reader is by now fairly conversant with the debate about "soft" and "hard" news. Books are written about the processes of the "news industry." Magazine articles appear about "news personalities" and "news trends," new developments in "news formats" and "news styling." Sometimes even television talk shows warily discuss the "role of media": for example, the "role of media" in national, state, or local elections: were "issues" given prominence, or merely "images"?

Of course, a great many of the nation's less concerned citizens appear to be resolutely uninterested in this fascinating new topic. Thus, television news managers have been able to point to the contentedly viewing, or dozing, mass public as signaling approval of the news fare that is being given it, and so continue about their business, which often seems to be little more than engaging in old-fashioned circulation wars with one another and then taking out ads in *The New York Times* to announce how many "households" have been captured. That this contentedly viewing mass public is more or less the same public that, throughout history, vaguely "keeps up" with the news and for its modest pains is then surprised out of its wits every few years by one or another of life's logically predictable disasters should probably give somebody pause by now, but it doesn't seem to. There may even be some kind of case to be made that being surprised out of one's wits is the mysterious ingredient that makes life in a democracy tolerable, though I'm not sure that the families of men and women killed in wars or calamities that "just suddenly happened" would all agree. Some might agree, to be sure: if God (or Walter Cronkite) had known that *that* was going to happen, He (or he) would have warned us! But a sizable number, I imagine, would not insist that the element of surprise in democratic life was all that endearing, or all that necessary. Even simple people, after all, have a powerful instinct not only for self-preservation but for the preservation of the family and tribe. Consider, for example, the familiar story of the farmer who laughs at his unfarmerlike, collegiate son for his newfangled ways, though he in fact was the one who scraped enough money together to send the fellow to college in the first place. The son, one might say, is the father's emissary to the future: the old man's outrider, dispatched not merely into space but into time in order to represent—however reluctantly or clumsily —the father at some higher level in the future.

The mass public in its response to news, it seems to me, is not altogether unlike the farmer. On the one hand, the mass public appears not to care, not to give a damn about anything, as the sayings go, that lies beyond the purview of its wallet or garden. Often it scoffs at newfangled methods or appears actually to obstruct progress. But on the other hand it cares enough to send its own outriders into the future: that oddly chosen minority of the supposedly educated, who are required, by a kind of social logic no less than by genetics or ambition, to ride out ahead of the great trudging columns of population and reconnoiter what lies on the horizon. Granted that it is part of this strange social compact that, more often than not, the outriders' scouting reports are for a maddeningly long while ignored and even ridiculed. The public never thanks its outriders, at least not at the time, for depressing or "boring" it to death about, say, the danger of the rise of Adolf Hitler in the nineteen-thirties or the hazards of our involvement in Vietnam in the nineteen-sixties. But in the end, and just in the nick of time, so it would seem (though perhaps the trudging columns see time differently), the new messages are accepted: the trudging columns imperceptibly change course, doubtless now heading for yet another distant pitfall; and that in itself is usually thanks enough.

So, once again, it would seem, the outriders of our society are sending back a new set of messages. Some are about energy; and the equations of population and hunger. And some, too, are about "the news." All these messages—however skillfully or lovingly packaged by the intellectuals riding out ahead—appear to bounce off a solid wall of initial public uninterest. But clearly something is up. Even in the seemingly esoteric area of news communications, clearly the complaints and murmurs about the processes of news are keyed to something important that will have to be reckoned with later. The outriders have found the shape of the problem: call it the form of the news. But what is the problem itself? On the surface, it appears to be defined by the debate about "soft" news and "hard" news. Thus, where not so long ago television broadcasters were criticized for trivializing news, for confusing news with entertainment, lately both newspapers and magazines as well as radio and TV stations have been outscrambling one another to make news more "fun." Even the once stately (and soporific) *Times* now seems to publish more column inches of recipes, wine tips, and interior decoration than of old-fashioned news reports. Similarly, the news magazines, *Time* and *Newsweek*, have each revamped their format to make themselves prettier and more "accessible," which means fewer words, more white space, and many more pictures, especially of entertainment figures. In fact, throughout every news organization it's as if a palace revolution has taken place, with the old king of the conventional hard-news story having been toppled from his granite throne, and with the chamberlains now running about the kingdom proclaiming first one leader and then another, apparently not yet quite willing to actually crown the charming Prince of Entertainment, but without the conviction to really crown anybody else instead, and with the general populace generally delighted at not being governed at all. "Everything is news!" a network news executive breezily announced not long ago, explaining why his evening news show had devoted an appreciable amount of its air time to an interview with the coach of a high-school basketball team—and who is to deny it? On a rival channel a few evenings later, there was a lengthy "report" about some swans in Maryland that were eating too much underwater grass.

These were network programs, too, and not local news, which for some time has been the chief repository of the soft, or the softheaded, or (to put the best face on it) the human-interest story on television. Indeed, one of the things that seems to be happening is that the big boys at the networks have taken to copying the small-fry at the local stations. Not that network news doesn't still play it pretty straight: straight and true: straight and solemn: the basketball coach as well as the swans were both chatted about in the same "Is it your opinion, Dr. Kissinger . . . ?" sonorities. But the hardness of the network news programs is being rapidly eroded. A striking, though perhaps aberrant, example of this trend was the bringing of the redoubtable Barbara Walters to ABC News, where she was first uneasily paired with Harry Reasoner (since departed to CBS's *60 Minutes*) and then unleashed on her own. More typical has been the institutionalization of the feature story on all three networks, the results of which range from the superficially informative (like Ted Koppel's educational-primer disquisitions on SALT II for ABC) to what is sometimes not much more than the proverbial Sunday-supplement once-over (like some of NBC's *Segment 3* features about the 1979 gasoline shortage). As for the rest of the twenty-four-minute packages of network evening news, these still come across pretty much as they have in the past. In times of crisis, one continues to marvel at the extent and directness of the coverage. But on the majority of evenings when no certified crisis is known to exist, it seems to me that the once stiff and straight-backed news increasingly slides off into waffle. Thus, in a recent week, the networks devoted sizable chunks of their precious news time to such subjects as an international conference for "iceberg utilization"; the society aspects of a New York art show; a droll analysis of expense-account lunches; an inventor who had waited twenty-five years for a patent; the dangers of liquefied-natural-gas fires, which mainly showed impressive glimpses of previous fires; the space shuttle, which mainly showed impressive glimpses of the space shuttle; and a story, of indeterminate point, about a sculptor in Arkansas whose house was overrun by squirrels.

The reasons for the shift to soft news by the networks are fairly well known. First, the popularity, at least among certain station managers, of news consultants such as Phil McHugh and Frank Magid, who have raised the ratings of a number of news programs by "personalizing" the newsroom and by emphasizing entertainment features. Second, the success of CBS's *60 Minutes*, with its appealing combination of dramatic interviews and magazine-type features. On the whole, ABC, which was the tardiest of the three networks to build up a competent news organization, seems to be the most eager to follow the new trends. Sometimes this newly acquired energy, unfettered by past conventions, has resulted in inventive news programming, especially in the *Close-up* documentary series, which often reveals a more confident feel for film than do the traditional documentaries of the two other networks. But, more than its rivals, ABC seems to indulge in the recent vogue for blurring news and entertainment values. Thus, the notorious Ms. Walters is determinedly presented by the network more as a "news personality" than a news-person, and she herself often doesn't seem to understand the difference in *tone* between an interview with a foreign minister and one with a hairdresser. Similarly, the heavy-tongued Howard Cosell spins dizzily from network sports programs to network news programs. The morning talk and information program *Good Morning America* is anchored by a personable and intelligent man, David Hartman, but by training he is an actor, not a newsman, and despite his charm, an unsettling amateur note often creeps in when he is asked to deal with a hard-news story.

NBC, on the other hand, is rather like the old lady in tennis sneakers, tripping over her feet trying to learn the new dance steps. In the past, though NBC News never quite matched the élan of CBS News, it frequently employed fine correspondents and produced solid news programs, at one point backing up the anchor team of Huntley and Brinkley with Frank McGee, Edwin Newman, Sander Vanocur, and John Chancellor, which was as good a quartet of working TV correspondents as then existed. But that was a while ago, and now Huntley and McGee are dead, Brinkley is semiretired, Vanocur is at ABC, Newman is a media star in his own right, and though John Chancellor still works up front, night after night projecting his calm, bespectacled reasonableness, one has the feeling that he has never been quite at ease since he started using his face muscles more than his leg muscles. The *NBC Nightly News* isn't a bad program, as network news programs go; it covers pretty much the same ground that the others do, and its share of competent correspondents is still fairly high. But it seems to know less about what it's doing, or what it should be doing, than its rivals. And perhaps because of internal morale problems, the documentary unit seems, for the time being, remarkably uninspired and lacking in drive. Most of its recent documentaries, in fact, have been of the pseudo-documentary variety: essentially, editing jobs (and usually hasty ones at that) of standard network news clips of a given subject—say, the Pope's visit, or the latest crisis in the Middle East—which are then spliced together and sent out into the world with the help of a dignified narration by an NBC correspondent and a full-page ad in the major market newspapers.

CBS News probably remains the best of the network news organizations, but one can sense that its news standards, which were still being ironed out at the end of the Vietnam War and the beginning of Watergate, are coming under fire from a new direction—from inside the company. Spokesmen for CBS are forever remarking nowadays that the *CBS Evening News* is one thing and *CBS Reports* is another thing and *60 Minutes* is yet another thing, and never the three shall meet—or, at least, inflict themselves on one another. But even the casual viewer can detect that *CBS Reports* has pulled in its horns considerably—in fact, is sometimes scarcely visible—while the popular *60 Minutes* goes sailing ahead; and that the effect of *60 Minutes* on news programming in general, even on the saintly *CBS Evening News*, is substantial in all sorts of ways, producing an emphasis on personality and features as well as an "investigative" (i.e., prosecutorial) manner of interviewing where often none is called for.

Obviously, there should be room for all sorts of programs: for *60 Minutes* as well as *CBS Reports*; for hard-news stories and documentaries as well as soft-news features and interviews. But that is not the way television seems to work. There are trends; the trends point toward dollars; and the executive rabbits follow the trends. Traditionalist newsmen as well as traditionalist viewers profess concern at the new wave sweeping over what is, thus far, still the beginnings of broadcast journalism, but at the same time they are painfully aware that youth must be served and that while it is bad enough to be old, it is usually worse to be old and to be caught clinging to old concepts. Maybe "everything" is news, after all? Does it matter, in the end, what type or weight or flavor of news one reports on: the king himself, or the state of the kingdom, or how the king's jester spent Saturday night? The outriders naturally write ponderous and gloomy reports about the state of the news, heavy with statistics indicating the amount of air-time minutes devoted to this and not devoted to that. Just as naturally, the mass public throws away the reports before reading them, sometimes wrapping their fish in the statistic printouts to show their interest. The broadcasting proprietors and managers then point to the apparent contentment of the public and continue doing what they wish.

But what have the outriders really seen that causes them to fuss and worry about the relative softness or hardness of the news? Surely it can be nothing so simple, or reactionary, as the dangers of progress. For, beneath all the flurry about what "the news" is doing or not doing, a shift in the logic of television journalism has definitely been taking place. As a result, what might be termed television's special strengths, which all along have tended toward portraiture, anecdote, and intimacy (and which, for years, were resisted by network news organizations when they were largely staffed by print-oriented journalists), are now finally being employed and exploited by network managements in order to ensnare a wider and more profitable audience. Aside from the logic of commerce, there is thus a logic of form and technique that supports this shift. Why shouldn't television do what it does best, and let print journalism do what *it* does best?

Is that all there is to our concern about the changing nature of the news—another overcautious response to the march of progress? In some ways, probably yes. The old ways are hard to give up, and the new ways hard to stomach. Consider, too, the unmixed blessing of some of the old ways: hard news, for example. Surely, hard news hasn't always been such a delight, such a national treasure. In the era of the cold war, hard news gave us mostly surfaces, deceptive surfaces, too, and all-too-simple polarizations. In the era of Vietnam, hard news gave us the Strategic Hamlet program, and the Pacification program, and the Vietnamization program, and the troop buildup, and the body counts. Hard news has often been boring: that is, alienating, authoritarian, bureaucratic, difficult to connect with, or to accept emotionally. Hard news didn't help us much—either in the mass or as minorities—to stumble through the past decades, and so now we are trying soft news. There is much to recommend the change, at least on the surface. The softer style seems so much more natural to television, and even to other media. How accessible those glimpses of personality seem to be! The faces of the newsworthy! Those personal, offhand moments caught—but caught so gently —by the camera! The parade of individuals and of individuality through the news seems such a diversion from all those officials, and official meetings, and official statements, that the old news gave us.

But there is a further thought, a further possibility. I wonder if the gradual institutionalization of soft news into a form that is becoming as rigid in its way, and as omniscient, as was once true of hard news doesn't lead to a perspective that is regressive, even "pastoral," and thus intrinsically confusing to the public. In other words, to say that the new, casual type of news is unauthoritarian begs the question. It is only that the locus of the authority has changed: from the dream of bureaucratic power to the dream of individual power. Thus, old-fashioned hard news tried to tell us (through its world view) that the official acts of statesmen, bureaucrats, governments, and world bodies were the only permissibly effective acts in the world, which, of course, was false: impossible to relate to, when our eyes and ears increasingly told us how the actions of individuals, of unofficial groups, of informal bodies were altering the march of great events. But now soft news threatens to turn us backward, into some garden, some Arcadian fantasy where individuals now count for *everything*—individuals smiling, talking, expressing their opinions, which is perhaps, for the modern world, just as false a perception. In short, it may well be that we can't, or won't, resolve the great dilemmas before us (of which geopolitics and energy are only two of the most visible), either as faceless proles or through the impersonal grunts and heavings of giant bureaucracies. But are we likely to resolve them any better, or any sooner, or at all, through the dream or world view of the single, candid, personally expressive individual face? I suspect that it is *this* image that the outriders have found, not knowing what they have found, and so, for the present, they mutter nervously about "the news" as they watch the close-ups proliferating on the screen, as they observe the soft gauze of personability descending on great events, as they become aware, perhaps, even of a soft-news President who leads us. It wouldn't be the first occasion, after all, when it wasn't so much the times that were out of joint as the way we looked at them.

(1977)

THE GOVERNOR'S BRIEF
BRUSH WITH LOGIC

In 1945, in a lecture at Princeton University, the German philosopher Ernst Cassirer remarked on the reemergence of myth as a primary force in politics after its long banishment by the rationalists of the eighteenth century. Not only had myth reappeared, Cassirer noted, but in the twentieth century a wholly new type of myth was in evidence. For, instead of slowly evolving out of centuries of experience, myths were now actually being designed according to specifications and manufactured on request. "From now on, myth was no longer allowed to grow up freely and indifferently," said Cassirer. "The new political myths were artificial things made by very skillful and cunning artisans. To put it bluntly we may say that what we see here before our very eyes is a new type of a completely rationalized myth." At the time, Cassirer was referring to the startling and powerful appearance of myth in Hitler's Germany, and to the then novel mythmaking techniques of such early media technicians as the radio propagandist Joseph Goebbels and the filmmaker Leni Riefenstahl. Clearly, a different situation obtains today. Our leaders are centrist and affable instead of wicked and totalitarian. Our myths of leadership are fairly modest and unassuming (not Lincolnesque, or even Kennedyesque) instead of grandiose and Wagnerian. Our mythmakers are no longer remote and sinister Svengali figures, operating out of the shady recesses of smoke-filled rooms, but hardworking professionals, trained in political science, laden with polls and samplings, all too happy to sit down and visit for a moment on the evening news and chat about their work. In fact, the only thing that seems to have stayed the same is that Cassirer's "rationalized myth" has gradually become so much a part of our overall political experience that we now take its presence pretty much for granted, and not merely in the obvious areas of political propaganda or paid advertising but in the news.

It's a truism, of course, that in the past two decades television has communicated political news increasingly on a mythic bias, with the networks making occasional and dutiful attempts at interviewing candidates according to old-fashioned rationality (for instance, sitting them down and asking them logical questions about issues and positions), but for the most part being all too content to present them as part of an ongoing dramatic pageant. Thus, this year in the primaries, Senator Kennedy was regularly shown embattled and pugnacious on the streets of Eastern and Midwestern cities; George Bush (whose political fortunes were perceived by the mythmakers as perpetually declining) was usually glimpsed as a solitary jogger, trotting along in the early-morning hours in his jogging suit, or else seated by himself on an airplane, silently studying reports, returning from the Southern primaries; meanwhile, recent television news of independent candidate John Anderson has not had much to tell us about his controversial positions on nuclear power but instead has persistently shown how he shakes hands in Illinois: generally in a raincoat, one gathers, and in a friendly, modest, but somewhat startled manner, as doubtless befits a mythic underdog.

Indeed, the once excessively rational news seems now to be so wrapped up in the fashioning of mythic vignettes that it no longer has time for facts or issues. But a new displacement is taking place: paid political advertisements are being used more and more to discuss the rational aspects of political elections that the news ignores. The theory behind this trend, one imagines, is that, with so much myth being communicated by the news, there is a danger that candidates for election will soon lose all identifying marks, all political texture, all intrinsic differences (save, of course, for the purely mythic ones), unless they step in briskly, put down their money, and etch in their political identification marks themselves. The only trouble with this fine new attempt to rerationalize American political perceptions in the mythmaking era is that political candidates may not be the ideal sources for the kind of impartial, logical information about themselves that the citizen-voter is supposed to be in need of, any more than oil-company advertising may not be altogether the best source of information for an understanding of the energy situation. Even so, there was Senator Kennedy on the TV screen in Pennsylvania a few days ago, pumping away about monetary economics and the inflation rate in a series of commercials, while the nightly news blathered on about his "troubled personal history" and his "faltering campaign," showing him once again bustling down some busy urban thoroughfare. There, too, in the same week was John Anderson, looking all spruced-up and presidential in a new thirty-second spot. No more raincoat, no more lonely-man-at-the-airport vignettes. Instead, it was candidate Anderson, standing tall in a grownup suit in front of one of those baby-blue TV studio curtains, giving us some straight talk about oil-import taxes, natural-gas decontrol, and the balance of payments. And perhaps strangest of all, there was Ronald Reagan, the former Governor of California, campaigning by commercial in Connecticut. Since the beginning of the primaries, television news reports on Reagan have steadfastly avoided virtually any serious examination of his governance of California (which is, after all, a state the size of a major European nation), concentrating instead on the intriguing issue of how well he was running compared to the other Republican candidates: "just ahead," or "well ahead," or "with the nomination all sewn up." In Connecticut, Reagan had paid for time in which to present his views on our mishandling of the Iranian crisis and on the hazards of being too soft toward the Soviets.

But not all television news is myth-oriented. Little ghettos of old-fashioned rational journalism still exist, such as on the Sunday-afternoon interview programs, where last week, on ABC News's *Issues and Answers*, a fairly fascinating exchange took place between ABC correspondent John Laurence and the amiably mythic Governor Reagan himself. Laurence had been questioning Reagan about his anti-inflation program, which apparently included a thirty-percent tax cut, and then began preparing the ground for another question by referring to a recent Reagan commercial. "You've been saying in your television ads that you didn't always agree with President Kennedy," said Laurence, consulting a transcript of the commercial, "but that he found that a thirty-percent tax cut helped almost everybody in the country, and if you were elected President you would cut taxes the same way he did."

Reagan shook his head affably but firmly. "No, I don't know what the rate of his tax cut was. I said that he went for a broad-based cut in the income tax. I don't know what the percentage of that cut was but that it was contrary to all the economic advice being given and that it did result in an increase in revenues."

Somewhat surprised, Laurence persisted. "If I can quote from your own ad, you're saying on camera"— now Laurence read from the transcript—" 'I didn't always agree with President Kennedy, but when his thirty-percent federal tax cut became law, the economy did so well that every group in the country came out ahead. If I become President, we're going to try that again.' " He asked Reagan, "Do you remember saying those words?"

Reagan once again agreeably shook his head. "I don't remember saying that, because I honestly don't know what the rate of the tax cut was."

"Well, perhaps someone else wrote them for you?" said Laurence.

"I'm sure they did," said Reagan. "But I don't even remember reading that."

Now another ABC correspondent, Bob Clark, got into the act. "Coincidentally, I saw them in print this week, with your media adviser—the fellow who puts together your media commercials—giving out the text, I believe."

"Well," said Laurence, "that raises the whole question of how familiar you are with the television ads that you do and—"

But Reagan was having no part of that knotty question, either. "Sure, I do them," he said. "I read them. And I suppose in the process of a whole afternoon, as you know, sitting in front of the camera and doing these things, and each one several times over, that I maybe just went by that one without thinking the thirty-percent figure was familiar to me." The governor smiled affably at his inquisitors.

The ABC correspondents, nonplused, drifted on to other subjects, and the little exchange disappeared into the void of transcript files and videotape libraries. For a brief moment, though, the curtain had been tugged back on our political mythmaking process to reveal (not unsurprisingly!) the busy figure of the Wizard of Oz declaiming into his microphone and blowing smoke out of his smoke machine. Then just as quickly the curtain had been drawn closed again, leaving the Wizard, so it would seem, happily fiddling with his magical devices, and the merry old land of Oz (apparently ever more comfortable with wizards than with logicians) once more to look out for itself.

(1980)

ADRIFT IN DOCU-DRAMA

TRY as I might to be open-minded toward the lavishly elaborate Nixon–Watergate mini-series, *Washington: Behind Closed Doors*, I'm not sure that I was really ready, just yet, to see the Nixon gang depicted on the screen with the sweep and pageantry of a chronicle play. The petty deeds that were hatched some years ago still seem to be petty deeds today, despite the crisp, ironic dialogue that the screenwriters have spread around between passages from the public record. The tin-plated emotions of the Nixon team still sound as tinny as before, when we were picking them up from live interviews in the press, though Jason Robards, a veteran player of Eugene O'Neill's tormented misfits, did a fine job filling out the soul and body of our recently retired President. Robards never stooped to mere impersonation, it should be noted, but deftly caught the character's neurotic moodiness as well as his playful, discordant, almost touching lack of humor.

All told, this journalistic melodrama was a capable, professional piece of work. Our motion-picture and television crafts have rarely been as well stocked with skilled actors and competent screenwriters as they are today, and both vocations were nicely represented on the week-long program. No longer are there only a handful of actors trained well enough to play a variety of roles at a distinguished level of performance; lately there seem to be hundreds of such men and women, even boys and girls. Good screenwriters, too, have multiplied, which means that stories of increasing complexity and literateness are being produced. In other words, the technics were never better. The surfaces are in good shape. The question worth raising at this stage is what's underneath.

Underneath, it seems to me, exists a powerful though still unresolved preoccupation with the *real*: real life, biography, actuality, documentary, what really happened. This is hardly a new preoccupation of humankind, but what is relatively new is its steady intrusion into the areas of entertainment narrative that for several hundred years were largely ruled by fiction. First, by the almighty novel; then by the even more almighty movie, whose energy and style were fictional no matter that the film's subject might have its origins in a biography or a newspaper column. Imperceptibly, at first, this began to change. Movies, while still doing pretty much as they pleased, made more of a show of being historically accurate. Details were paid attention to; costumes were got right. The real push toward nonfiction, however, came from television, with its gradual institutionalizing of the docu-drama.

This hybrid form is too various to be described by exact definition, but generally speaking a docu-drama is a story whose energy and focus has shifted from fiction to what is supposed to have actually happened. Although the word itself is split down the middle and neatly hyphenated, the weight of a docu-drama is not spread evenly between the two forms. The message of these stories is that they speak the truth.

In the past few years, docu-dramas have proliferated on television. The life stories of athletes, statesmen, musicians, and a whole list of public figures, dead or extant, have provided material for these new *vérité* entertainments, and not surprisingly their success in some quarters has raised in other quarters a discussion bordering on argument as to the proper relationship of fact to fiction, as to the permissible employment of fiction with fact. It is not an unreasonable subject to be arguing about, although some of the dialectics doubtless become a bit tedious through repetition in the Sunday-newspaper entertainment sections, and are even irritating to those who believe that such concerns have no place in the supposedly simple transactions of mass entertainment. Even so, there seems little to be gained (certainly by a critic) in being fastidiously tight-lipped on the issue, or in going along too agreeably with the currently prevailing view: namely, that anything short of actionable libel becomes legitimized by its power to give the audience a "feel" for a true story.

Let us reopen the discussion (admittedly on a rather one-sided basis), employing *Washington: Behind Closed Doors* as our somewhat distant text, by considering that one of the distracting side effects of the fact-vs.-fiction colloquy has been its tendency to polarize the public into a contest of sorts between competing life views. Thus, fussy, conservative, and presumably old people are supposed to care excessively about whether Napoleon rode a bay horse or a black horse or a motorcycle at Borodino, whereas loose, free-spirited, and presumably young people are supposed to care only whether the character feels right, whether the story seems believable. Docu-dramas have also provoked a variety of equally polarized political responses concerning the rights of audiences. On the one hand, there are those, some of them unlikely figures to be donning the threadbare garments of fighters for academic freedom, who see in demands for greater accuracy a threat to the American public's inalienable right to see whatever it pleases. On the other hand, there are those who detect an essential vulnerability in this great audience and believe that ways should be found to protect it, at least from false facts and images.

Among exponents of the looser, freer, more youthful point of view, the names of such redoubtable authorities as Tolstoy and Shakespeare are periodically invoked in defense of screen and television writers who, while using actual events or persons in their creations, sometimes feel at liberty to bend or invent details to suit a larger artistic perspective. Shakespeare and Tolstoy are undoubtedly a splendid duo to have on one's side, though it seems to me that there is reason to wonder if the two worthies would line up that way so readily on their own. Surely, the function of Tolstoy's Napoleon was to portray character and not to provide historical or journalistic information. Surely, no one reads or listens to Shakespeare's histories in order to obtain an accurate political understanding of Tudor or Plantagenet England. Indeed, since Shakespeare didn't take much time to check the second- and third-hand sources he was borrowing from, it would be an unwary scholar at best who hoped to pick up some incidental current-events information by sitting through *Coriolanus* or *Henry V*. In most docu-dramas, however, the point of the story is that the audience believes that it is seeing the real thing. In *Washington: Behind Closed Doors*, for example, the public was invited not only to empathize with the characters and find them believable (as might also be said of the BBC's *Upstairs, Downstairs*) but to specifically identify them as figures in the Nixon Administration, engaging in real historical events (as might not be said of the BBC's fictitious Lord and Lady Bellamy). Nor was this deliberate encouragement to view *Washington . . .* as a *roman à clef* confined to mimicked gestures or suggestively similar names: e.g., Richard Monckton for Richard Nixon, or Dr. Carl Tessler for Dr. Henry Kissinger, etc. Whole events were carefully transplanted from the real world to the make-believe world. Thus, while a real Kissinger once negotiated China policy, a make-believe Tessler also negotiated China policy; while a real Nixon once visited war protesters at the Lincoln Memorial, a make-believe Monckton also visited war protesters at the Lincoln Memorial; while a real Nixon once secretly escalated the Vietnam War into Cambodia, a make-believe Monckton also escalated a war into a "nearby neutral country," and so forth. The real world of past events and the make-believe world of television fiction were made to overlap and merge, with no harm to anyone, one might say—except that, in this blurry context, when Monckton plans a secret political undermining of the Twenty-second Amendment so that he may be free to run for a third term, who knows whether this significant little detail was real or also make-believe?

Then, too, there was the problem of the CIA syndrome in *Washington . . .* This was the central plot gimmick which the docu-drama producers had apparently bought from former Presidential assistant John Ehrlichman, when they bought his novel, *The Company*, for television. With novel in hand, the docu-drama people had then apparently strengthened considerably the anti-Nixon bite of the original Ehrlichman story, which could be considered tough on Nixon only if you took into account that the author once had been his loyal assistant; this stronger anti-Nixon coloration became the primary point of view of the television series. But, all along, Ehrlichman's novel had held that there were really two crimes committed in the pre-Watergate decade, and that only one of them had been Nixon/Monckton's small-scale burglary. The other crime, fully as great as Watergate, had been committed by former President William Curry, the handsome, popular, explicitly Kennedyesque figure who had secretly ordered numerous assassinations of politically troublesome foreign leaders, here and abroad. This novelistic assassination thesis was transferred intact to the docu-drama, where it became the series' principal story line. What secrets did Curry's protégé William Martin—now Monckton's CIA director—know about the dead President? What secrets did he also carry with him about those assassinations? Obviously, this is not the first time that CIA assassination theories have been voiced about President Kennedy. There is certainly a fashionably appealing resonance to such conjectures. But are they true? Or only somewhat true, or slightly true, or just a little bit true, or not true at all? And does any of that matter? Does it matter that, in an entertainment fiction that nonetheless lays deliberate claim to authenticity, unproved rumor about President Kennedy's involvement in CIA assassination schemes is casually paired with President Nixon's proved penchant for illegal activities and the abuse of power? Or are we supposed at that point to be watching "just a story"?

It's hard to see that it doesn't matter a great deal, although there are different aspects to the overall question raised by *Washington* . . . and other docu-dramas, which probably require different answers. Obviously, too lawyerly a view of what is portrayable in a person's life is likely to produce too narrow and artificial a portrait. There should be room in our chronicle plays for such an evocative, though not precisely factual, interpretation as Robards's Nixon, where the actor's skill and subtlety brought us closer to human truth. At the same time, however, for major television producers to be so spaced-out by the present Entertainment Era as to intentionally fool around with the actual life of an actual man, even of a discredited President (or even of a former CIA director, for there were several similarities between William Martin's career and that of former CIA director Richard Helms), seems irresponsible and downright shabby.

Still, this fictional-factual confusion is a problem that is easier to take sides on than to understand or see very clearly. For instance, can one really be against the right of audiences to watch what they want to watch, short of libel? Probably not, in a constitutional sense. On the other hand, the right of audiences can surely be pushed toward foolishness, lunacy, and self-destruction, and if there is one worthwhile and overriding right remaining in the world, perhaps it is the right of humankind not to destroy itself or even make itself any more foolish or spaced-out than necessary; at least, not without first checking with posterity.

At the same time, the right of drama guardians to protect or safeguard audiences from fictional facts or factional fictions sometimes seems to make no better sense, though the role of guardian probably has certain parental features that appeal to persons of a controlling disposition. The real likelihood, in any case, is that in the docu-drama's present habit of fooling with facts about important people some deeper, cyclical effect is bound to be at work. Some generations ago, the tide of political and personal sensibility flowed happily toward authority, inundating passersby, so to speak, with uniforms and titles and official statements. In recent years, the tide has reversed itself, rushing with equal velocity (and irrationality) against authority and deference to high station. In short, the public's earlier myopic regard for the self-importance of established truth has been supplanted by its present blurry vision of life as an arena of entertainment and entertainingness, and there is precious little that the hapless observer can do about it for the time being except call out the direction of the tide and try to avoid getting soaked in the process.

Besides, the root of the problem is clearly elsewhere, having only superficially to do with the license of fiction or the ethics of nonfiction. After all, for some time now, we have been resolutely marching into a period of biographic playfulness. Journalists today increasingly play with details of fact: the "unimportant details." Popular novels play breezily with the lives of public and semipublic figures. Movies play with biography and also journalism, and commercial television has created the ambiguous docu-drama. We have had docu-dramas about Lee Harvey Oswald, General Douglas MacArthur, Vince Lombardi, Harry Truman, Karen Silkwood, and a dozen others, and this is clearly only a beginning. The public evidently likes these stories, with their convenient touchstones of actuality and their easy slipping between fact and fiction, and so it will have them. Nor does it seem to matter in the least that some viewers are troubled by this mixture of fact and fancy, any more than it matters that other viewers profess to have "really learned something" from these programs. Really learned what? About stage design and acting? About how things actually were? Which things, then, since so many of them were made up and so never were?

What is happening, one imagines, is that we are restless with fiction and fearful of fact. We toy, we fiddle, we poke around with the real, sometimes enhancing it but often dishonoring it with modish carelessness. The other day, a writer of docu-dramas gravely observed that there was no such thing as "absolute truth." One wonders what had led him to consider such an abstraction in the first place. The point about truth, one always thought, was trying to get close to it. In any case, the chances are that the current trend of randomly hostile playfulness in real-life entertainments will turn out to be just as illogically motivated as the reverence for official facts that went before. In other words, *Washington: Behind Closed Doors* is part of our uncertain age: well ordered, superbly professional, attentive to detail, and disrespectful of life (that is, of the *bios* in biography). The idea now is to learn how to stay here, knee-deep in the surf like old Canute, waiting for the tide to change.

(1977)

STUNT MAN

A chapter from yet another ironic, knowingly detailed
Hollywood novel, written after watching one too many
TV shows and TV movies in which the protagonists
appear to be various types of motor vehicles
and their drivers

THE CALL had been for seven in the morning, but Mulloy
had taken his time, as usual, stopping off at the Krazy
Kaptain for eggs and a Michelob and a quick look at
the trades. Then the not altogether unpleasant, not entirely smog-choked drive down Sepulveda to the studio.
"Hey, Mulloy," said the guard with the whiskers and
the walrus nose. "I seen you two nights ago in *Thunder-
clap*. A class show but lousy ratings. I hear they got
Biemiller's ass on the line."

"Best place for it," said Mulloy.

The guard put his face close to Mulloy's. "I knowed
it was you, Tuesday night," he said. "I knowed it on
account of the eyes. I called my wife—I said, 'Hey,
that's Mulloy stuntin' for Drew Danby!' She came
runnin', but by then you was gone."

"*Vita brevis*, Pops," said Mulloy. He swung his
aged Mustang around to the parking lot on the right,
found an empty spot in the middle of what seemed to
be a family reunion of chocolate-brown Mercedes, and
ambled over to check in with Pruitt.

"You're late," said Pruitt. Like all executive producers, he sported a solid-gold Swiss army knife from
Hermès on a belt loop of his Cacharels.

"Well, I hope you didn't hold things up on my account," said Mulloy.

Pruitt tried one of his scowls that never came out right. "You should be so lucky," he said. "Get suited up in Wardrobe. You come on at the end of the big Interstate scene."

"We had a big Interstate scene last week," said Mulloy.

"Last week was the Freeway Hijacking," said Pruitt.

"My mistake," said Mulloy.

He walked down the hall to Wardrobe and got fitted into the top half of a state-highway patrolman's uniform. "How come I don't get to wear the britches?" he said.

"I guess because they ain't gonna *show* your britches," said the wardrobe girl. "Who're you stuntin' for today?"

"Garson," said Mulloy.

"Tommy Garson?" said the girl. "I thought he did his own stunts."

"Not the ones he needs me for," said Mulloy.

Outside, the sound of engines—car engines, truck engines, motorcycle engines—filled the air as Mulloy made his way to the set, wearing his own trousers and the top of the patrolman's uniform. Over in front of Makeup, two red LTDs and a police commissioner's limo waited to get their trim retouched. Behind the wheel of the limo, wearing at least the top half of a police commissioner's uniform, slouched the unmistakable figure of Jimmy Lee Loomis, smoking a suspicious-looking cigarette and reading the car-ad section of the L.A. *Times*. Once upon a time, Mulloy reflected, Jimmy Lee Loomis was *Truck Patrol*. Once upon a time, Jimmy Lee Loomis just about *owned* Wednesday night. But that was three years ago. The guy could have had anything then. They offered him a five-year renewable. They offered him his own golf tournament. They offered to tape the whole show right from the highway in front of his mother's house. Even today, nobody really knew what had happened. Some said it was on account of artistic differences with his co-star, Lance Laidlaw. Others said it was because Jimmy Lee was already beginning to lose it in the skid scenes. Anyway, one day Jimmy Lee Loomis walked. He made a Grand Prix musical with CheeWee Degener, which the critics liked but nobody saw. He went to Japan to make a motorcycle comedy that was too kinky to get out of the country. Finally, he came back. As a favor to his agent, they tested him for *Truck-Drivin' Lawyer*, but it was true: he'd lost it in the skid scenes. So now he lived with a grounded Eurasian stewardess out in the Canyon, taught a class in engine maintenance at film school, and took an occasional guest shot when it came up. Hollywood was a tough town, Mulloy reflected.

"Hi, old buddy," Mulloy said to Jimmy Lee.

"Hey, Mulloy," said Jimmy Lee. He always spoke real slow, like a football player; that is, before football players started to study sports announcing. The makeup man was busy daubing some red dust on the right front fender of the limo. "Not too heavy with the dust, Eddie," said Jimmy Lee.

"We need plenty of red, Mr. Loomis," said Eddie. "That Prentice is gonna zoom in very tight on the fenders at the cloverleaf."

"You're lookin' good, Jimmy Lee," said Mulloy, which was no less than the truth. Even after the passage of three years, Jimmy Lee's straw-yellow hair, pale-blue eyes, and superlatively tanned forehead were as splendid as ever.

"I'm readin' scripts," said Jimmy Lee.

"I bet you are," said Mulloy.

"I got a whole garageful of scripts, but they ain't got a *full-size* machine in one of them. Just them itty-bitty things and them pickups and them ambulances. The other day, this guy at Parsifal called me down to audition for some new father-and-son paramedic pilot. Heck, they wanted me to play the *father*. I told 'em to try Walter Pidgeon."

"You keep 'em flyin', Jimmy Lee," said Mulloy, starting to head over toward the set.

"You know the trouble with this town, Mulloy?" said Jimmy Lee. "Ain't nobody can write a simple three-car pileup anymore."

Over by the set, everything was chaos and bedlam, as usual. They had been working on the Interstate scene since early morning, with Peter Prentice, the director (stern and unforgiving but beautifully in control, as always), riding in the camera boom above the "Interstate"—another of Cy White's masterpieces, designed to replicate the stretch of Arizona I-98 midway between Tucson and Scottsdale—while below him Johnston, the assistant director, rehearsed the extras on the motorcycles. "Gentlemen, let's run through it one more time," said Prentice through a bullhorn. "Where *are* those motorcyclists?"

"Let's go, you guys," said Johnston. "Remember, this is a state patrol. Both wheels on the asphalt."

Now, on cue, far down the long strip of highway, a

green Toyota sedan appeared, cruising at a good seventy-five, followed by a red-and-white ambulance. As the ambulance moved inside to pass, the Toyota feigned a blowout and spun toward a ramp down which a huge Diamond Reo semi was accelerating. Now there was Tommy Garson in the patrol car, coming up fast, followed by the motorcycles: Garson weaving beautifully, first slipping by the ambulance on the outside—with the ambulance skidding off toward the green Toyota—and now coming up toward the big Diamond Reo, appearing to go head-on against the Diamond Reo but suddenly spinning again (a full-vector Manfredi in four lanes of traffic, as only Tommy Garson could do it), knocking down four of the cyclists, squeezing in between the Diamond Reo and the Toyota and an onrushing Pontiac Trans Am before crashing to a stop against a "Food and Fuel" sign beside the road.

"Okay, okay," said Prentice through the bullhorn, cool as a cucumber. "Billy, I'm afraid you're forcing that skid a little. What I think we want here is more a *suggestion* of a skid. *Comprenez?*"

The red-and-white ambulance sped over to the camera boom, and Billy Taylor leaned out the window—all goggled and silver-suited, like a spaceman. He lifted off his goggles and shook his glossy dark hair free and blinked his dark-brown eyes—eyes like a deer's after it has been stuffed and mounted, as an unfriendly New York critic had once remarked. "He's not giving me time to downshift," he said.

"Billy, I don't *want* you to downshift," said Prentice, with exaggerated patience. "I don't believe I read 'downshift' anywhere in the script."

"I'm telling you it just doesn't feel right this way," said Billy Taylor. "I always downshift. I downshifted in *Rear Axle*."

Prentice groaned aloud to Pär Lagerkvist, the cameraman. "Now he's back on *Rear Axle* again."

Lagerkvist pretended not to hear.

"Billy, *Rear Axle* was a nice series," said Prentice. "A nice little series. But just a shade *unsubtle*, don't you think, with all those tires screeching, and those unmotivated drawbridge jumps?"

"You call a forty-two share *unsubtle*?" said Billy Taylor, blinking his deer eyes as if he were close to tears.

"I call it unsubtle, coarse, unmotivated!" snapped Prentice. "Mr. Taylor, let me remind you we are not dabbling in audience share here. We are making *television*."

Billy Taylor shoved the goggles back on his head, jammed the ambulance into gear, and drove off, narrowly missing Johnston and the motorcyclists.

"God save me from actors," said Prentice.

"Ve are losing the light," said Lagerkvist dourly.

Prentice noticed Mulloy standing nearby. "Nice of you to show up," he said sarcastically.

Mulloy waved.

"Are you ready? Did you get the new pages last night?"

Mulloy nodded.

"All right, everybody!" Prentice called on the bullhorn. "This time, we're going to do it. Five minutes."

Two men ran out onto the set with cans of paint and paintbrushes and began painting over the skid marks while others attempted to straighten out the "Food and Fuel" sign. Mulloy stood in the sun watching the activity, listening to the engines throbbing around him but scarcely noticing any of it as he retreated to that deep space inside him, trying to psych himself up for the part. About thirty yards away was the talent tent, an elaborate roped-off area that contained the principal vehicles and the principal actors, who were now loitering in the shade of the overhanging canvas, sipping Gatorade and talking contracts: a dozen men, variously in driving suits or policemen's uniforms, standing about with helmets under their arms, somewhat like warriors —each one either tanned and yellow-haired or paler-skinned with dark, wavy locks. Beautiful, muscle-bound bastards, Mulloy thought contemptuously. Sometimes, in moments of weakness brought on by too many Michelobs, Mulloy asked himself if he still envied the talent. It was a question there was no point in wasting time over. He remembered trying out years ago for a minor cop show, with no race-car experience, no stock-car experience, not even motor-pool experience—just three years at Yale Drama School and six months at the Kennedy in *The Cherry Orchard.* "But what can you *do*, kid?" they kept asking. Water over the dam, Mulloy thought. He'd made his peace. Now one of the tall yellow-haired men—this one in the full regalia of a state-highway patrolman— left the enclosure of the talent tent and walked slowly in Mulloy's direction.

"Hi . . . Mul . . . loy," said Tommy Garson. He spoke the words, as he always spoke, in a strange, low monotone, with no inflection and with equal pauses between syllables—the result, someone had said, of his once having taken voice training at the American Airlines Institute for Passenger Representatives in Fort Wayne, Indiana.

"Hi, Garson," said Mulloy. "I hear we got the big one comin' up."

"Yes . . . we've . . . got . . . the . . . big . . . one . . . Mul . . . loy," said Garson, in the same weird, stately voice.

"No sweat, Garson," said Mulloy. "I've done it a hundred times."

"I . . . en . . . vy . . . you . . . Mul . . . loy," said Garson. Mulloy watched Garson's face closely. At the right side of his mouth, as if by a Herculean effort, a single muscle briefly twitched, and the barest trace of a smile passed across Garson's noble, impassive countenance, only to disappear as quickly as it had come. Mulloy was tempted to say, "Garson, that and five hundred bucks will buy me one week of pool consultation with Mr. Trang." It never paid to ruffle Garson, though. Instead, he just said, "Sure, Garson."

But now there was no stopping Garson. "I . . . real . . . ly . . . mean . . . it . . . Mul . . . loy," he said. Clearly, he had attempted to inflect the word "mean," but the attempt hadn't quite succeeded. "You . . . do . . . the . . . tough . . . parts . . . Mul . . . loy . . . but . . . every . . . body . . . thinks . . . it's . . . me."

Not *everybody*, Garson, Mulloy thought. "Look, Garson, there's a dozen guys who do what I do, but there's only one of you. I mean, there's not another actor in town could have done a Manfredi right there in the inside lane and come out of it alive."

Garson tried another smile. His whole jaw heaved

mightily and finally locked into place, so that a few teeth appeared. "That . . . was . . . a . . . good . . . Man . . . fredi . . . was . . . n't . . . it . . . Mul . . . loy?" he said.

Just then, Johnston's whistle sounded, and the principals started to buckle themselves into their various vehicles. "Take . . . care . . . Mul . . . loy," said Garson. His beautiful blue eyes stared straight ahead. He raised his right hand to his highway patrolman's helmet in a salute and strode away toward his car.

This time, the scene went without a hitch, with the green Toyota and the ambulance coming on fast, and the big Diamond Reo thundering down the ramp, and Garson, gleaming and invisible, like a medieval knight, beneath his goggles and helmet, whipping down the lane, scattering the extras on their cycles, moving up on Billy Taylor's ambulance—but this time Billy Taylor did something quite marvelous. He sideslipped: not a skid at all; not even a suggestion of a skid. A sideslip—perfect. And then Garson was head-on against the Diamond Reo. "Jesus," Mulloy muttered. "He's left the Manfredi awfully late. He hasn't given himself enough room." But suddenly the patrol car was spinning—one spin, a second spin, a *double* Manfredi—then straightening out, then skidding. Now came the Pontiac Trans Am—sideswipe. Now the Toyota sedan—a frightful rending of bumpers. Now the final spin toward the "Food and Fuel" sign.

"Okay, okay," came Prentice's voice on the bullhorn. "Where in hell is Mulloy?"

Mulloy walked slowly toward the smoking patrol car, which was resting, half tilted on its side, against the nearly demolished sign. Pruitt, together with Garson's agent, was helping Garson out of the car. "Beautiful, Tommy. A very powerful moment," the agent was saying to Garson.

"You want a hand?" Pruitt said to Mulloy.

"Not from you," said Mulloy. The left window of the wrecked automobile was open, so Mulloy slithered in, turned himself around inside, squeezed in beneath the steering wheel. A propman reached in and handed him Garson's helmet and driving glasses, and also Garson's white silk scarf—his trademark. Mulloy buckled himself into the seat belt and took a couple of deep breaths.

Outside, the second-unit camera was now in place.

"I vant more head and shoulders," said Naumhoff, the second-unit cameraman, who was actually Danish but affected an irresolute Swedish accent out of deference to Lagerkvist. A sound man reached into the car and tucked a tiny mike, out of sight, into the folds of Mulloy's scarf.

"All right, Mulloy," said Prentice, now standing behind the second-unit camera. "You know what I want. Let's make it good. Everybody quiet. Everybody ready. Lights. Camera . . ."

Even behind Garson's thick glasses, Mulloy could feel the lights. The lights always excited him. He blinked his eyes, using up a few seconds, letting the script recede in his memory, letting the lines flow into his head as if they had always been there.

"Roll 'em," said Prentice.

On cue, Mulloy began the grin, at first pushing his mouth into it, then feeling his face relax, feeling the grin take over, wide now, not too wide, keep control—a stupendous grin. Jesus, wouldn't Garson have liked to pull off a grin like that! Now the laugh. What did the

pages say? A reckless laugh? Mulloy let the peals of
laughter erupt, hearing them reverberate inside the
patrol car, pushing the laugh, driving the laugh higher,
looking for the right place. *Now.* He held it, counting the
seconds, letting the recklessness take over, letting it seem
as if the laugh were suddenly in command, as if he
couldn't handle it, and then began to taper it, bringing
it down—not too fast, not too abruptly—softening the
high notes, lowering the laugh to a register where his
voice began to catch. Where was the catch? There! His
voice caught beautifully. The laugh now slipped, now
glided effortlessly into the beginning of a new sound:
at first, the merest hint of a sob. Then two sharp, quick
sobs. Watch out for a sneeze, Mulloy said to himself.
Now go for it! A real sob. Mulloy brought his right
hand to his face—a touch not in the script, but now he
was well into the part, deep into character, remembering, as if he had been the one behind the wheel, the
sideswiped Pontiac and the thundering Diamond Reo,
recalling the thud of the motorcyclists bouncing off the
back fender and the gallantry of the green Toyota, feeling the mysteries of life and death, the ambiguities of
speed and slowness, the challenges of falling rocks and
no passing on the right, the excitement of the center lane,
and the unbearable sadness of the access roads . . . With
an effort, Mulloy reached for the police microphone that
dangled from the dashboard of the car and brought it
to his lips. Dimly, he was aware of the lights boring in
upon his helmet, piercing his glasses. He could sense
Prentice somewhere out there. The rest of the crew. Let's
make this one good, he thought. Aloud now, in a firmer
voice—shaken but still proud—he said, "Zero-two-niner.
Zero-two-niner." Then softer, quieter, not yet a whisper,

though with an unmistakable resonance of hope: "Tell Sue-Ann I'm *comin' home*." Then he slumped forward onto the steering wheel.

After they pulled him out of the car, he handed the helmet, glasses, and scarf back to the propman. Johnston was smiling, and gave him the thumbs-up sign. Even Prentice, in a rare moment of warmth, came over and draped a cardiganed arm around his shoulder. "Nice work, Mulloy," he said. "It made me *weep*. The recklessness of that laugh! It made me *weep*." He removed the arm. "Okay, everybody, we've got work to do. The canyon leap next. Mulloy, I'll be seeing you."

As Mulloy walked away from the car, he spotted Garson standing all by himself at the edge of the now empty "Interstate." "Hi, Garson," he said.

"Lis . . . ten . . . to . . . this . . . Mul . . . loy," said Garson, taking a deep breath as if he were about to dive underwater, and then carefully and metronomically enunciating the words. "Tell . . . Sue . . . Ann . . . I'm . . . com . . . in' . . . home."

"Hey, not bad, Garson," said Mulloy.

"Ze . . . ro . . . two . . . nin . . . er," said Garson, once again clenching his face into that impenetrable look. "Ze . . . ro . . . two . . . nin . . . er."

"You just keep working on it, Garson," said Mulloy. He put his hands in his pockets and headed for the parking lot. Sooner or later, they all wanted to do their own stunts.

(1980)

ON GIVING
THE DEVIL HIS DUE

THE GREEKS called it "song drama"; we know it as melodrama, and it's undeniably a still potent form of storytelling which seems ideally suited to movie and television screens, where passages of romance and adventure appear with a vividness and "reality" that the printed page and even the technically resourceful modern stage find hard to equal. But, on the whole, much of the melodrama one sees on the television screen is disappointing: not in the bourgeois cultural sense of being too lowbrow or popular, but because television melodramas rarely seem to succeed on their own terms as emotional entertainment. TV romances and adventures are usually jammed with incident and give the appearance of dramatizing basic conflicts, but, as with the proverbial Chinese dinner that leaves the diner hungry afterward, there's all too often an emotional thinness to the stories which makes them finally unsatisfying.

A fairly typical case in point was a two-hour made-for-TV movie called *Murder by Natural Causes*, which appeared a while ago on *The CBS Saturday Night Movies*. Made-for-TV movies have improved perceptibly in the last couple of years, and clearly this one was no slapdash cops-and-robbers quickie, for it had a recognizable cast of capable actors (among them, Hal Halbrook, Katharine Ross, and Barry Bostwick), and from the smartly paced opening moments of the action it also appeared to have a script (by Richard Levinson and

William Link) of more than average interest and literacy.

Indeed, the story begins with a fine mixture of suspense and authority. First, one sees Hal Holbrook making a long-distance phone call to a hospital computer to check the pacemaker on his heart. Then one finds out that Holbrook is Arthur Sinclair, a world-famous mentalist, or mind reader, who is about to appear on a television talk show. Then, in the talk-show anteroom, Holbrook receives a phone call from his apparently loving wife (Katharine Ross), though the camera reveals that she is in bed with another man as she makes the call. Then Holbrook appears on the talk show and proceeds to dazzle the host and the studio audience by "reading" not only the combination of a safe that has been brought on-stage but also its contents.

So far, so good. We are evidently in the hands of professionals who are about to give us a good time. The dialogue is lively. The short scenes with Holbrook have energy and work well; there's an astringent cleverness to his part, and also a generosity that loosens us up. Holbrook seems right as Sinclair. It's a verbal-ego part, and Holbrook has generally been strong in such roles, projecting the force and charm of the verbal ego as well as whatever may be unsettling or unreliable about such a personality. But already a soft, or, rather, a flat, spot has appeared in the texture of the story: the wife. We've seen only a little of her, and from all appearances she's a bad girl, which might be promising. But there's no subtlety here; she doesn't seem interestingly or even convincingly bad—just *bad*: bitchy, dishonest, and unfaithful. Also, in contrast to the light touch with which Holbrook is directed in the opening sequences, there's something soggy about the scene in which Katharine Ross is talking on the telephone from the conjugal bed; there's a clumsiness in that old-fashioned, stilted way of panning the camera to reveal the lover in bed beside her. Still, sex and wickedness are arresting, and it seems reasonable to expect that the wife's affair with the young man will tell us something interesting about her, and presumably about her relationship with her husband, so that what seemed at first to be merely meanness will turn into character.

This never happens. As the story progresses, Holbrook's character continues to evolve: his dazzling mind-reading act, for example, is shown to be something of a fake. But the characters of the wife and her lover remain frozen at pretty much the point where we first found them. Not that there is no change at all: whereas the wife started out mean and bitchy and vaguely murderous, she gradually becomes meaner and bitchier and more explicitly murderous; and the young lover (whom she keeps trying to bully into murdering Holbrook), who began weak and petulant, now becomes even weaker and more petulant. At any rate, an unintended split develops in the focus of the narrative. On one side, there is Holbrook, the fascinating mentalist: clever, humorous, something of a charlatan, and decidedly ambiguous. And on the other side is the decidedly unambiguous duo of the mean wife and her churlish lover and their nasty murder plot. The wife is an especially sour note; I have never been a great devotee of Katharine Ross as an actress, but I doubt whether the legendary Duse herself could have done much with a part of such simpleminded meanness. Except when she is being stagily insincere, the lady never has a kind word for anyone; she wishes to bump off poor Holbrook for no better-developed reason than that she's a greedy girl and has "expensive tastes"; she doesn't like her young lover any too well; later in the story, another lover turns up whom she doesn't seem to like much better (he is Holbrook's lawyer: yet another blandly squalid and homicidal role). Thus, though there's quite a bit of clever twisting and turning to the plot, the movie never really develops any impact as melodrama, because one can't get involved in the emotional life of any of the characters: that is, one might be able to be involved with Holbrook, but the wife and her young lover (and her lawyer lover) are so thinly drawn that their lack of plausibility and substance aborts the human flow of the story before it gets started. In short, it's hard to generate much emotional electricity for exchanges between a "real" character and cardboard cutouts—which is a shame in a case like this, when a certain amount of talent and skill must have gone into the creation of the Holbrook character.

This is a kind of failure in the dramaturgy of modern melodrama, I think, which recurs time and again, and usually in the same place: in the character—or perhaps the lack of characterization—of the villain. One sees it often in routine movie thrillers, and even more often in commercial television adventures, where wickedness seems to be consistently painted in monochrome colors of such flatness and predictability as to make a meaningful or interesting connection between good and evil almost impossible. Consider the parade of modern villains who march across our screens: for the most part, they are only superficially different (sometimes a white banker, sometimes a black pimp; sometimes a gangster or a Southern sheriff or a government official); essentially, they are all alike—fashioned from the same psychic mold and sharing the same quasi-chivalric adherence to a code of simple malice. Evil is theatrically fascinating and exerts a powerful attraction on audiences, but nowadays, in those regions of the popular entertainment world where Satan is allowed to cast his shadow, wickedness seems largely to have degenerated into a one-dimensional and textureless meanness—more often than not, a cool and facile cruelty, pruriently tiptoeing on the edge of outright sadism until those moments when the plot, or lack of plot, causes the evildoer to tumble off the edge into fits of viciousness or mayhem.

Now, it might be argued that this criticism of modern-entertainment villainy asks too much of melodrama. Weren't the villains of traditional melodrama always one-dimensional bad guys who wore stovepipe hats and sneers, and tied helpless heroines to railroad tracks? This simple rationale, I think, misses the point. No one is suggesting that a villain in a modern television melodrama should be constructed with the same richness as Iago, but only that the evildoer (or negative charge) in a popular story might be given the same dramatic plausibility and potency as the hero (or positive charge), so that the two forces between them will produce enough tension and energy to make the story interesting. A hundred years ago, a one-dimensional villain in a stovepipe hat made sense in melodrama, because he invariably played opposite a one-dimensional hero: equally unambiguous and untextured—as good as the villain was bad. But this unambiguous hero hardly exists anymore, even in popular entertainments. True, one now and then comes across a young cop or paramedic of such unalloyed nobility as to infect the drama around him with irredeemable silliness, but by and large the heroes of most modern melodramas have been drawn with an increasingly realistic brush: they have quirks, crotchets, and sometimes more than petty weaknesses; their once perfect purity is all too visibly flawed—in other words, they are ambivalent, in tune with the revealed sensibility of modern man. Back in the nineteen-fifties, when the traditional one-dimensional, unambivalent hero made one of his final appearances, in the person of Alan Ladd as Shane—wearing a pale buckskin jacket and a demeanor of medieval saintliness to do battle with black-vested Jack Palance beneath the Grand Tetons—he was already something of an anachronism: a storybook figure whose chief appeal (as in the case of a more recent anachronism, *Rocky*) was less to anything as vigorous as living myth as it was to the softer, fuzzier, more charm-conscious contemporary demands for juvenilia and nostalgia. By contrast, many of the most successful heroic figures in modern melodrama (whether played by Dustin Hoffman, Al Pacino, Clint Eastwood, or Jane Fonda on the movie screen, or by Robert Blake, Peter Falk, Alan Alda, James Garner, and many others on television) are men and women whose capacity for doing good—far from being lacking, as the vogue description "anti-hero" seems to imply—in fact persistently surmounts, in classic heroic fashion, the obstacles not only of the plot or situation but of the ambiguities in their own characters. As a small footnote: though it wasn't a hugely profitable movie, it seemed both pleasing and well suited to the spirit of the age that when, a few years ago, the screenwriter James Goldman reworked the legend of Robin Hood into *Robin and*

Marian, he should have reincarnated Robin Hood
(played by Sean Connery) as a middle-aged, overweight,
doubtless decent but somewhat slow-thinking medieval
chap—obviously no match at swordplay or vine-swinging
for John Barrymore, Douglas Fairbanks, or Errol Flynn,
but a role that nonetheless made a kind of honest, un-
camped sense to modern audiences which the earlier,
more glamorous, and less grainy interpretations could
surely not have provided.

Thus, it seems that our popular modern heroes often
connect to the evolving psychology and sensibility of the
contemporary audience but that our modern villains
rarely do so. Why, one wonders, with all the attractions
of wickedness they have going for them, are they so
frequently uninvolving, insubstantial, without past or
future, without enough humanity or even "background"
to relate plausibly to the other characters in the story?
A mean and homicidal wife—or drug pusher or CIA
agent—is usually simply that: mean and homicidal,
with occasionally a line or two of antiquated "psychological" exposition about a deprived childhood thrown
in as an afterthought. These thinly sketched traits of
personality—one as banal as bitchiness and the other
as uncommon (at least, according to crime statistics) as
murderousness—are supposed to coexist as naturally
as eggs and bacon, and represent not just the limits of
character but character itself. What else (the melo-
dramatists seem to be saying) do we need to know about
evil beyond a certain surface nastiness, beyond the
modern show-business *look* of evil, with its reliance on
modish, though simplistic, signature effects? For example, in *Murder by Natural Causes*, just before the lawyer
lover takes a shot at Holbrook, in order to make clear

to us his utter wickedness he slips on one of those dainty little black gloves, as worn originally by Jack Palance in *Shane*, and by five dozen movie and television bad guys since—presumably the contemporary equivalent of the stovepipe hat.

But if it's easy enough to spot the failures of dimension in modern melodrama villains, it's another matter to understand why this should be so. Do villains lag behind heroes in ambivalence and plausibility—in substance—simply out of nostalgia for the old forms? That seems unlikely, for there is a force behind the new creations which surely comes from something less weakly narcissistic than mere nostalgia. And yet it doesn't seem to be the stronger, more vital force of observed life and experience. I wonder, in fact, if the men and women who create popular melodramas—those stories for the public—haven't for some time now been taking a shortcut, away from life and into literature, for their source material for evil. As Richard Slotkin pointed out several years ago in his book *Regeneration through Violence*, the role of serious eighteenth- and nineteenth-century American literature was crucial in embedding in the public consciousness the artistic idea of the redemptive killer—the classic murderer hero of the American fictional landscape, who kills to save his soul, and whose family tree, originating in early Puritan fiction, reappears in Hawthorne and Melville, and has since spread its progeny as far afield as *The Virginian, High Noon, Shane*, and countless Westerns and detective stories. So the influence of literary art (with its habit of sometimes reordering and sometimes falsifying experience) has been felt on popular fiction and melodrama for many years, especially in the creation of morally ambiguous heroes. More recently, though—at least since the Second World War—a new secondhand influence has interposed itself between the mass audience and those who must turn out entertainments for this audience: namely, the so-called modern novel, whose masters are admittedly a law unto themselves but whose imitators and second- or third-rung practitioners have been disbursing steady quantities of cool, ironic, alienated, existential, or nihilistic figures onto the impressionable contemporary scene. The moral line these "artistic" literary creations tread is usually so faint as not to exist; thus they are often called "amoral"; thus they can serve as role models for either heroes or villains—but especially the latter, for the audience for popular melodrama is generally not so baffled or overeducated as to accept willingly an absence of moral character as heroic ambivalence. And so a new family tree has evolved. This one begins, at a far remove, with such literary writers as Hemingway and Camus and Graham Greene (whose creations, however much they may artistically falsify reality, at least originate in life, or in some particular moment in life), and branches out with all the trendy imitative novelists and then with *their* vast progeny—the "serious" detective-story writers and the "serious" screenwriters—until the final growth is reached, in the television entertainment factories. At this point, the original, laconic Hemingway killer has usually degenerated, through excesses of secondhand "art," into a deaf-mute, sadistic gunman, and Camus's alienated *étranger* has become a disaffected teenage ganglord. In other words, the outer form of villainy has been retained, while the interior substance—the humanity—that gave shape and energy to the form has been dropped or forgotten. Depictions of evil in modern melodramas often have this strange, cartoonlike quality because they are in fact cartoons, not so much of life but of literature. The character of the villain is expressed in hasty, unrevealing flicks of the pen. The actor fills the part as best he or she can, but the part is usually all surfaces: an art director's conception of evil as a composition of looks and gestures. Of course, it is difficult for all but the greatest artists to stare evil in the face and re-create it in human terms—to render it as human as it is—which is probably why so many screenwriters and popular novelists either give us the remembered outlines of the creations of great writers or else keep escaping into fantasies (totalitarian, conspiratorial, sexual, and so forth), where their souls are safe.

(1979)

HOSTS AND GUESTS

EVEN AT a time when ambivalence is being raised to the level of a national virtue, that was a mighty odd program emanating from the television set a while back, entitled *The Barbara Walters Special*, whose particular flavor was only hinted at in a large—in fact, huge—newspaper advertisement: "Tonight, the private homes and private thoughts of Jimmy and Rosalynn Carter, Barbra Streisand and Jon Peters are revealed on the Barbara Walters Special! You've never seen these people like this before!" Actually, the content of the revelatory program turned out to be fairly harmless, even rather cozy; though what might have been dismissed in another era as mere women's-magazine gossip was now supposedly being elevated, before our raised journalistic consciousnesses, into news—or, at least, into feature—by Ms. Walters's asking of the newsperson's "tough questions."

In this regard, Ms. Walters seemed on her way to creating a new interviewing form all her own, consisting of a synthesis—to put the matter in the best light—of the two basic interviewing styles of the great Edward R. Murrow. Mr. Murrow, as students of television know by now, was compelled in his later years by the commerce-minded executives of CBS to split himself into two people: one, the Higher Murrow (so named by the television critic John Lardner), who conducted serious journalistic interviews on *See It Now*; and the other, the Lower Murrow, who on *Person to Person* wandered vaguely and elegantly about in the homes of celebrities making small-talk and discussing interior decoration.

Ms. Walters's contribution is to combine the features of the two Murrows in the persona of a single interviewer on a single program. Thus, the other evening, a chatty, even fluttery Ms. Walters addressed herself to household details, as when entering the Streisand–Peters dwelling: "Oh, Jon, it's *nice*. Listen, this place is *terrific*. I expected, you know, a ranch, a mansion. This is very *small*." Then, in an aside to the audience: "He sold his lucrative hairdressing salons for six figures. The rest of the house is dominated by the family room and bits and pieces from Barbra's famous Art Deco collection. She feels comfortable with her treasures near. Now, this is Barbra's bathroom . . ."

At other times, however, a more formidable, nononsense Ms. Walters fired away with the tough questions, handling poor Mr. Peters as if he were of no greater consequence than an Assistant Secretary of Defense on *Meet the Press*: "Do you feel you're any good? . . . Why? . . . How do you know you're not going to ruin Barbra Streisand? . . . Were you in reform school? . . . Why? . . . *When* did you straighten out?" In her visit with the President-elect and his wife, Ms. Walters's artful new interviewing technique was equally in evidence, though it seemed that her success with the form was less pronounced here, owing perhaps to the greater artfulness of the Carters in appearing not to notice the difference between the two styles. "It's a lovely portrait," the chatty Ms. Walters would say prior to launching the tough question, such as: "Is your husband a good dancer?" The Carters, however, greeted all the sallies or salvos with equal good humor. Doubtless, they had been warned in advance by the Streisand–Peterses.

But what was oddest by far about the program was something that had little to do with the people who were on it, or even with the matter of interviewing styles. One might explain it as economically as possible by saying that there seemed to be a general confusion from the start as to who was host and who was guest. For example, the program opened with Ms. Walters standing in her own New York apartment, all dressed up to receive company in the accepted manner of a television hostess, but informing us that she was going to be taking us *out*, so to speak, "into the private homes and private thoughts of two couples." Then, the Streisand–Peterses were shown acting as hosts to Ms. Walters. Then, there was an intermission of sorts, during which Ms. Walters —transported back to her apartment and her original hostess role—proceeded to take us, as her guests, on a tour of her various art objects and souvenirs. Then, we were off to Georgia, where the Carters were clearly now the hosts and took Ms. Walters through *their* house. In conclusion, we returned to New York with Ms. Walters, who signed off by saying, "I'm so pleased you could join us in your homes. Good evening from mine."

At this point, a classics scholar, or even anyone famil- iar with a good dictionary, might remark that in all these comings and goings *The Barbara Walters Special* was only being faithful to the original ambiguity of the Latin root word for hospitality, *hospes*, which means both host and guest, and also stranger. That could be, although judging from the continually shifting asser- tions of hosthood and guesthood throughout the program, one would have to guess that classical ambiguity was only dimly or inadvertently being attended to. The prob- lem in any case was not the confusion of roles but the underlying insistence that someone should always be host and someone should always be guest, which is an insistence that has permeated much of American television since its beginnings.

Nowadays, hosts and guests abound on television to such a degree that their presence is taken for granted; in fact, these television role definitions have been passed outward into society—into academic circles, for example, where I recently read of a university professor's "hosting" a classroom discussion. Most talk shows have little structure, certainly little conversational structure, beyond this simple dramaturgy of host and guests. Entertainment programs regularly have hosts and guests. Even a routine detective series has guest stars, who do not so much appear as make "guest appearances." I was about to say that news programs seem immune from this ongoing drama of hospitality, but there are obvious exceptions to this on soft-news programs, such as the *Today* show, and lately I've noticed that some local evening news programs have started to use guests as well as the "guest interview."

Admittedly, our language is full of obsolete or old-fashioned nomenclature (for instance: master of ceremonies or maître d'hôtel) whose present meaning often bears only the haziest relation to the original meaning, and so it's probable, to some degree at any rate, that our television *host* and *guest* are simply words which have a loose though vaguely appropriate sound to them. Even so, it's interesting that broadcasting as a whole, and television in particular, should have been so eager from its inception to present itself as a pageant of hospitality. The early days of radio, for example, witnessed countless hosts, such as the sinister Raymond of *The Inner*

Sanctum, and even the President of the United States, Franklin D. Roosevelt, who modeled his Fireside Chats on the popular radio shows and became the first Presidential host. Later, with the beginning of commercial television, virtually no drama program existed without its (usually movie-star) host: Ronald Reagan on *General Electric Theatre*, Dick Powell on *Four Star Playhouse*, Robert Montgomery on *Robert Montgomery Presents*. Today, drama series have more or less disappeared from television (except, perhaps, for public television's *Masterpiece Theatre*, which retains Alistair Cooke as host—himself the former host of *Omnibus*), but the roles and connotations of host and guests seem to be as firmly embedded in the medium as ever.

At first, what one notices about all this hosting and guesting is the perfunctoriness of the procedure. After all, what is a television host in most cases but a professional entertainer who conducts a program on which other professional entertainers, or celebrities, or merely newsworthy persons, appear by mutual arrangement and for their mutual benefit? Sometimes the attempts at simulating hospitality are so slight or abbreviated as to be virtually nonexistent. On a recent evening, for example, I watched a public-television discussion program about European Communism on which the designated "hostess" (or interviewer) sat primly in a modernistic chair, facing four designated "guests" (or experts), who were arrayed side by side in four similar chairs. The program opened with the hostess and guests grimly facing one another, after which different members of the guest "group" held forth in stern, high-minded monologues, though remaining frozen in their respective positions, rather in the manner of strangers warily con-

versing across an airport lounge. At other times, notably
on the popular talk shows, the rituals of hospitality are
far more definite and ambitious. For instance, on most
such programs the host is shown already *in situ* in his
territory (usually a sound stage, which is in fact more
significantly occupied by technicians than by him),
which the guest is shown in the process of entering or
approaching. At this juncture, there are handshakes,
kisses, even hugs—though in most cases guest and host
have just been introduced backstage—after which the
guest is invited to sit down, either beside the host in the
place of honor, or beside the other guests who have
already been welcomed into the host's domain. Then
follows the interrogatory catechism of the stranger's
initiation: Whence has the stranger journeyed from?
(He was on location in Puerto Vallarta.) How fares the
stranger's family? ("Linda's just fine. She'll be joining
me in Hawaii for the weekend.") What is the extent and
nature of the stranger's good will? ("It's just great to be
back here, Ted! Just great!") The only important aspect
of hospitality that seems to be missing is an offering of
food or drink, but that is soon metaphorically supplied.
"So, tell us about the new movie, Bill," the host will say
at the appropriate moment, with the bored courtesy of a
tribal chief watching yet another roast pig of a free
network plug being set before a hungry visitor.

On these programs for the mass audience, the little
dramas of hospitality often come across as far more
than mere byplays of outmoded nomenclature. Merv
Griffin, for instance, seems to act the part of the professional man as host: the doctor or lawyer who has
been more or less trapped into giving a party but is still
trying to have a good time. He would like to be friendly

and sociable, but what he is mainly hoping for is that the event "go well." Also, since his wife is never around —probably out in the kitchen, making canapés or crying —Merv has to make conversation with the guests, most of whom he doesn't really know very well or feel at ease with. Still, he is game, a regular guy. He smiles a lot, not very convincingly, but still a guy's smile. He is the kind of man for whom parties often start out on an unnatural and unsustainable high note of ain't-we-got-fun, which quickly fades as reality sets in. "I *love* it!" Merv called out the other evening, for no apparent reason, before an audience which then dutifully applauded. "*I love it!*" he repeated, bowing from the waist, compelling the audience to applaud some more. "Isn't that *nice*?" he said. And, "Isn't that *really nice*?" And, "Okay, *let it all out*!" Then, abruptly, as if there were now too much emotion in the air, or perhaps too little control, he shot out a cold, flat question. "Where did you get *that*?" he asked a woman in the audience, apparently referring to her hat, with an inflection of barely amused disapproval which now caused the audience to turn its attention to the hapless woman. The audience as well as the woman giggled nervously. The host was back in control, perhaps wondering why he was giving this party anyway. Would it really be good for business? "Ladies and gentlemen," said Merv, with a tight smile, "please greet Miss Dody Goodman."

Dinah Shore, on the other hand, plays not so much a professional man's wife as the wife, or widow, of some grander, absent chairman of the board. As such, she is a little above the hurly-burly of the world, though she clearly likes to keep in touch and has a fondness for people. The chairman has his friends, of course, and she has hers. The important thing is that she loves her home, loves entertaining in her home—loves having people just "drop by" without a lot of fuss and pretense. Even so, she always manages to dress up for the occasion (usually in a hostess gown), unlike Merv, who rarely seems to get back from the office in time to change for the party. And her home is always so nicely arranged, not a lavish place, but comfortable, with a quiet look of prosperity about the furnishings; money definitely went into it. A big, inviting sofa sits in the middle of the room; plants and flowers are placed all around. Dinah herself is invariably gracious and personable, maybe compensating a bit for the absent chairman, who is doubtless a nice fellow but with no flair for people. "Do you mean that you went out on the Met stage *all by yourself?*" said Dinah one afternoon to a singer named Melba Moore. It was just a friendly, more or less flattering comment such as one might expect from an accomplished hostess, but not without its subtle element of hostesslike control. For not only must the flattery be acknowledged by the guest, usually in higher coin—in this case, by a whole series of appreciative murmurs—but the guest must also accept and play her part in a little game designed by the hostess's ego, wherein both parties pretend to be unaware that the charming hostess herself has spent much of her life on numerous stages, all by herself, probably to even greater acclaim.

Johnny Carson's approach to hosting on the *Tonight Show* is more complex, and is perhaps truer to the mixed nature of hospitality. In effect, the program employs dual hosts. On one side, there is Ed McMahon, who symbolizes the traditional warmhearted host. He is the generous-spirited host of folklore, in some tales renowned for the hospitality of his table, though commonly made fun of for his lack of guile. On the other side, there is Carson, who symbolizes the trickster host. He plays the King to his guest's Scheherazade. Will Johnny be pleased by Scheherazade's latest story, and treat her kindly, and ask her to return at a future date? Or will he have her head chopped off with a look of boredom or a sarcastic remark? It is an interesting relationship that exists between these two host figures, for while McMahon is clearly of lesser power than Carson, he is vital to the show; indeed, though Carson is frequently replaced by substitute hosts ("guest hosts"), McMahon remains a fairly constant presence. Also, the show has an elaborate hospitality ritual that extends even further than Griffin's or Shore's. Here, not only is the host revealed in his domain, with the guests compelled to bring themselves to him, but at the start of each program the host is shown asserting the right to his position. Carson's arrival is formally announced, not by an off-screen voice, but by none other than the guileless alter-host, Ed McMahon. Then Carson makes use of the host's prerogative not merely to extend a greeting but to deliver a speech: the nightly monologue. The vulnerability of the moment is illusory, for the assemblage can do little else but listen. The King has opened Parliament. Then, sometimes, to press home the reality of power, or to make it appear more playful than it really is, Carson will make jokes about his court and retinue. McMahon, the guileless host, now allows himself to become the Jester. The musicians become the Fiddlers Three. Moreover, this host is not one to mingle too freely with the guests, as does the gracious, less powerful hostess Dinah, who has to share her couch. The Carson host requires a throne, an article of separation: in fact, a desk. Does the King here bestride his desk or hide behind it?

It is probable that the origins of human hospitality go back to the beginnings of life. Biologic organisms, for example, are receptive to certain organisms different from themselves and rejective of others. Animals are variously hospitable or rejective, as in the different social responses of the dolphin and the porcupine. Not dissimilarly, human beings are continually drawing together and flying apart. But what is notable about the human response to these biological or chemical flows and ebbs—this instinct for connection and rejection—is that human beings have designed literary formulas, or myths, with which to organize the process artistically and for the larger human benefit. As such, probably the first known myth of hospitality, at least in the West, is the story of Philemon and Baucis, as transcribed by Ovid. In this account, the gods Jupiter and Mercury (or, sometimes, Zeus and Hermes), bored with life on Olympus, make it a practice to come to earth from time to time, looking for adventure. On one such trip, the two gods come to Phrygia, and there, disguised as poor travelers, they wander around the land knocking at the doors of rich and poor alike, all of whom treat them unkindly and turn them away. Finally, the gods arrive at a little hovel and are warmly greeted by two old peasants, Philemon and his wife, Baucis, who welcome them and give them freely of the little food and drink they have. The gods are pleased, and, in return for their hospitality, Philemon and Baucis are permitted to become priests in Jupiter's temple. Furthermore, at the end of their lives, they are granted their ultimate wish of being allowed to die at the same time, at which moment their bodies are transformed into two trees, a linden and an oak.

Clearly, this story can be read in two ways. Taking it at face value, it seems to show mankind's traditional admiration for the ennobling virtue of hospitality, for the need to maintain social intercourse. But, peering into the innards of the tale, one sees a somewhat darker story, for what surrounds the isolated act of generosity of the worthy Philemon and Baucis is a world where fear and hatred of strangers apparently prevail: what the Greeks described as xenophobia. The opposite of xenophobia is obviously hospitality; but just as clearly it is an antidote that does not so much remove all traces of the original poison as coexist with it and work against it. Thus, for thousands of years, a tension has existed between the antisocial force of xenophobia and the socializing dynamic of hospitality, between the rituals designed for welcoming strangers, or even visitors, and the deep-rooted fears and hostilities that these rituals were intended to assuage. Backward peoples, for example, possessing few other social ceremonies, practice elaborate rituals of host and guest; as do certain advanced peoples who live in intrinsically defensive societies, such as the American antebellum South or prerevolutionary St. Petersburg—or even in anxiety-ridden modern communities. Children, however, when they are very young (and might be said to have the fewest defenses), seem to practice very little in the way of hospitality. Aside from occasional tears or scrapping, little kids easily mingle in one another's homes without recourse to the niceties of ritual. For instance, at a small child's birthday party it is rarely clear who is host and who is guest—at least, not without the insistence of an adult that the distinctions be made clear. So, one wonders, does the need for hospitality come into the human consciousness with the end of innocence? And do the rituals of hospitality—as with the great host who showers his guest with food, drink, and even one of his wives— then not tell us as much about human fear of our own dark natures as they do about our desire to do right by company?

Ironically, television, which persistently plays to the defensive, overcivilized aspects of society, with its charades of hosts and guests, at the same time has done much to connect people with one another, to demystify strangers, to deisolate backward communities, and especially to help break down the walls that often exist between individuals as well as generations and that have caused so much hostility (whose Latin root word, *hostis*, is coincidentally so small a variant of *hospes*) in those trapped behind them. Predictably, it would seem, many people today lament a decline in the rituals of hospitality among the young. Young people, one hears, don't always show a proper respect or understanding for the structure of parties. Guest lists are distressingly fluid. People wander hither and yon, sometimes arrive at all hours of the evening. Now and then the host or hostess is absent—has stepped out for an hour or two—or there are numerous hosts. This so-called uncivilized confusion is often upsetting, and even appears antagonistic, to those who grew up obedient to different rules. But there seems more than a slight possibility that young people— freed by television, not entirely but in great measure, of some of the defensiveness that led to the need for rules and rituals in the first place—are in fact gradually evolving patterns of behavior that may make up in true sociability what they seem to lack in conventional civility.

Nor has this movement of liberation through loss of ritual been confined to the young. Where television has come into backward rural communities—for example, in the South—or into isolated mountain communities— for example, in the Rocky Mountain states—among the first signs of change to appear (invariably regarded as loss, especially by outside observers) has been a decline in the social or hospitality rituals of the region. Slowly, and sometimes swiftly, the quaint, parochial customs of social intercourse disappear. There are no more quilting bees and fewer village barbecues. Barn dances are no longer the attraction they once were—nor the occasion for night-long and often violent drinking; bar life generally becomes more subdued. There is less desperation, and so less ritual, in social gatherings. Old people, too, no longer live in stark, albeit picturesque, isolation but now have the opportunity at least of communing with *As the World Turns*, Merv, Mike, Johnny, and even Walter Cronkite. Strangely, one of the areas where the new socializing influence seems to have made itself least felt is *within* television. Otherwise, why all these hosts and guests? Why this constant playacting of hospitality? Why the need for rituals and control? One wonders inevitably which stranger these hosts are so afraid of. Could it be *us*?

(1977)

TALKING BACK

From time to time, I've found myself writing about the largely authoritarian role that so much television broadcasting has assumed in our era. The monochrome and monotone "voice" of the networks has been frequently alluded to, as has the framing or focusing authority of most of the news programs. Indeed, "power" on the part of the television establishment and "passivity" on the part of the audience have been perhaps the two key words, or concepts, with which to consider the influence of television up to now in our society. On a different, more emotional level, intimations of Orwell's Big Brother have surrounded us in the air (and on the airwaves) since the first exploitation of broadcasting by national authorities, in the early part of this century; and, with these intimations, there has often developed in members of the public a feeling of resignation and inescapability concerning such distant and intangible matters.

What I would like to do here is temporarily to reverse positions, because, while the present state of broadcasting is undeniably authoritarian, the present also contains the future, and the future (which we are beginning to deal with now) contains at least the possibility of something very different. In short, I should like to risk talking for a while on a subject that nobody in the television audience has had much apparent interest in: that of space satellites and satellite communications. For modern satellites and their ground receiver-transmitters have already reached a level of technical competence and economic practicality which has brought them further and further into the arena of political decisions. A number of political decisions concerning them have already been made, and, in fact, there is much about the current satellite situation which is roughly comparable to what obtained in regard to television broadcasting in the nineteen-thirties: that is, much of the basic technology is already in place, and the rest of it is in the process of development. What remains is to make the final, hard-to-reverse political decisions that will determine the shape of future satellite communications in the nation as, back in the nineteen-thirties, decisions were made that determined the shape of our present commercial television service. As it happens, the token reason, or news peg, for my belated attention to satellites is a substantial, and not altogether impenetrable, document that I have lately been reading, which is titled simply: *Description of Public Broadcasting Satellite Interconnection Plan.* Briefly, what this proposal encompasses is the nation's first satellite television network, wherein the Corporation for Public Broadcasting will be empowered to lease three, and eventually four, transponders (or channels) on Western Union's Westar I satellite, and also to construct about a hundred and fifty-five ground receiving stations, of which five will have the ability to transmit as well as receive. It is a fine, ambitious plan, and is currently under active consideration by the FCC—circumstances that provide, I think, as good an opportunity as any for trying to understand, or perhaps unbore oneself about, these new devices and the new kinds of communications they make possible.

We might as well start at the beginning. For practical

purposes, satellites might be said to derive from what was surely one of the most important and ghastly inventions of the twentieth century: the rocket that was known by the Germans (who first launched it at Peenemünde in 1942) as the Aggregate-4, and later by the British, whose cities it assaulted, as the V-2. The second step followed logically from the first. In 1957, employing a rocket derived from the Aggregate-4, the Soviet Union launched and orbited the first satellite: Sputnik. Since Sputnik, literally thousands of satellites have been put into orbit, most of them by the Soviet Union and the United States, and with roughly ninety percent of them in the service of the military: the "guardians of our skies," as our own are sometimes referred to in defense-contractor advertisements. The metaphor is doubtless accurate, though not entirely reassuring, especially since in these matters insufficient notice is usually paid to the American citizen, whose taxes furnished the $85 billion that provided the space program that evolved the rocket and communications skills that resulted not only in our landings on the moon and Mars but also in the present multitude of "guardians" orbiting above us.

Here, though, we shall consider only civilian communications satellites: that is, those few satellites now in the air that are the property of American communications companies. Some elementary questions come to mind. For instance, what is special about satellite communication? What are its advantages over present standard forms of communications? The basic answer is deceptively simple, and easy to gloss over: satellite communication is more efficient than ground communications. Consider, in the matter of transoceanic communications, that twenty years ago the only way of speaking by telephone between New York and London was via radio, which was expensive and, because of atmospheric conditions, undependable. When the first transatlantic telephone cables were put in operation in 1956, the service became more dependable, but it was still expensive and the transmission was far from ideal. The cables could carry sixty phone conversations simultaneously, but no television. The extent to which a present-day satellite supersedes cable technology is as follows: the cost of orbiting the satellite is a fraction of the cost of cable laying; a satellite can handle fourteen thousand phone conversations simultaneously, with high dependability and fidelity, or relay twenty-four color-television programs simultaneously. Similarly, in the area of transcontinental communications, whether by phone or television signal, the advantage of a satellite system is so great in terms of cost, multiplicity of access, and fidelity as not to be usefully defined by the catchall term "efficiency." At present, for example, most telephone and television communication is carried along the telephone company's vast and expensive network of cables, or else is beamed along the newer microwave system, which requires line-of-sight transmission and reception, and thus the construction of receiving-and-transmitting towers at around thirty-mile intervals across the country. With either microwave or cable communication, the cost and difficulty of sending a voice or a television signal over long distances involve not only a huge outlay for construction and maintenance but also an elaborate amplifying apparatus for boosting the original signal along its way, which must be built into the system at regular intervals and which frequently produces less than satisfactory fidelity. With satellites, however, the basic communications structure is far simpler, involving not thousands of miles of cable, or towers with all their attendant switchers and boosters and maintenance, but orbiting devices of enormous sensitivity, with a multiplicity of channels, and with ground sending or receiving terminals of ever increasing simplicity and cheapness. For instance, many ground receiving stations still require antennas of up to a hundred feet in diameter, and might cost nine million dollars to build. But some such stations can now be served by antennas no more than thirty-three feet in diameter, and cost around three million dollars; and the Japanese have recently developed a prototype TV receiver (dependent on new satellites with increased transmitter potency) that costs fifteen hundred dollars and could probably be marketed eventually for a good deal less. Technically, home ownership of a direct-broadcast satellite television receiver is virtually within reach.

The first of the civilian (or commercial) communications satellites was Telstar I, which was put in orbit in 1962, and which was paid for and owned by A.T.&T. By present standards, Telstar was a fairly primitive device. Admittedly, it could handle one TV signal or a hundred phone conversations simultaneously, compared with the sixty conversations of the first transatlantic cables, but there was a built-in limit to its overall effectiveness in that the satellite's orbit around the earth was elliptical and low. Since television signals travel in straight lines, this meant that a program could be beamed from Point A, received by the satellite, and amplified and transmitted to Point B only at a time when the satellite was in direct line of sight with both A and B. If Telstar sped out of this line of sight too soon, or if the timing was inconvenient, program transmission had to wait until the satellite had returned after orbiting the globe. An alternative, which was not tried, would have required a continuous, revolving parade of as many as thirty Telstars in orbit, with one of them always in range.

The reason that this costly and cumbersome method was not attempted derives from an imaginatively simple solution proposed by Arthur C. Clarke, who is an engineer as well as a successful author of numerous books of science fiction. Clarke's solution was based on the calculation that a satellite placed in orbit at 6,830 mph at an altitude of 22,300 miles above the earth would take nearly twenty-four hours to circle the globe. Thus, it would be "geosynchronous" with the rotation of the earth; that is, the speeding, orbiting satellite—appearing to stand still—would remain in line of sight constantly. Also, the height of the orbit would be much greater than that of Telstar, and would therefore permit a vastly greater number of sending and receiving points. In fact, no more than three satellites, properly placed, could provide a global communications system. In 1963, Syncom II, the first working geosynchronous communications satellite, was built by the Hughes Aircraft Company and was launched by NASA. The Hughes Company built three Syncoms that were launched by NASA and one, launched in 1965 and named Early Bird, that was operated as a civilian communications satellite by the International Telecommunications Satellite Consortium, or Intelsat.

As in a Biblical family tree, Telstar in 1962 begat Comsat (or the Communications Satellite Corporation), which begat Intelsat. For, as a result of the success of

A.T.&T.'s elliptically orbiting Telstar, one of those important debates occurred in the upper reaches of government and business which go largely unnoticed by the public. This one dealt with the question of whether a civilian satellite communications system should be kept in the hands of the federal government or be handed over for development to the "private sector," or business. Business prevailed, and Comsat was established in 1963, supposedly as a partnership between the large communications corporations and the public, with fifty percent of the stock in the new company owned by A.T.&T., ITT, RCA, Western Union, and more than a hundred smaller companies, and the remaining fifty percent being sold, through the New York Stock Exchange, to "the public." Since A.T.&T. was a main force in the origins of Comsat, and since A.T.&T. already had an immense investment in ground communications facilities in the United States, it was decided that Comsat would concentrate its attention on international communications. Hence the organizing, in 1964, of Intelsat, which has since grown to encompass ninety-four nations, five satellites, and a hundred and nineteen earth stations around the world. Intelsat is an operating organization that leases its satellites and facilities to each member nation's designated representative—which in the United States is Comsat.

Within the past few years, there has been a second major debate, also largely unnoticed by the public, which has resulted in the orbiting of several Domsats, or domestic satellites. This debate had to do not with the important question of whether the public or the private sector should control the new domestic satellites but merely with whether these satellites should be a monopoly of Comsat or be owned and operated by other communications companies—the assumption, at least in certain quarters, being that Comsat already half represents the public. In 1972, following its bent for pseudo-populist communications programs, President Nixon's Office of Telecommunications Policy proposed an "Open Skies" policy, which stated, roughly, that any applicant possessing suitable financial and technological capacity might launch and operate a communications satellite, and in due course this policy was adopted by the FCC. So, while Comsat handles international satellite communications for the people of the United States, a new procession of familiar corporate giants is entering into control of domestic satellite communications. Western Union and RCA have both launched their own satellites, as have A.T.&T. and G.T.&E., which have also joined with Comsat on satellite projects. And several more (including a recent application by Hughes Aircraft) are waiting in the wings.

There are further decisions in the making, however, and the Corporation for Public Broadcasting's Satellite Interconnection Plan marks another step along the way —a step in the right direction, it appears from the current proposals. First is the obvious, and not at all unimportant, question of cost. Despite the expense of leasing satellite channels and constructing ground facilities, CPB's satellite system should be cheaper in the long run than any comparable system based—as is virtually all television transmission, commercial or public—on the leasing of A.T.&T.'s so-called long lines. But more important even than cost, and buried within the concept of efficiency, is the significant potential— the essence—of satellite communications: namely, that they represent the first visible, plausible promise of what might be clumsily called intercommunicative broadcasting, of broadcasting that does not always, or inherently, proceed in one direction: from the broadcasting authority to the public.

Today, most television programs flow in a more or less direct line, along A.T.&T.'s cables or microwave stations, either from west to east or from east to west. Television-broadcast traffic across the continent is thus limited, in a manner comparable to the limitation on railroad traffic, by the sheer expense of laying track as well as by the difficulty and cost of dispatching programs in various directions. It is technically possible for a network to originate a nationwide broadcast of a football game from Dallas or a news story from Boston, but the cost runs high and the traffic-scheduling problems are considerable; even for wealthy networks, there are clearly limits to the number of times it can be done. Public television's proposed satellite system will not seem at first to make any drastic change in the present arrangement, but it will *begin* to make true interconnective programming possible. It will begin to do away with the old "railroad track" system, and perhaps, along with it, certain assumptions by the audience and the station managers as to what constitutes broadcast traffic. At the heart of the new system, after all, is the fact that the satellite is already up there, apparently "parked" in the sky, though in fact speeding along with the spin of the earth, making occasional, slight course adjustments by means of tiny engines, and usually accompanied by a twin: a backup satellite, to be brought into operation if the first one should somehow fail. Thus the rigid, limited network of the long lines is replaced by a space-age trigonometry, with the result that it is no more difficult, electronically, to dispatch a television signal from Minneapolis to Miami than from Minneapolis to St. Paul. Also, the variety of signals relayed is defined not by the dimensions of an unchangeable cable but by the leasing of transponders on a satellite. With CPB's satellite system, individual public stations will have far greater flexibility in their programming—choosing, alternately, between regional broadcasts and the national feed. Most important, too, CPB's five proposed transmitting stations will not simply permit but encourage a degree of regionally originated programming (that is, programs not from New York or Los Angeles), which now remains at the mercy of leased lines, high costs, and "feed" schedules.

Admittedly, there is a problem in talking about the future, for the future usually involves technical progress, and this progress is often presented in such unreal or utopian terms as to be oppressive—what laymen defensively call "boring." One likely result of CPB's satellite system, at least for the first few years after it comes on-stream, is that Thoreau's mid-nineteenth-century demurrer on the subject of the nation's first transcontinental telegraph line will seem to have new pertinence. What, we soon may have cause to ask, if Houston has nothing better to relay, via the heavens, to New Rochelle than yoga instruction or *Mister Rogers*? However, I suspect that the significance of the proposed development will go far beyond the merits or demerits of specific programming. For it seems to me that these new and as yet unmade satellite systems, even when stripped of the glamour of cost statistics and the futuristic jargon-poetry of scientific utopias, represent nothing less than man's most potent tool, to date, for reversing—or, at least, holding his own against—the supposedly irreversible thrust of technological society, which has been carrying us steadily forward in this century toward greater homogeneity, and thus the dangers of totalitarianism.

The evils of a technological world are commonplaces by now, and appear to be accepted by many people because they can conceive of no plausible alternative— the exception being those brave, poignant, guerrilla-type counterattacks by the young, who storm the redoubts of technology armed with little more than sensibility and handmade jewelry. In addition, the baby-and-bathwater argument is much used, or leaned upon, by those who try to feel hopeful about the general drift of modern societies. That is: is it not necessary to give up certain amenities or freedoms in exchange for, say, polio vaccine, computer billing, and the boneless chicken; and might one not altogether lose the "new" in trying to regain the "old"? It is not too much to say that the people of advanced societies, such as ours, have been largely immobilized before technology: on the one hand, enjoying its benefits and repeating its pieties, and, on the other hand, giving increasing evidence of nervousness, interior dismay, and a propensity for mild rebellion against the very technologies—whether of politics, communications, or merchandising—that they have assisted in creating.

Consider only broadcasting technology. Broadcasting did not create our technological society, but in this century it has accompanied the shaping of our country, and the form we have permitted broadcasting to assume in our midst has had much to do with the evolving relations of the mass of people to authority. Broadcasters periodically make much of the deference they pay the public, but in reality this occasional deference is paid either to the authority of the state or to the rival authority of business. The form or "message" of broadcasting, especially that of the powerful television industry, has been for years that of a central transmitting authority (albeit divided into several companies), which "speaks" one-way only, to the mass. What is it, after all, that explains the popularity of CB radios except a delight on the part of the public in employing economically accessible technology for talking back—for demassifying itself. What are all the phone-in radio shows but attempts on the part of the audience to de-audience itself —to intercommunicate and participate? The truth is that, by and large, our vaunted Communications Era has been in many ways a strange, depressing period during which a massed citizenry, no longer assembled in city squares attending to a voice from a loudspeaker, instead has been assembled before one hundred million television sets, looking at and listening to distanced presences that transmit but never receive. It is an unnatural state of affairs—in some ways, a kind of slavery—and one that doubtless poses great unseen burdens on society. Surely, the condition of alienation (and its related disorders) that occurs in so many parts of the advanced world derives to some degree from the ongoing and unrelieved process of being talked to by authorities—however seemingly benign, or even cheerful—and never being able to talk back.

Satellite communications on a scale proposed by CPB will obviously not reshape the emotional structure of the world. But there is much at stake here in the principle of two-way broadcast transmission and in the public's right and need to have access to the new technology: to get its voice back. Also, there is a certain element of political risk, and even danger. How will governments govern when a capacity exists for a nearly instantaneous citizen response—to a new strip-mining bill or to some hostile action by a foreign power? One result of a greater interconnection might be that governments will finally be compelled to reconsider in whose behalf they govern anyway. But the larger hazard facing the new communications systems probably is that the authorities in their role as parents will be reluctant to turn them over to the children, who are us. Temporizing reasons will be found in order to at least slow down the process. The national security must be protected, or the corporations entrusted with national communications must not be second-guessed; in other words, the new toys should be kept in a safe, parental place, since the children will only misuse or break them. Already I notice that in the matter of the relatively modest CPB proposal, Western Union has petitioned the government for the right to use public broadcasting's earth stations for its own benefit. Apparently, no authority ever gladly lets anything go.

All the same, there is something deeply stirring about the new possibilities. There is a logic behind them, one senses, that will sooner or later put them in the hands where they will do the most good: the hands of the public —that multitude of nonchildren. In the end, perhaps what is most stirring of all is the glimpse that has just been provided of man's ability to extricate himself from some of the trouble that his technology has brought him. To put the matter another way, the year 1984 is not so far away and it sometimes seems that the grim futuristic fantasy, *Nineteen Eighty-Four*, that George Orwell published some thirty years ago has turned out to be mainly prophetic. Newspeak and Big Brother have certainly made their appearance in different sections of the globe. But the larger, social message of the book, with its depiction of a gray world weighed down by a mass of passive, obedient, and shabby "proles" (a projection, as Raymond Williams has pointed out, of Orwell's own private pessimism and class views), has so far turned out to be essentially unprophetic. At least, it seems in no significant way to resemble the world we are living in, whose recent history, for all its chaos, bloodshed, and hunger, has still one claim to nobility in its favor: namely, the continual and often indomitable attempts by men and women all over the world—in large countries or small, in large numbers or small—to oppose the forces of oppressive authority with their own brave voices and lives. Much misery and alienation have come to pass in this century, but there are no signs yet of Orwell's elegant nightmare of passivity and resignation. In fact, what is probably most needed now, at least in this prototypical and pioneering technological nation, is not so much physical bravery as something that in some ways is even more difficult to provide: acts of faith and consciousness. That is, we should compel ourselves to stay awake and not be oppressed—or "bored"—too easily by the seductive and sometimes inaccessible clangings of our new technologies. Technology, after all, is still man's handiwork; man is the one to keep an eye on.

(1976)

POSTSCRIPT

Four years after this essay was written, public television had completed the switch from a long-lines network to satellite transmission. The results of the new interconnection don't yet seem all that visible to the naked eye, though I noticed recently that a group of independent filmmakers was trying to arrange funding for a project that would feed locally originating telecasts into the national system for a single day's experiment—America broadcasting to itself, so to speak. Doubtless, it will take time for real benefits to make themselves felt, but it's already apparent that when new technology begins making an established system more responsive to particular needs there are plenty of people waiting around with stories they want to tell and songs they want to sing.

Generally speaking, the employment of satellites in broadcasting has been increasing rapidly each year, especially in the growing field of pay-cable television. Not all that long ago, for example, Time-Life's Home Box Office service was a money-losing operation, limited to a few hundred thousand subscribers in the greater New York area. But after signing an agreement with another communications giant, RCA, to use its Satcom I satellite, Home Box Office has been available all over the country, wherever a cable system chooses to set up an earth station to receive the HBO signal from the satellite. Currently, HBO reaches about four million households and its ratings are sometimes competitive with network programs. (It should be noted that the cost of earth-station equipment has been dropping steadily, to the extent that Neiman-Marcus, the Dallas department store, advertised a saucerlike receiving antenna for home

use at $36,500.) Other satellite programming services
have been quick to follow suit, and at the moment there
are Viacom/Teleprompter's *Showtime*, ESPN's all-sports
service, the Christian Broadcasting Network's *Ministry
in the Sky*, and several others in the works.

Naturally, a number of cautionary voices have been
heard to complain that the cultural levels of the new
satellite-cable services are scarcely higher than the
marshmallow-to-midcult content of traditional network
programming. But cultural levels don't seem to be the
point right now. They're not unimportant to a nation
over the long run, but in the first place a little patience
is probably called for as the new satellite-cable systems
find their audiences. In the second place, it's a fair
measure of our fundamental alienation from the concept
of culture that so many people assume it can somehow
be produced by opening a valve or turning a spigot or
even by parking a satellite overhead in the sky. In the
third place, although it's difficult and usually unwise to
try to impose culture on a mass public for the benefit
of a few, it's likely that the new technological developments provide the best chance we have had in a long time
for a broadcast system that will be responsive to the kind
of particular needs and tastes which, in fact, produce
authentic forms of culture.

At any rate, satellite and cable technology has caused
broadcasting (especially television) to shift what had
seemed to many to be an inalterable course in its relationship with the public. First, that is, we had the national networks, which fed programs to the rest of the
country along the phone company's lines or via their
microwave towers, and as a result became enormously
wealthy and so were able to keep buying the best talent.

Then we had cable systems, which originally were local grid systems—locally responsive but without the resources for buying top programming. Now, more recently, with the advent of satellites and with the decline in the cost of earth receiving stations, we have the new satellite-cable systems (sometimes also called networks), which transmit nationally but to people with more specific interests. The old networks will doubtless continue to exist, and even prosper, but no longer will Americans be primarily dependent on their homogeneous, low-common-denominator programming for broadcast services.

These new satellite-cable services, of course, do not provide a true interconnection with the audience, in that the audience still can't talk back. There is one much smaller operation, however, that does provide what is known in the trade as the "response factor." This is Warner Communications's Qube system, which was installed in Columbus, Ohio, in 1977, and which will soon be offered in Houston and Cincinnati. Qube costs its subscribers a current rate of $10.95 per month, for which each household gets access to thirty channels: ten of these bring in regular commercial and public television programs; another ten are community channels, originating local talk shows, children's shows, and so forth; and ten are "premium" channels which bring in special movies and entertainment programs, for which subscribers are charged extra. Even so, Qube's most interesting feature is the little hand-held console that each subscriber receives, and on whose panel are not only thirteen white buttons for program selection but also five black buttons for "response signals." In the course of watching a local variety hour or municipal budget meeting, Qube subscribers may be asked to indicate their opinion of what they have just heard or seen, which can be done by pressing one or another of the five black buttons—indicating such still simple responses as "agree," "agree strongly," "disagree," etc. An electrical signal travels back along the cable from the individual subscriber's home to the Qube computer, which a few seconds later correlates all the other answers and flashes the results on the home television screen. So, apparently, in this small way, the future is already here. Is this new instant responsiveness dangerous? Undoubtedly—though the Qube subscribers in Columbus seem to have gotten along fine with their consoles and limited two-way dialogue. The truth is that inevitably we learn the new languages of technology; we learn to deal with telephones and voting booths and computer printouts as if we had been living with them all our lives. The catch is: In what direction does each new technological advance point—toward a life that is more humane or less humane? Right now, for a change, there seems to be some modest evidence in the air that the new broadcast technology leads away from that dream of homogenized, generalized passivity that we have been living through and toward a greater responsiveness and particularity—and, if so, there can be little harm in that.